Isaiah 1–39

INTERPRETATION
A Bible Commentary for Teaching and Preaching

INTERPRETATION

A BIBLE COMMENTARY FOR TEACHING AND PREACHING

James Luther Mays, *Editor*
Patrick D. Miller, Jr., *Old Testament Editor*
Paul J. Achtemeier, *New Testament Editor*

CHRISTOPHER R. SEITZ

Isaiah 1–39

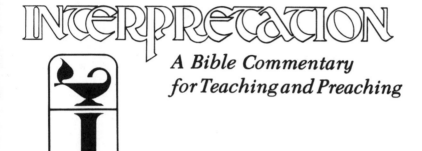

A Bible Commentary
for Teaching and Preaching

John Knox Press
LOUISVILLE

Library of Congress Cataloging-in-Publication Data

Seitz, Christopher R.
    Isaiah 1–39 / Christopher Seitz. — 1st ed.
        p.   cm. — (Interpretation, a Bible commentary for teaching and preaching)
    Includes bibliographical references.
    ISBN 0-8042-3131-1 (cloth : alk. paper)

    1. Bible. O.T. Isaiah I–XXXIX—Commentaries. I. Bible. O.T. Isaiah I–XXXIX. English. 1993. II. Title. III. Series.
BS1515.3.S34   1993
224′.1077—dc20   93-3263

© copyright John Knox Press 1993
This book is printed on acid-free paper that meets the American National Standards Institute Z39.48 standard. ∞
10 9 8 7 6 5 4 3 2 1
Printed in the United States of America
John Knox Press
Louisville, Kentucky 40202-1396

SERIES PREFACE

This series of commentaries offers an interpretation of the books of the Bible. It is designed to meet the need of students, teachers, ministers, and priests for a contemporary expository commentary. These volumes will not replace the historical critical commentary or homiletical aids to preaching. The purpose of this series is rather to provide a third kind of resource, a commentary which presents the integrated result of historical and theological work with the biblical text.

An interpretation in the full sense of the term involves a text, an interpreter, and someone for whom the interpretation is made. Here, the text is what stands written in the Bible in its full identity as literature from the time of "the prophets and apostles," the literature which is read to inform, inspire, and guide the life of faith. The interpreters are scholars who seek to create an interpretation which is both faithful to the text and useful to the church. The series is written for those who teach, preach, and study the Bible in the community of faith.

The comment generally takes the form of expository essays. It is planned and written in the light of the needs and questions which arise in the use of the Bible as Holy Scripture. The insights and results of contemporary scholarly research are used for the sake of the exposition. The commentators write as exegetes and theologians. The task which they undertake is both to deal with what the texts say and to discern their meaning for faith and life. The exposition is the unified work of one interpreter.

The text on which the comment is based is the Revised Standard Version of the Bible and, since its appearance, the New Revised Standard Version. The general availability of these translations makes the printing of a text in the commentary unnecessary. The commentators have also had other current versions in view as they worked and refer to their readings where it is helpful. The text is divided into sections appropriate to the particular book; comment deals with passages as a whole, rather than proceeding word by word, or verse by verse.

Writers have planned their volumes in light of the requirements set by the exposition of the book assigned to them. Biblical books differ in character, content, and arrangement. They also differ in the way they have been and are used in the liturgy, thought, and devotion of the church. The distinctiveness and use of particular books have been taken into account in decisions about the approach, emphasis, and use of space in the commentaries. The goal has been to allow writers to develop the format which provides for the best presentation of their interpretation.

The result, writers and editors hope, is a commentary which both explains and applies, an interpretation which deals with both the meaning and the significance of biblical texts. Each commentary reflects, of course, the writer's own approach and perception of the church and world. It could and should not be otherwise. Every interpretation of any kind is individual in that sense; it is one reading of the text. But all who work at the interpretation of scripture in the church need the help and stimulation of a colleague's reading and understanding of the text. If these volumes serve and encourage interpretation in that way, their preparation and publication will realize their purpose.

The Editors

CONTENTS

viii

FOREWORD

This series defines as its goal the production of commentaries "designed and written as a resource for interpreting the Scriptures in the church." It is not surprising that a good number of the commentaries that have already appeared have distinguished themselves by emphasizing an interpretation geared to the present form of the text or the final shape of a biblical book. It is, after all, the final form of a biblical book that is read in liturgy, Bible study, or private devotion.

A commentary on First Isaiah, the first thirty-nine chapters of the larger Book of Isaiah, might require some explanation on this score, since it is only a section of the final form of the book. Moreover, while a commentary on the present form of a biblical book might be logical and right in the case of narrative texts, prophetic books appear less amenable to a focus on the final form of the material, with their seemingly random movement from this oracle to that. And the Book of Isaiah is an especially good example of a prophetic book that is resistant not only to comprehension of final form but also to comprehension of individual units within the final shape of the material. Two more recent attempts at traditional historical-critical interpretation have produced results that could not be further divergent (Hayes/Irvine; Kaiser). How can one describe the present shape of the text when there is such utter disagreement about its constituent parts?

In fact, much of the shift to interest in final form has proceeded out of a general weariness with traditional critical work, its frequently tedious historical reconstructions and literary-critical operations. But if interpretation is not simply to fall captive to this or that whim of readership—either historically oriented or one tired of its hegemony—then the appeal to final form must itself be well grounded, as having to do with the text's own intentions and not just the predilections of readers zealous for simplification or another new approach.

In this commentary I have sought to argue that the final form of the Book of Isaiah, and therefore derivatively its first thirty-nine chapters, is both an intelligible and an intended result of the efforts of those who gave shape to the present form of the book. I have spoken of the "presentation" of Isaiah, by which I mean the way in which the prophet and his message have been shaped for posterity. In trying to establish the coherence of the final presentation of the Book of Isaiah, I have frequently paid more attention to arguing for the coherence of larger structure than to any individual pericope in isolation. I hope that the argument for final coherence does not overshadow a concern for more specific interpretation and application, but I readily admit the threat is there.

My hope is that the shift of focus to the final form of the text will cause the interpreter to pay more attention to the biblical text itself and especially to the larger context that surrounds—and I believe influences—individual passages. It has been my experience as a preacher that all too often modern lectionary schemes, rather than broadening our vision on the wider biblical narrative, actually encourage selectivity and individual focus—a sort of "pericope preoccupation," if it might be called that. Admittedly the preacher's time is limited, and broadening the scope of interest to surrounding texts might seem like a call for yet further study and historical reconstruction. Instead, I am simply making appeal to a time-honored principle for teaching, preaching, and general biblical interpretation: let the Bible interpret itself. In the context of this commentary on Isaiah this means, let the interpretation of individual passages be guided, above all, by attention to larger context and the final presentation of the book as a whole. Not only do I follow such an approach in the commentary, I also attempt to justify this procedure as consistent with the very forces and concerns that have gathered the traditions of the prophet Isaiah, given shape to the Book of Isaiah, and then bequeathed that book to Israel and, by extension and confessional assent, to the church.

My own firm belief is that congregations and Bible study groups, while aware of the historical dimension of the text and its emergence from a time and a culture distinct from our own, nevertheless see these sorts of concerns as somehow penultimate. More negatively, they are seen as capable of diverting our attention from a more abiding and somehow more direct hearing of the Bible, or they testify to the even more problematic conclusion that the Bible is after all outmoded and incapable of speaking either a direct or an oblique word to modern men and women. My hope is that this commentary will simply encourage the reader of Isaiah to read Isaiah again, beginning in chapter

1 and continuing on through the nations material (chaps. 13—27) right up to the sparing of Zion and the pregnant account of Babylonian visitors who come to inspect Hezekiah's treasures (chaps. 36—39). My instinct is that there is a sense about this presentation, however elusive, and that this sense is unlocked once one is willing to take context, larger shape, and movement seriously. My other instinct is that this larger coherence represents the intentional and cumulative wisdom of many, many hearers of Isaiah's original word, who have then presented that word and its resonating consequences to a posterity that includes us.

A commentary cannot do everything. If I have made a coherent and stimulating proposal for reading the Book of Isaiah in its present form, I will be satisfied. At the same time I hope new directions might be opened up for interpreting other prophetic texts along similar lines. As such, this commentary is a modest attempt at defining method even as it seeks to interpret a significant portion of the Book of Isaiah within the framework of this commentary series and its specific goals.

ACKNOWLEDGMENTS

I acknowledge with gratitude the generous support of the Alexander von Humboldt Foundation in Bonn which enabled me to take a leave from my teaching responsibilities and devote full attention to writing this commentary. My host at the University of Munich, Professor Dr. Klaus Baltzer, and his wife, Jo, made my stay as warm as possible. I take this opportunity to express my deep appreciation to both of them.

I have learned much about the Book of Isaiah in the classroom at Yale Divinity School, teaching both Master of Divinity and doctoral students. I remember with particular fondness a seminar on Isaiah 1—39, where we wrestled with the peculiar shape of the prophet's vision. I learned much from the visions of my students on that occasion.

Two names stand out as I reflect on my own changing attitudes toward reading the Book of Isaiah, those of Peter Ackroyd and Ronald Clements. I have learned much from both of them and wish to acknowledge my indebtedness particularly to Ron Clements, with whom I am in ongoing dialogue and occasional appreciative disagreement. He and Ackroyd have thought about the larger Book of Isaiah in interesting new ways, even as they have not sought to sever lines of connection with older approaches.

Colleagues at Yale Divinity School also helped make this leave possible, chief among them Deans Aidan Kavanaugh and Thomas Ogletree, as well as my Old Testament faculty colleagues Brevard Childs and Robert Wilson. I gratefully mention my debt to them here.

To the Editors of this fine series I also want to say thanks. They read my first drafts in timely fashion and made innumerable helpful comments. If the commentary fails at any point, it probably has to do with not heeding their sage counsel.

Finally, and most important, I want to thank the many Munich friends who helped me pretend I was living a normal life during the writing of this book. To members of the Church of the Ascension, the EFM study group, older friends from my university days in Munich, Gaby Holzer and Sabine Zucker, Klaus and Jo Baltzer, Dee and Dick Pattee, and my "family" in

Schwetzingen, Linni and Werner Heimburger—many thanks! My father and mother provided much-needed phone conversation and support, but my debt to them is already beyond tallying. Without my good friend Dinah Wells I am sure the vision of Isaiah would have engulfed me completely, as it threatened to do to the prophet (21:1–4). Sally Belle Hamilton proved a worthy proofreader and page corrector, and I am grateful for her last-minute help. And while it might sound strange to those who do not enjoy the companionship of animals, I have to thank my dog Bror, who dragged me out for daily walks through the Isartal. If you cannot thank a dog, it is only because they are loyal by instinct and relentlessly good-natured, unlike some authors I know.

This book is dedicated to my brothers Tom, Mark, and Peter. "Successus Fidelitate" and "An endless Alleluia!"

Introduction

The Character and Position of the Book of Isaiah

Isaiah can rightly claim a place of prominence among Israel's prophets, though the reasons for this are varied and frequently unrelated. First there is Isaiah's signal position in the canon, heading up the collection of Latter Prophets (Isaiah, Jeremiah, Ezekiel, and the Twelve). Since on historical grounds others could lay better claim to this position—Amos or Hosea, for example—we must search elsewhere for the reasons behind Isaiah's first-place status. To speak of the Book of Isaiah's large size is simply to beg the question, Why has this prophet attracted such a sizable collection of oracles? Further, we know of one prominent rabbinic listing that locates the Book of Isaiah after Jeremiah and Ezekiel. Yet even in such an arrangement Isaiah is said to be distinguished by dint of containing "nothing but salvation," thus rounding off and bringing to completion Jeremiah's opening message of judgment and Ezekiel's half-judgment, half-salvation proclamation. Here, last is every bit as important as first. The Book of Isaiah has the "last word" and is appropriately conclusive.

Not unrelated to such an interpretation of Isaiah's importance is that of the Christian church before the modern period. Then the emphasis was not so much on Isaiah's salvific character as it was on Isaiah as a book that spoke of the future, generally, and of salvation through the agency of the Messiah, Jesus Christ, specifically. So it was that the church fathers (Eusebius, Theodoret, Jerome, Augustine) regarded Isaiah not just as the first and greatest prophet but as the first apostle and evangelist.

Though the reasons for this may be clear from the standpoint of the New Testament, which cites Isaiah more than any other book in the Old Testament, the testimony of Isaiah is itself not so univocal. When asked by Augustine which book of the Bible should be read first, Ambrose responded "Isaiah." Yet Augustine was thoroughly confounded in his attempts first to read the book on its own terms and had to come back at a later

1

day, at which point he returned to the New Testament's construal of Isaiah as the best guide to its interpretation. Whatever else it may mean, Isaiah's prominence has never translated into ease of interpretation! Luther may well have had Isaiah in mind when he commented: "The prophets have a queer way of talking, like people who, instead of proceeding in an orderly manner, ramble off from one thing to the next, so that you cannot make head or tail of them or see what they are getting at" (Von Rad, p. 33). Let the commentator, ancient or modern, beware.

In the modern period the literary complexity of the book has been probed using the tools of historical analysis, leading one to conceive of Isaiah's prominence in very different terms. The attempt to penetrate the logic of the book's presentation on historical grounds has led to the division of one Isaiah book into three separate collections (chaps. 1—39; 40—55; 56—66), presumably originating in the public proclamation of three discretely inspired individuals or schools, spanning a period of several centuries, if not more—right up to the Christian era itself. Especially measured against the more historically circumscribed books of Jeremiah and Ezekiel, this massive extension of Isaiah's message into later periods is unique. Whatever else one makes of it, it bestows on Isaiah a certain prominence, though clearly of a different character than traditionally expressed. It also means that in the context of a commentary on First Isaiah one must wrestle with the puzzle of the Book of Isaiah's development, as one unique feature of the larger book in which chapters 1—39, more narrowly conceived, now form only the opening section.

That the Book of Isaiah's larger literary development affects how we read the first thirty-nine chapters can be readily demonstrated on literary, theological, and even historical grounds. Interpreters now agree that one can see within chapters 1—39 evidence of literary additions—at times sporadic, on other occasions more comprehensive—supplied by editors under the influence of Second Isaiah chapters and the wider experience of the fall of Jerusalem and the exile; one speaks of a "Babylonian" or "exilic" redaction of chapters 1—39. Such a view reverses the position held by Bernhard Duhm a century ago whereby First and Second Isaiah were to be kept strictly separated. Still others have argued for a later redaction in chapters 1—39 made with an eye toward Third Isaiah material (chaps. 56—66). Points of contact can be spotted, for example, between chapters 1 and 66, the first and last chapters of the wider Isaiah collection.

Prior to these observations concerning literary and historical linkages among the "Isaiahs," interpreters had noted key theological concepts and terminology that bound together the (then held to be) discrete sections of the book, including an emphasis on Zion, God as "the Holy One of Israel," and themes of sin and forgiveness. New linkages across the Book of Isaiah have been put forward recently. They include deafness and recovery of sight, plays upon the name Isaiah in Hebrew and the promise of salvation for Israel, exodus motifs, and even divine council and prophetic commissioning language. The focus on Zion and its final destiny has received renewed attention in the present climate of Isaiah studies, as a concern shared by every generation of Isaiah editors. The argument that Second Isaiah chapters have developed within a context broader than the historical circumstances of Babylonian exile, and in close exegetical connection to developing First Isaiah traditions (especially Childs and Clements), shows just how far the mood of previous interpreters has been altered in recent years. Indeed, it would be fair to say that the future for Isaiah studies is only gradually becoming clearer, as the quest for unity in the Book of Isaiah—and a proper understanding of the nature of that unity—replaces a narrower historical approach that was concerned to read the book against reconstructed historical backdrops. In the Book of Isaiah, this was an undertaking that was and still is notoriously difficult, producing the most widely divergent results (cf. Hayes/Irvine and Kaiser).

For all that, the historical dimension will not, and should not, go away. Newer literary and "reader-oriented" approaches that insist on multiple meanings and the impossibility of determining intentionality apart from the influence of the reader are now also seeking to replace the older historical readings (see now Conrad). Yet even in so complex a book as Isaiah, the interpreter must still face an important theological question whose difficulty has to do with historical factors: Were Israel's religious texts shaped in such a way that correct theological interpretation was wholly the function of readership and not inherently part of that literary shaping as such, time-bound and concerned with specific matters of history and historical interpretation? It is at this point that historical questions resurface, not from the standpoint of "revelation in events" as the biblical

3

theology movement meant it, but from a concern to understand the intentions of biblical authors, however elusive and multifaceted. By "authors" we mean not just the original prophet but also and especially those who heard his message and "presented" him to posterity as Isaiah, prophet both of judgment and of salvation (Ackroyd, "Presentation").

In this commentary we are committed to an approach that does justice to the historical roots of the message of Isaiah, on the one hand, and the present literary context in which that message is found, on the other. The final form of the material, with its own presentation of the prophet Isaiah and events of the eighth century, need not stand in absolute opposition to events of history as these might be reconstructed in the modern period (e.g., what really happened during the Assyrian siege of Jerusalem in 701 B.C., as compared with the literary presentation of that siege in chaps. 36—37? or, what was Isaiah's specific word for and against Ahaz, and how has that word been presented to us in chaps. 7—9?).

We reckon with editors who worked under two constraints: faithful hearing of the message of Isaiah as it confronted them in their own age and the shaping of a text that would broker that message within a much broader historical and theological perspective (including the Babylonian exile and the challenge it presented for the faith of Israel). That we can recognize the difference between these two aspects of the Book of Isaiah (original situation and secondary interpretation) is a testimony to conclusions reached in the past two centuries of Isaiah research. What is called for now is a reading of the Book of Isaiah that acknowledges and then moves beyond the tension between historical prophet and canonical presentation in order to recover something of the theological coherence available to precritical readers. That such coherence remained mysteriously veiled for even so zealous a reader as Augustine gives one pause. Yet the task of theological interpretation confronts each generation with its challenges as well as its rewards.

Why a Commentary on First Isaiah?

As recently as ten years ago this sort of question would have been viewed as idiosyncratic. Yet given the interest that Isaiah's larger unity now holds for interpreters, a commentary on chapters 1—39 would seem to require some justification. Does the term "First Isaiah" continue to have any relevance, in either a literary or a sociohistorical sense?

What sharply distinguished interpretation of First Isaiah from that of Second Isaiah was the conviction that chapters 40—55 emerged from the specific circumstances of Babylonian exile and were therefore removed historically from the prophecies of Isaiah by approximately a century and a half—to say nothing of their distinctive geographical, sociological, and form-critical identity. Interpretation of chapters 1—39, therefore, was occupied with (1) the search for authentic oracles traceable to the prophet Isaiah, (2) a description of the prophet, his office, and the times in which he preached based on this analysis, and (3) a literary-critical evaluation of which oracles belonged to which historical backdrop and how the present chapters reached their final form. The fact that interpretation had moved beyond the quest for the historical Isaiah, narrowly conceived, is evidenced by those works which sought to determine later settings (the reign of Josiah, e.g.) as possible periods in which Isaiah's prophecies were secondarily edited, filled out, and shaped toward new historical and theological ends (see Hermann Barth's work).

Yet even in these instances of concern with secondary amplification and presentation, no bridge was seen to link First Isaiah to later chapters in the book, so that interpretation of First Isaiah was kept quite separate from Second Isaiah work. At best, the final form of Isaiah was made to conform, externally and rather artificially, to an alleged tripartite organization said to be found in Ezekiel, in the Greek text of Jeremiah, if not also in Zephaniah and the Greek text of the Book of the Twelve. In such a structure, indigenous oracles of judgment (chaps. 1—12) are said to be followed by oracles concerning foreign nations (chaps. 13—24), themselves followed by oracles of salvation (chaps. 25—39). With Peter Ackroyd, we would say that the scheme is arbitrary, poorly evidenced in the text, and a modern invention necessitated by a theory gone awry. More telling is the fact that proponents of such a tripartite structure disagree over whether it embraces the entire book or just First Isaiah chapters. When Duhm made reference to the theory, he had chapters 1—39 in mind; that is to say, he spoke of First Isaiah *as a book,* with a conclusion drawn from Kings (cf. II Kings 18:13—20:19 and Isaiah 36—39), on analogy with the Book of Jeremiah (cf. Jeremiah 52 and II Kings 25).

5

Recent work, however, has shown that such a description of First Isaiah's independence is grossly overstated. Not only have chapters 1—39 undergone a "Babylonian redaction" whereby Assyria is interpreted as a type for the later Babylonians and the sparing of Jerusalem in 701 B.C. is seen as just a postponement of the prophet's larger vision of judgment; First Isaiah chapters have also had a forward exegetical influence on Second Isaiah. The links between Isaiah's commissioning scene (chap. 6) and the opening chapters of Second Isaiah (chap. 40) are only now coming into clearer focus. Ronald Clements has argued for a wider array of thematic connections as well, including deafness and recovery of sight (Isa. 6:9–10; 29:18; 35:5; 42:16; 43:8; 44:18), rejection and election (2:6; 41:8–9; 43:6–7; 44:1–2), and devastation and restoration (6:11; 44:26). What we see is not an external, artificially imposed organization based on an alleged tripartite structure but an organic development based on a process of careful exegetical amplification and a straining to hear the word of God across several centuries (see Clements, "Beyond Tradition-History").

So, why a division at chapter 39 if not for the reasons traditionally associated with First and Second Isaiah interpretation? The answer is that those who shaped the traditions into their developing and then final form appear to have marked a significant boundary at chapter 39, and for that matter at the larger tradition block now found in chapters 36—39. Here we hear of the sparing of sinful Jerusalem (chaps. 36—37) and of a death sentence reversed by dint of royal petition and obedience (37:16–20); of a king who does hear and understand and whose heart is not so fat that he cannot turn and be healed (cf. 6:10 and 38:1–6). But then we learn that in days to come the Babylonians will carry off the royal house and serve as replacements for the Assyrians as agents of judgment (see 39:5–7; cf. 13:1–16; 23:13). Hezekiah could only postpone a sentence of judgment and have "peace and security" in his days (39:8). Chapters 40—66 look back on the sentence of judgment as completed (40:2) and on the decree for judgment as one of the "former things . . . of old" (43:9, 18; 44:7). The final victory over God's agent of judgment—a theme introduced in 10:15–19—is also one of the former things announced of old (45:21); in Second Isaiah this involves God's calling of Cyrus vis-à-vis Babylon (cf. 13:17). So, even while within First Isaiah chapters there are foreshadowings of later days and anticipations of themes more fully developed in chapters 40—66, the actual sentence of final judgment is not announced as completed until after chapter 39. So one has strong grounds for holding to a division between First and Second Isaiah sections of the larger Book of Isaiah, mindful of the changed climate in which an appreciation of the "reciprocal relationships" (Rendtorff, p. 199) within the larger Book of Isaiah has properly come to the fore. We will have more to say about the actual "conclusion" of First Isaiah in the commentary proper.

Literary Structure

If the evidence for a tripartite structure is less than perspicuous in either First Isaiah or the entire book, what can one say about possible literary organization in the final form of Isaiah? This is not merely a literary question if one judges the final shaping of the material to be neither accidental nor arbitrary, but meaningfully executed, with the intention of conveying some final theological message. It was with such an expectation, for example, that the nineteenth-century conservative interpreter K. F. Keil, commenting on the structure of Isaiah, spoke of "a test sent from God for Judah and the house of David, in which it was their duty to decide in favour of faith and confidence simply in the omnipotence and the grace of the Lord; instead of which, they placed their confidence in the earthly worldly power of Assyria, and, as a punishment, were given over to this worldly kingdom, and by it were drawn into the secular historical process of the heathen nations, in order that, being purified by severe judgments, they might be led through deep sufferings to the glory of their divine calling" (Keil, pp. 286–287). Here one should be able to recognize the lineaments of the larger Book of Isaiah, moving from chapters 1—12 to 13—27 to 28—66, within which structure Keil identified, yet further, theologically relevant subsections in the Book of Isaiah.

Opinion has long been divided over the principles governing the larger arrangement of the book, some opting for chronological (Jerome) and others for thematic movement (Vintringae). In an attempt to articulate his own position, Keil described the organization as "neither purely chronologically in the order of time, nor merely in the material order according to homogeneousness of subject-matter; but according to a prin-

7

ciple of successive unfolding of his prophetic activity" (Keil, p. 285). Here one sees what kind of subtlety is required in order to do justice to the material in the form in which it presently exists; not for nothing have certain critics judged the present structure of Isaiah as meaningless. In the modern period a convincing description of the final structure of the book remains a desideratum for those who argue for some form of unity of presentation in the larger Book of Isaiah.

Within First Isaiah chapters, most have generally recognized the following groupings: chapters 1—12; 13—23 (24—27); 28—32; 33—35; 36—39, with further discussion especially in the section that comprises chapters 28—35 (does chap. 33 belong with 28—32 or 34—35?). On closer inspection, several complications upset even this rather bland classification. Following hard upon what appears to be a superscription for the entire collection (1:1) is an additional opening rubric (2:1); chapter 1 is frequently regarded as an overture that rehearses major themes of the whole book. Does this mean that 1:1 is a superscription for the entire book, only for chapter 1 (cf. Hab. 1:1), or only for some other subsection (chaps. 1—4; 1—12; 1—39)? Various views have been held. Isaiah 2:1 introduces a unit (2:2–4) that appears in almost identical form in the Book of Micah (Micah 4:1–4). But most troubling for some—especially proponents of a chronological arrangement—is the delayed appearance of what most regard as the call narrative of Isaiah, found in chapter 6 (cf. Jeremiah or Ezekiel). The problem is further complicated by the fact that this narrative, together with a longer prose section (7:1—8:22), appears to have been placed squarely in the middle of a section of text connected by the refrain "For all this his anger is not turned away, and his hand is stretched out still" (5:25; 9:12, 17, 21; 10:4) and a series of seven woe oracles (5:8, 11, 18, 20, 21, 22; 10:1).

Similar problems attend a closer examination of other subsections. The nations oracles section (chaps. 13—23) does contain distinct superscriptions for foreign powers: Babylon (13:1), Moab (15:1), Damascus (17:10), Egypt (19:1), the mysterious Wilderness of the Sea (21:1), and Tyre (23:1). Assyria appears to be subsumed under Babylon (14:24–27) and Philistia connected to the death of Ahaz (14:28–32); Persia (the Medes) plays the important role of bringing Babylon's reign of judgment to an end and appears in the context of that oracle (13:17–22). Yet the order of the nations is not entirely clear. And it would be wrong to classify the material as oracles *against* nations, since salvation can finally attend their fate (see especially Egypt and Assyria in 19:19–24); other sections of Isaiah, consistent with themes introduced here (18:7; 23:17–18), clearly envision the ultimate worship of Israel's God by foreign nations (esp. 2:1–5). Other oracles are also found here: concerning the Valley of Vision (22:1–14) and Shebna the steward (22:15–25). Should the following section (chaps. 24—27), which concerns a cosmic judgment, also be included with chapters 13—23? The answer turns in part on one's evaluation of the mysterious city mentioned at several points (24:10; 25:2; 27:10).

These and other questions arise when one attempts to probe the logic of reasonably distinct sections of the book. It is not clear, for example, whether chapters 28—35 represent a distinct unit in Isaiah, similar to chapters 1—12 or 13—27, or only heterogenous material loosely collected and placed between chapters 27 and 36. In favor of the former is the repeating phrase *hôy* found at the head of chapters 28; 29; 30; 31; 32 *(hēn);* and 33. What this repetition means in more precise terms, however, is not so clear. Moreover, since most regard the material in chapters 28—32 as rooted in Isaiah's own historical ministry, why have these oracles been separated by the nations oracles (chaps. 13—27) from other material closely associated with the historical prophet (e.g., chaps. 1—12)?

Until recently, chapters 36—39 were regarded as belonging in the first instance to the Books of Kings (II Kings 18:13—21:9) and only secondarily transferred to Isaiah, in order to form a conclusion to the "First Isaiah Book" (cf. Jeremiah 52). This view has been called into question for a variety of reasons, the most significant tied to the observation that chapters 36—39 play a clearly integral role in Isaiah, one that is all but unrecognizable in Kings: these chapters accomplish a transition from the Assyrian to the Babylonian period, thus introducing chapters 40—66. The curious order of chapters 36—37; 38; 39 is explicable in the context of Isaiah, but it finds more difficult explanation in Kings.

What can one say in conclusion? First, if there is an order to the Isaiah presentation, it is less than clear. This observation stands as a testimony to the fact that the Book of Isaiah—even in an edited form where one might expect coherence—has not lost the marks of tradition-historical development. Second, while it is possible to isolate groupings or subsections in the

9

larger book, it is not clear what relationship these have one to another. It is easier to identify developments that have taken place within the context of these smaller groupings, modifying and reshaping them as such; what this means for the larger structure of the book is more difficult to say. This does not exclude the possibility that one was meant to get some larger sense of the movement across individual sections, only that the primary context for editorial development remains the individual sections.

It might be helpful to find a fitting metaphor for the shaping process in the Book of Isaiah, and one that has been suggested is an orchestral score—with the one proviso that this is a piece of music with quite a few composers. In an orchestral score one can grasp certain key repeating themes that help unite the work and give it meaningful structure (Zion; the outstretched hand; God's plan of old; the "thorns and briers" motif). So too there are discrete developments and nonrecurring motifs that appear in the context of an individual movement alone (the reunification of Samaria and Judah). Not only does the opening chapter present us with a sort of overture, as has been frequently proposed, it also moves us ahead to one key episode in the larger book, involving the destiny of Zion. In so doing, it gives us an important clue as to an overarching concern of the many composers responsible for this work. We will have more to say about this concern and the structure of the larger book in the course of the commentary. I must admit that aspects of Keil's description of the larger movement of the book (made at an earlier period out of a different apologetic concern) seem not so farfetched. It is also clear that this movement is not chronological, even as it is concerned with events in history; nor is it strictly thematic, even as one can occasionally detect smaller groupings around one specific topic. When Clements described the Book of Isaiah as possessing one of "the most complex literary structures" in the canon, he had recognized an integral feature of the book in its present form (Clements, "Beyond Tradition-History," p. 98).

Historical Structure

10   Consistent with our interest in the present structure of the book, we will review historical factors as these play a specific role in the final form of First Isaiah (cf. Seitz, "Isaiah").

Superscription and Call

At 1:1 we learn that Isaiah prophesied to Judah and Jerusalem during the reigns of Uzziah, Jotham, Ahaz, and Hezekiah. Though debate continues about the proper dating system for biblical records, this general notice places Isaiah firmly in the eighth century, perhaps from around 740 to 700 B.C. The last significant historical event recorded in First Isaiah, the siege of Jerusalem (chaps. 36—37), took place in 701 B.C.

Several things are significant about the superscription. First, it grants to Isaiah an approximate forty-year career, analogous to that assumed by the Book of Jeremiah (Jer. 1:1–3) for the prophet Jeremiah (627–587 B.C.). A forty-year career for two of Israel's major prophets is consistent with the status they are finally accorded in the canon (Seitz, "The Prophet Moses"). Second, the notice was probably appended to the book after it had already reached mature form. Yet since Jotham is never mentioned and there is no explicit reference to preaching in the period of Uzziah but only the death of that king (6:1), it is puzzling why the superscription includes these two figures. This is especially problematic if one is prepared to accept chapter 6 as a call narrative of Isaiah; it is dated to the "year King Uzziah died" (6:1).

Frequently the suggestion has been made that the prophetic superscriptions were supplied by the Deuteronomistic Historian, so it would make sense to inquire what kind of significance this grouping of kings might have had in the Books of Kings. What is traceable to the reign of Uzziah of Judah (and Menahem of Israel) is the beginning of the Assyrian threat, in the person of Pul (Tiglath-pileser). When he "came against the land," King Menahem paid him one thousand talents of silver "that he might help him confirm his hold on the royal power" (II Kings 15:19). The Deuteronomistic Historian is interested in episodes of foreign alliance and traces the downfall of Judah and Israel in part to them. Israel's classical prophets are understood as having stood firm against such alliances (so Isa. 7:4–9). It is not surprising that, quite apart from its claim to historical fact, the superscription sees as coterminous the beginning of the prophetic career of Isaiah and the rise of the Assyrian threat to Israel, Judah, and Jerusalem. By modern reckoning, Tiglath-pileser's accession year was 744 B.C.

More difficult to determine is whether the Book of Isaiah

contains oracles that can be clearly dated to the reign of King Uzziah—or Jotham for that matter. If one follows a loose chronological model, then such oracles would precede chapter 6. This would in turn require that the call narrative be differently interpreted: as a critical prophetic commissioning episode. Such a move would also ease some of the strain on the very difficult command to the prophet to "make the mind of this people dull" (6:10), less theologically difficult if following upon a period of warning and exhortation (e.g., chap. 5). This option for interpretation will be discussed in detail in the commentary itself.

The Syro-Ephraimite Coalition (734–732 B.C.)

The Book of Isaiah is itself interested in two specific historical events: the attempt by the Northern Kingdom and Syria to force Ahaz of Judah to join their coalition (the Isaiah text at 7:1 refers to this more simply as an attack against Jerusalem) and the 701 B.C. invasion by Sennacherib of Assyria, during the reign of Hezekiah (also an assault on Jerusalem, see 36:1, 2, 15). The similarity of these two prose accounts (chaps. 7—8; 36—39) has been noted by scholars; it is of such a nature as to suggest direct editorial influence, in both directions, in order to draw out the contrast between Ahaz and Hezekiah.

We can assume from ancient Near Eastern records that the coalition of Rezin of Syria and Pekah of Samaria (Ephraim) was formed in order to ward off Assyrian hegemony and that together they sought to include, forcibly if necessary, Judah and King Ahaz. The Isaiah record, however, eliminates such complexities. Rezin and Pekah came to "attack" (7:1), to terrify, to conquer, and "make the son of Tabeel king" in Jerusalem (7:6). Ahaz refuses to trust in Isaiah's counsel (7:4–9), and in a stroke of irony, God delivers him anyway: through the agency of the king of Assyria (7:17). This same king will deliver Jerusalem from the hostile coalition, but at great cost (7:18–24). God will use this Assyrian king as an agent of judgment until he reaches up to the neck (8:8). Israel will have to endure his arrogant onslaughts until God himself intervenes (8:10; 10:12–19), and until that time Israel must face difficult hardships, conspiracy, and occasions of stumbling and testing (8:11–22). For the entire period following the Syro-Ephraimite war, Judah is overshadowed by Assyrian threat, through the reigns of Shalmaneser V (726–722 B.C.), Sargon II (721–705), and Sennacherib (704–681).

12

In 721 the Northern Kingdom falls to mighty Assyria, leaving only Judah and Jerusalem amidst the nations. Not long thereafter, in 715 B.C., King Ahaz dies (Isa. 14:28) and is succeeded by Hezekiah (715–687).

King Hezekiah and the 701 B.C. Debacle

Opinion is divided over the proper evaluation of Hezekiah's reign. On the one hand, one sees the clear contrast that has been established between him and his predecessor Ahaz. In chapters 36—37 we return to "the conduit of the upper pool on the highway to the Fuller's Field" (36:2), to the same fateful spot where Ahaz rejected the prophetic counsel (see 7:3), thereby unleashing the assault of Assyria and the nations. But here we see a king who responds in prayer and penitence (37:1–4, 14–21), who seeks prophetic counsel, and whose request and prayer are honored by the prophet Isaiah (37:21–35). Where before we saw the awesome might of Assyria unleashed, here we see a blasphemer thwarted, hunted down, and slain by his own sons (37:36–38), in fulfillment of the prophetic word there (8:9–10) and here (37:6–7). Chapter 38 continues the contrast by depicting Hezekiah as recipient of a prophetic sign (38:7; cf. 7:10–12), as near death but ultimately delivered. Indeed, the narrative appears to suggest that the royal house, when it stands firm in the promises to David, has the power to reverse a prophetic sentence of death and save the city through proper intercession (38:1–6).

At the same time, another view of Hezekiah has been put forward that relies on information from ancient Near Eastern historical sources and especially II Kings 18:14–16. The latter notice, which is strikingly absent from the otherwise synoptic account in Isaiah 36—37, has been granted objective historical status and set in contrast to the Isaiah account and the remainder of II Kings 18:17—19:37. It tells of a pre-siege payment by Hezekiah to Sennacherib and is customarily linked to the Annals of Sennacherib, which likewise depict a relatively obedient king of Judah (though with important divergences from II Kings 18:14–16). Such a view of Hezekiah, obedient vassal of Assyria, stands in considerable tension with the description just provided, based on chapters 36—38 of Isaiah. It would seem as though II Kings 18:14–16 and Isaiah 36—38 stand in irreducible tension over their respective evaluations of Hezekiah.

This tension is usually resolved when one views the Isaiah

13

tradition (and its counterpart in Kings) as a secondary theological interpretation of a core historical record. Still, one is left to wonder just how such a development, so at odds with the original tradition, could have taken place. Support for such a reconstruction is said to exist in other sections of Isaiah, especially in chapters 28—31, where condemnations of political alliances are clearly to be found (30:1–5, 15–17; 31:1–4). Yet it is striking that Hezekiah is never mentioned by name; rather, the text condemns various leaders and unnamed officials. Why is there no explicit mention of Hezekiah when at other points there is no reticence in naming King Ahaz? Finally, apart from its obvious criticism of the royal house in the person of Ahaz, the Book of Isaiah is remarkably free of antagonism toward the Davidic line (cf. Jeremiah 22 or Ezekiel 17) and indeed includes some of the most powerful rhetoric in support of kingship in the Old Testament—hence the interest in Isaiah from the side of the New Testament (see Isa. 9:2–8; 11:1–9; 32:1–8).

However one should interpret the Assyrian records (themselves hardly free from tendentiousness), it should be emphasized that, apart from the notice of II Kings 18:14–16, the biblical account is relentlessly positive in its assessment of King Hezekiah, both in Kings (II Kings 18:1–7) and in Chronicles (II Chronicles 29—32), but particularly in the Book of Isaiah. The contrast between Hezekiah and Ahaz forms one of the clearest theological structures in this otherwise complex literary presentation. Indeed, this contrast has urged not a few interpreters to regard the messianic oracle of 9:1–7, coming hard on the heels of the denunciation of Ahaz (7:9, 17), as directed toward the figure of Hezekiah. This in turn may have given rise to the interpretation of Immanuel (7:14) as a royal figure, if not Hezekiah himself—a reading otherwise troubled by chronological factors (Hezekiah appears already to have been born before the Syro-Ephraimite debacle).

The last recorded episode in First Isaiah concerns the visit of an envoy from Merodach-baladan (Marduk-apla-idinna), prince of Babylon (chap. 39). Most link his rebellious incursions into the region before Sennacherib's 701 B.C. invasion (chaps. 36—37), but in this final literary position the account prepares us for the transition to Second Isaiah chapters. The grim prophetic word foretells Babylonian exile, if not the end of the royal line itself (39:7). Not only does the chapter help link First Isaiah chapters to the later period of Babylonian exile presup-

14

posed by Second Isaiah, the reverse is also true: Second Isaiah chapters are linked back in time to the period of the historical Isaiah (the "former things"). Chapter 39 reminds the reader that, however mysteriously, Babylon was already at work within God's plan for Israel and the nations, when it was still far overshadowed by the Assyrian empire.

Theological Structure

Within the complex literary and historical presentation of the Book of Isaiah a certain theological structure and perspective begins to emerge. Twelve chapters (chaps. 1—12) precede the nations oracles section (chaps. 13—27) in which Israel and the house of David are put to the test, especially during the events of the Syro-Ephraimite crisis (chaps. 7—8). Ahaz, representative of the royal line, fails to trust in Isaiah's counsel and as a consequence Assyria is brought within Israel's borders, saving Judah from a Syro-Ephraimite assault but at the cost of the fall of the Northern Kingdom and, ultimately, with serious repercussions for Judah and Jerusalem itself. We have a fairly clear sense of this seriousness already in the opening chapters (chaps. 1—4). The hand that is stretched out against that part of the vineyard that is the house of Israel (5:7) "is stretched out still" (5:25) against Judah and the royal house (9:12, 17, 21), so that what was done to Samaria, Jerusalem can expect as well (10:11).

Yet also within the presentation of these chapters, Isaiah appears as prophet of both judgment and salvation (Ackroyd, "Presentation"). The judgment on Jerusalem will lead to ultimate cleansing and the worship of the nations (2:1-5). A doubting and cautious king will be replaced by one called "Wonderful Counselor" (9:6) who will establish and uphold the throne of David forever (9:7). Enmity between the Northern Kingdom and the Southern Kingdom will give way to unity and peace within the broader circle of nations (11:11-16), themselves gathered around the ensign of the root of Jesse (11:10). In that day, the only proper response will come in the form now provided in chapter 12: "You will say in that day: 'I will give thanks to you, O LORD' " (12:1).

On the other side of the nations oracles we confront another twelve-chapter complex (chaps. 28—39). The nations oracles depict the final worship of Israel's God by those who had challenged Yahweh's existence and sovereignty (chaps. 13—23). But before this time the nations, and Israel, must experience a cosmic scene of judgment reminiscent of the days of Noah (chaps. 24—27). This nations panorama remains the central panel in the larger Isaiah presentation, reminding the reader that God, having assigned for Assyria and the other nations a role vis-à-vis Israel, also envisions their final conversion and obedient worship in the company of his own people Israel.

Chapters 28—39 return to the present (historical) period of the prophet Isaiah. As in the initial section (chaps. 1—12), so too here foreign rapprochement is condemned as an attempt to replace trust in God with trust in military might or in a Zion theology unconditioned by personal faith. As in chapters 9 and 11, so here too we see a description of how Israel's royal house is to conduct itself (32:1–8), thus anticipating the final episodes where Hezekiah's deportment plays a critical role in saving the city. Chapters 33—35 envision the coming debacle and, within it, God's special attention to David (33:17) and Zion (33:20), the turning back of the nations (34:1–17), and the final return of his people (35:1–10). The final chapters (chaps. 36—38) describe Jerusalem's miraculous deliverance, the turning back of Assyria, and the proper deportment of the royal house, offering a clear contrast to the events of 734–732 and fulfilling Isaiah's word of salvation (8:9–10; 9:1–7).

The final chapter (chap. 39), about which we will have more to say in the commentary, presents a complex picture. It clearly depicts the coming Babylonian threat and the exile itself, but the degree to which Hezekiah is held responsible for these events is by no means clear (Ackroyd, "Babylonian Exile"). The Chronicler judges this to be a time of great testing for Hezekiah, to see how he would react to the prophetic word of judgment (II Chron. 32:31). In the Chronicler's eyes, Hezekiah passed this difficult test (32:32) and, like Josiah after him (II Kings 22:20), is therefore granted "peace and security" in his own lifetime (Isa. 39:8). He was able to postpone the Babylonian judgment, but God had yet a further purpose in mind for this foe from the north, his "consecrated ones" (Isa. 13:1–16).

It is clear that the final editors of First Isaiah have seen an important correlation between Assyria and Babylon and the events of 701 and 587. This probably explains why we hear of two great scenes of judgment (chaps. 24—27 and 33—34), the first linked to the more massively destructive events of 587, the

16

second anticipating the events of 701. But here one also sees the paradoxical nature of their relationship. For 701 events were the culmination of a wave of Assyrian destruction, a reaching up to the neck (8:8) that included the annexation of the Northern Kingdom and the destruction of Judah (36:1); but in the final episode, Assyria is turned back, decisively and at considerable cost. Even the mention of Esar-haddon reigning in Sennacherib's stead (37:38) is far overshadowed by the dramatic and final way in which the mighty Assyria falls before the angel of Yahweh (37:36).

If the 701 B.C. tradition (chaps. 36—38) ever formed the conclusion to First Isaiah, vindicating Isaiah's message of salvation, it has been transformed in the final form of the book to a powerful example of what the royal house can accomplish when a king like Hezekiah occupies the throne. In the final form of Isaiah, 701 B.C. traditions offer only a glimpse of the salvation finally to come after the 587 B.C. debacle. Isaiah's judgment tradition is extended beyond the destruction of the Northern Kingdom, beyond the destruction of Judah and a reaching to Zion's neck, to include even Zion itself (40:2; 49:14—55:13). The effect within First Isaiah is registered at those places where the deliverance of Zion is mentioned, but viewed as an act calling for further penitence and a new righteousness on the part of Judah and Jerusalem. The Book of Isaiah clearly opens on this note (chap. 1). It is also the note on which it closes (chaps. 56—66).

In sum, Isaiah is a book of paradoxical linkages: Isaiah is a prophet of salvation but also of judgment; Zion theology is the guarantor of God's presence but as much for cleansing judgment as for protection or benefaction; Ahaz's caution is contrasted with Hezekiah's bold intercession; the Syro-Ephraimite crisis gives way to 701 events, in turn giving way to the 587 denouement; Assyria is replaced by Babylon, who is finally defeated by Persia.

So why read the Book of Isaiah? Merely to see a record of past events, with little relationship to the present? The Book of Isaiah presents another option. Here we see quite clearly an effort made on theological grounds to catch the inner significance of historical events across the ages, from Isaiah's preaching in the days of Ahaz and Hezekiah, to the events of 587 B.C., and beyond. The choice is not between history or apocalypse, between seeing the book as relevant only for the past, or having

17

only to do with the reader's present. Rather, a series of crucial historical events are held up and linked together in order to demonstrate God's ways with Israel and the nations, as much for the present and the future as for the past. Hezekiah's example in the events of 701 B.C. is not remembered only to honor the dead but also to provide an example of righteous leadership for ages to come (11:1–9). God's judgment over the nations is meant to lead to their final worship and obedience, so that "nation shall not lift up sword against nation, neither shall they learn war any more" (2:4). Even past events of salvation are not opportunities for nostalgic memorializing but reminders only of the grace of God showered on an unworthy people (1:10), making possible new occasions of both grace and duty. The shapers of the Isaiah traditions have worked with one overwhelming conviction: that God's word to Israel in the past was uttered to instruct present and future generations. "It shall accomplish that which I purpose, and succeed in the thing for which I sent it" (55:11). We read the Book of Isaiah to see how that purpose was accomplished, in order to know better how and where God's word shall speak to our own day and thereby finally accomplish that purpose for which it was sent.

PART ONE

The Presentation of Isaiah: Word and Prophet

Isaiah 1—12

Overview

Before examining individual passages and commenting upon them, we will first look at the broader structural organization of larger sections in Isaiah, beginning with chapters 1—12. We will follow a similar procedure with other major sections in the book (chaps. 13—23; 24—27; 28—35; and 36—39). Recently much interest has been shown in the unity of the Book of Isaiah. We are interested in a related question: Does the text in its present organization provide clues for the exegesis of individual passages? This is more a question of simple coherence than one of unity. Is the text in its present shape meaningful? Is the text's coherence to be sought primarily on the basis of historical reconstruction, whereby an individual pericope is placed within a setting in past history and then related to the present; or can an individual text be illumined by attention to the broader context in which it is found? As we shall see, if the answer to this last question is positive, then we have our work cut out for us. For if the larger structure of the text manifests a coherence extending beyond individual passages, read against a reconstructed historical backdrop, then that coherence is also quite elusive and requires a careful reading to be properly appreciated.

Introduction

19

It has often struck me as unfortunate that those who put the final touches on the biblical books did not supply us with a key as to how they were to be read: a kind of preface or instruction sheet, as it were. Presumably the final editors were also the first readers. The only keys available, however, have been supplied after the fact, in the form of midrash, New Testament interpretations, or in the ancient and modern commentary tradition. These various aids are of course based on clues provided in the text itself, though also with strong external principles that encourage certain types of reading (pedagogical; legal; christological; historical). At the same time, it is probably also of significance that such keys or instruction sheets have *not* been supplied within the presentation of the books themselves, in such an explicit sense. Apparently they were not seen as necessary for at least some portion of readership.

In the recent period one principal guide to interpretation has been based on a biographical model. This has been particularly true for the prophetic books. The interpreter seeks to understand the person of the prophet, the times in which he lived, and the end to which his prophetic activity was directed. The theological justification for this is clear: the prophets were inspired persons, and the closer one gets to the person of the prophet, the closer one stands to the revelation vouchsafed to him.

It became a commonplace in the last century to nuance this view of prophetic inspiration considerably in order to allow for the inspired activity of other forces at work in the making of a prophetic book. Due allowance was made for the derivative and at times contradictory nature of secondary inspiration, but on the whole this broader view of prophecy and prophetic books gained acceptance, in no small part because it seemed to be based directly on the evidence of prophetic books themselves. At several points we are able to glimpse in the biblical text clues as to how the original words of the prophet were transformed and reshaped—a process itself based on the conviction that the prophetic word had a vitality and relevance that outlived its own originating circumstances. A classic text in this regard is Jeremiah 36. The prophet's preaching is committed to writing, with the assistance of Baruch; after it is arrogantly destroyed by King Jehoiakim, the scroll is reconstituted by Baruch. Then we are told that "many similar words were added" to the words of the prophet Jeremiah (Jer. 36:32). So too the Book of Isaiah makes reference to the *process* of inspiration and the afterlife of the prophetic word, beyond the circumstances of its delivery (8:16–22; 29:11–12; 30:8). Unfortunately these various references in the prophetic books are random and, taken together, hardly form a comprehensive picture.

Prophetic Agency

It is no accident that in the Introduction a section on the life of the prophet was not provided. This is not because such a life, at least in some cursory form, is incapable of reconstruction from the Book of Isaiah itself; the evidence of commentary writing in this century clearly contradicts such an assertion. Rather, its omission is meant to signal the kind of proportion that interest in the person of the prophet is given by the Book of Isaiah itself. What does it mean, for example, that the book does not open with a call narrative of the prophet Isaiah? Instead, the reader must wait until the sixth chapter for the prophet to step boldly into view, and even here it is not clear that the chapter should be designated a call narrative in the same sense in which the opening chapters of Hosea, Jeremiah, or Ezekiel function.

In an intriguing study entitled *Pseudonymity and Canon,* David Meade has argued persuasively that matters of authorship, inspiration, and proprietary claim to "copyright" were handled much differently in antiquity than we might expect. The prophetic word was always at one remove from the prophet who uttered it; instead, it remained the "spiritual possession" of the one who inspired it, namely, Israel's God. As such it was capable of extension and reapplication, consistent with its own inherent authority and independence. Meade uses the Book of Isaiah as a classic example of this phenomenon, thus explaining in part how the massive extension of the message of Isaiah was accomplished and how the theological justification for "later additions" functioned. As noted above, this notion of the independent authority of the word of God is especially prominent in the Isaiah tradition (see the reference to the divine word going forth to "accomplish that which I purpose" at Isa. 55:11).

One might say that Meade has chosen the best example in the Book of Isaiah for his thesis. Other contrasting notions of the centrality of prophetic agency can be seen in the prophetic corpus. The Book of Jeremiah, for example, has developed into its present form with an explicit interest in the prophetic persona; one thinks of the laments of Jeremiah, the "biographical" narratives found especially in chapters 37—45, the figure of Baruch, the genuine interest in dates and specific events in history. Ezekiel and Hosea also come to mind, if not also Amos. In these books the final editors are clearly concerned with the biographical and the sociohistorical reality of prophetic agency in a way that can be contrasted with what we see in the Book of Isaiah.

This is not to say that the figure of Isaiah plays no role whatsoever. Peter Ackroyd has probed this dimension of the Isaiah tradition, specifically in chapters 1—12, in his essay "Isaiah I—XII: Presentation of a Prophet." The allusion to his essay in the title of this section is not accidental; neither is the slight modification we have proposed. Ackroyd is not so much interested in the historical prophet, even as "the Isaiah of that historic period . . . stands behind the message" (p. 45); rather, he is interested in the prophet *as he has been presented to us:* "Whether the prophet himself or his exegetes were responsible, the prophet appears to us as a man of judgement and salvation" (p. 45).

We will have occasion to look more closely at Ackroyd's actual reconstruction of the presentation of Isaiah in due course. What is of more interest at this juncture is the point that both Ackroyd and Meade wish to make about the presentation of the prophet specifically in the Book of Isaiah. Isaiah is less a prophet who presents himself to us than he is a prophet who has been presented by others to us. Prophetic agency in delivering the word of God is less central than the word of God itself and that word's own presentation of the prophet Isaiah. Here we may also find an explanation of why the book does not open with a call narrative of the prophet.

Isaiah 1—4: The Presentation of Word and Prophet

It would be more accurate to talk about Isaiah 1—12, the opening section of the Book of Isaiah, as concerned with the presentation of Isaiah's word as well as his person. This is made clear in the opening four chapters. We mentioned in the Introduction several sticking points that frustrate a clear interpretation of the structure of these opening twelve chapters: (1) two superscriptions (1:1; 2:1); (2) delayed call narrative (chap. 6); (3) interruption of two series of refrains (woe: 5:8, 11, 18, 20, 21, 22; 10:1; outstretched hand: 5:25; 9:12, 17, 21; 10:4); and (4) Isa. 2:1–4 paralleled in Micah 4:1–4. Other structural problems could be mentioned as well.

When one moves to the area of content and interpretation, these problems are compounded: Are all three children the prophet's (7:3; 7:14; 8:1–4)? Are the sign names positive or negative? Are the messianic oracles (9:1–7; 11:1–9) directed to historical or eschatological figures? Are they birth or accession oracles? Trying to assign oracles in these opening twelve chapters to specific historical periods is a daunting task, with practically every period having been suggested for the material in chapters 1—4 alone. If one considers it likely that Isaiah's historical preaching has been placed in a new framework of interpretation, then the historical problem is not so much solved as relativized. New questions arise. How are we to interpret even a secondary presentation of the prophet's word and person?

I will make the following provisional suggestions, aware that they are proposals only and ones that follow from a certain working perspective on the Book of Isaiah. In this perspective, the prophet's word and person have been abstracted from straightforward historical presentation (namely, the chronological unfolding of the prophet's career) and have been placed in another framework meaningful to later readers and interpreters. The opening chapter is not so much an overture of the contents of the Book of Isaiah in its entirety as it is a summary recapitulation of Isaiah's vision relevant to the period mentioned at 1:1. Indeed, with the only clearly "historical" reference occurring at 1:7–9, concerning Zion's besieged but surviving existence, it is difficult to avoid the impression that the opening chapter summarizes Isaiah's preaching from the perspective of the 701 B.C. deliverance—or better, from a penitential perspective following upon that deliverance. That is, the opening chapter directs us just beyond the latest period of the historical Isaiah's preaching, such as can be found now in chapters 36—39.

The superscription at 2:1 attributes the oracle that follows (2:2–4) to the prophet Isaiah (so Ackroyd) and in so doing insists that Isaiah's message was one of ultimate salvation and the worship of the nations (2:1–5) as well as one essentially of judgment and exhortation (1:1–31). A statement is not so much

23

being made about the Isaianic authorship of 2:2–5, as, say, against Micah authorship (contra Ackroyd), as there is a concern to spell out the widest range for Isaiah's preaching from the perspective of those shaping his message for posterity. In sum, we are arguing that the superscriptions found in 1:1 and 2:1 pertain to the material that follows them and specifically to that material. On the other hand, because 1:2–31 offers a summarizing statement of the prophet Isaiah's message in the form of a comprehensive vision, 1:1 also functions as a superscription for the entire book. What 1:1 states, however, is less a matter of authorship or proprietary claims made on behalf of Isaiah than it is a statement of belief, made on the part of those who shaped the Isaiah traditions, that what followed was a faithful rendering of the essence of Isaiah's preaching as vouchsafed to him by God.

The distinction is subtle, but it allows for the extension of Isaiah's message into the present textualized form, at the same time acknowledging important theological realities concerning continuity with Isaiah's preaching and the faithful representation of the word of God. Did Isaiah actually deliver the speech recorded in 1:2–31? This is impossible to determine with historical tools alone, standing outside the book's own presentation. Does the book present Isaiah as having delivered 1:2–31? Yes, though not with all the notions attending authorship and "copyright" familiar in the modern period. Here the observations of Meade are telling. The "vision" of chapter 1 remains the normative entry point for the Book of Isaiah, and because it is represented as a divine word (1:2), it also stands over the prophet Isaiah. It is not his "spiritual possession" but a divine word summarizing his historical preaching. We would also argue that it is meant to summarize that preaching from a very specific vantage point, namely, following the deliverance of Jerusalem in 701 B.C. See more on this below.

The next major section of Isaiah (2:6—4:6) is held together by the refrain "in that day" and a perspective directed toward the future. In the latter sense it shares something of the same perspective of 2:1–5. However, only the closing section (4:1–6) recapitulates the tone and content of 2:1–5; the rest of this complex is concerned with a coming day that will lay bare the sins of Judah and Jerusalem, and where the nation will encounter the terrifying glory of the Lord. The opening four chapters, then, present the divine word as a sort of "chiaroscuro by which the prospect of the future is set out against the background of failure and doom" (Ackroyd, "Presentation," p. 45). The future will be marked by salvation only after a cleansing "by a spirit of judgment and by a spirit of burning" (4:4). A vision for the future is set forth using a recapitulation of the prophet's historical preaching, based on the latest period of his activity (1:2–31). Marvin Sweeney has summarized the message of chapters 2—4 as concerned with "the cleansing and restoration of Jerusalem and Judah so that Zion can serve as YHWH's capital for ruling the entire world" (Sweeney, *Isaiah 1—4,* p. 134). This broader editorial perspective is based on a recapitulation of Isaiah's preaching during the reign of four Judahite kings, but it also ranges far beyond that preaching. This is the perspective that confronts the reader not just of First Isaiah but also of the wider book of sixty-six chapters. It is telling that the presentation of Isaiah 1—12 begins with a presentation of the prophet's word rather than with a presentation of the prophet as such. For that, we must wait until chapter 6.

Isaiah 5:1–30

Apart from the usual historical-critical argumentation, one can also detect several strong contextual reasons for interpreting chapter 5 as the historical proclamation of Isaiah, if not also the starting point of that proclamation in the presentation of chapters 1—12. In chapters 1—4 the focus remains on Judah and Jerusalem (1:1; 2:1; 3:1, 8) or Zion and Jerusalem (2:3; 3:16, 17; 4:3–6), a perspective that makes particular historical sense not just during the exile or in the postexilic period (Sweeney) but also following the fall of Israel in 721 B.C. The image of the vineyard is introduced in 1:8, yet it is a vineyard in which Zion alone remains "like a booth in a vineyard, like a shelter in a cucumber field, like a besieged city." So we stand somewhere after both the fall of the Northern Kingdom and the 701 assault on Judah and Jerusalem.

In the Song of the Vineyard, with which chapter 5 opens (5:1–7), the fate of the vineyard still hangs in the balance, even as a final decision of judgment is rendered (5:5–6). Explicit reference is made to the house of Israel as "the vineyard of the LORD of hosts" (5:7) and Judah, perhaps more narrowly, as "his pleasant planting." The "in that day" perspective of chapters 2—4 gives way to present indictment, as the woe refrain already mentioned is taken up (5:8, 11, 18, 20, 21, 22).

Is it possible to date the material more specifically? Several

25

factors taken together suggest that chapter 5 was intended to be read as pre-Uzziah-period proclamation, with a specific focus on the Northern Kingdom. Again it is helpful to examine the historical perspective, not of modern reconstruction, but of Israel's own records, namely, those found in II Kings.

Prior to any mention of the death of Uzziah (II Kings 15:32), we hear of Tiglath-pileser annexing portions of the Northern Kingdom and carrying their population "captive to Assyria" (II Kings 15:29). This occurs during the reign of Pekah king of Israel. Reference to the Syro-Ephraimite pact between Pekah and Rezin, and the assault on Jerusalem (Isaiah 7—8), does not appear until II Kings 16:5. Here, then, we find confirmation of the specific reference to exile given at Isa. 5:13 and the wider description of judgment. In very broad terms, the presentation of Isaiah at this juncture conforms to the perspective of the Deuteronomistic History. That the fate of the Northern Kingdom was meant to be a warning to Judah/Jerusalem is a theme shared again by that History (II Kings 17) and the Book of Isaiah (Isa. 10:10–11). Also held in common is the notion of a gradual assault by God on the sinful Israel, beginning with the Northern Kingdom, then extending to Judah, and finally culminating at Zion's neck (II Kings 17:18–23). Here we find an explanation of why the theme of the outstretched hand (5:25) is introduced prior to chapter 6, separated from identical references after chapter 8. God raised a signal for Assyria (5:26–30) before the Syro-Ephraimite debacle and before Isaiah's specific commissioning "in the year that King Uzziah died." His anger was first turned against the Northern Kingdom. And it is stretched out still (5:25).

Isaiah 6:1—9:7

Attempts have been made since the time of Karl Budde (1928), or Bernhard Duhm before him (1892), to see within these chapters elements of a first-person memoir going back to the prophet himself. If such a memoir once existed, it has been all but obliterated in the final presentation of the material. First-person elements are now "very spasmodic and partial" (Clements, "Immanuel," p. 227), and the function of the chapters in their present form is now far removed from that of a memoir. Even the notion that chapter 6 represents a call narrative of Isaiah is not without its problems; we have referred to

26

these in the Introduction. Moreover, it is difficult to link the first-person reporting of 6:1–13 with that which is found in chapters 7 and 8.

We suggested above the strong possibility that the placement of chapter 6 within the presentation of chapters 1—12 was not accidental but was undertaken so that the word of God, in more comprehensive form, might provide the broader context in which to understand the depiction of the prophet and biographical aspects of his activity. We have also referred to chronological aspects of the presentation of chapters 1—12 that speak in favor of interpreting chapter 5 as divine speech delivered prior to the death of Uzziah and the episode depicted in chapter 6.

Features within chapter 6 confirm such an interpretation. Most telling in this regard is the objection of the prophet (6:5). The prophet exclaims that he is a man of unclean lips dwelling in the midst of a people of unclean lips. To be sure, an element of this confession is predicated on the fact that the prophet recognizes himself as having been transported to the divine realm, where his eyes see "the King, the LORD of hosts." But just as surely, the confession is a statement of simple fact. That Isaiah dwells in the midst of an unclean people is confirmed by the testimony of chapter 5. Even the prophet's ejaculation "Woe is me!" recalls the sixfold woe refrain found there.

This interpretation also eases some of the theological strain on the commission to Isaiah to "make hearts fat" (6:10, RSV). There had already been a period of prophetic warning. The time had come for the mature deliberation of the divine council to be shared with Isaiah. Here, however, the concern seems pastoral and specifically connected with the prophetic office. Isaiah leaves the divine council preaching warning and exhortation, not smug announcements of doom (see chap. 7). But he knows that refusals to hear are not indications of the vanity of his preaching or the impotence of his God but that they are, rather, signs of the extent of Israel's deafness and the accuracy of the divine diagnosis. The prophet also learns the time frame for the message of judgment. This involves a massive judgment, the survival of a tenth, and the further burning of that tenth, until only a holy seed is left (6:13). Once again, the graded character of the judgment is made clear, consistent with the image of the hand that "is stretched out still" (5:25; 9:12, 17, 21; 10:4). If the language of 6:13 were to be more specifically inter-

27

preted, we would take the massive destruction to refer to the fall of Israel, the tenth remaining and then burned to refer to Judah, and the final remnant, "the holy seed," as the survivors in Jerusalem following the 701 assault. Confirmation of this interpretation will require further substantiation in the commentary and in our treatment of chapters 36—39.

Chapter 7 opens with a notice resembling that of the Deuteronomistic History (II Kings 16:5) which moves the presentation directly ahead to the crisis of 734–732. Also in the manner of Kings, Isaiah 7:1 indicates the final outcome of the crisis from Jerusalem's perspective: "but [they] could not mount an attack against it." King Ahaz is on the throne, but a more specific date is not provided. The chapter wishes to do more than record history. Instead, in Ahaz we see a rather egregious example of the refusal to hear (7:1–9) and see (7:12), as the prophet had been warned (6:10), all the more critical because Ahaz represents the house of David to whom special promises had been made. The three sign-name children (7:3; 7:14; 8:1), rather than serving as vouchers of God's deliverance in the Syro-Ephraimite crisis, become instead paradoxical signs (8:18), due to the refusal of Ahaz and "this people" (8:6) to accept God's word of promise (7:7–9). Assyria delivers Judah-Jerusalem from the Syro-Ephraimite threat but with a dark proviso: that of becoming the rod of God's fury against his own people. What deliverance Israel can now expect will follow only after the Assyrian assault (8:9–10) and a period of stumbling and testing (8:11–22). Only then will the oppressor be broken and Israel ruled by one worthy to claim the throne (9:1–7), in absolute contrast to Ahaz.

Isaiah 9:8—11:16

With this vision of future rule adumbrated, we then return to the chronological setting reminiscent of chapter 5. Explicit mention is made of the fate of the Northern Kingdom (Israel, Samaria, Ephraim) as the adversaries of Rezin (9:11) are raised up against them and Israel is slowly devoured (9:12). Yahweh's hand continues stretched out against Israel (9:12) until it is cut off "head and tail" (9:14). In the midst of their destruction they strike out, their own people devouring one another: "Manasseh devoured Ephraim, and Ephraim Manasseh, and together they were against Judah" (9:21). Here we have clear reference to the Syro-Ephraimite intrigue.

In the next strophes (10:1–11), the fate of Judah-Jerusalem at the hands of Assyria, "the rod of my anger" (10:5), finds expression as Jerusalem is threatened with worse treatment than Samaria received (10:11). Yet precisely in the midst of such hubris, God draws a line on the mission of destruction he has decreed for Assyria (10:12–19). God will send a "wasting sickness among his stout warriors" (10:16), leaving a remnant so small "that a child can write them down" (10:19). Do we have here clear reference to the record of Assyrian defeat in 701 B.C., now found in Isaiah 36—37? The chapter closes with a vision of reunion and a promise of Assyrian defeat (10:20–27) as the Assyrian march against the daughter Zion is halted. "The lofty will be brought low" (10:33).

Chapter 11 then begins with a messianic oracle reminiscent of 9:1–7, even more expansive in its vision of coming peace and natural harmony. This "root of Jesse" will stand as an ensign to the dispersed of Israel, wherever they are found. Enmity between Ephraim and Judah will end as the nation is again reunited with its lost people and with itself (11:12–16).

Isaiah 12:1–6

This chapter is best understood as a hymn of thanksgiving. It clearly brings to completion the themes of reunion and messianic peace articulated in the previous chapter as it speaks of divine forgiveness and comfort. What was not said in the Syro-Ephraimite crisis is now proclaimed boldly: "I will trust [in God], and not be afraid" (cf. 7:4–9 and 12:2). The hymn then gives way to expressions of pure joy and thanksgiving (12:3–6). On this note, the presentation of Isaiah, word and prophet, comes to a close. What follows (chaps. 13—23) is an extended treatment of the nations theme, as this was briefly alluded to in 11:12–16.

Conclusion

Several distinct conclusions can be drawn from this structural overview of Isaiah 1—12. Chief among them is the overriding sense that the presentation of these twelve chapters has a coherence and significance that is the result of conscious editorial efforts. The historical preaching of the prophet Isaiah has been secondarily interpreted and presented in a new literary format.

29

Historical Structure

There is little evidence in chapters 5—12 of late, postexilic interpretation. The isolated instances (11:11) establish the general principle. On the other hand, one can see a conscious effort to relate the preaching of Isaiah during the Syro-Ephraimite crisis to the later events of Assyrian hegemony in the region, and especially the 701 assault on Jerusalem by Sennacherib. That assault, and its signal failure, underlie much of the text's concern to set a specific limit to Assyria's role as instrument of judgment. One also sees clear evidence that following that deliverance—which stood in such contrast to the events of 734–732—distinct hopes were expressed for the reunification of Israel and the return of the dispersed. What Assyria had begun even before the Syro-Ephraimite debacle, our text affirms will be reversed in equal measure. Assyria will only "shake his fist" at Zion; finally, all Israel will be restored.

On the other hand, the opening chapters present the deliverance of 701 B.C. and its abiding significance rather differently. Chapter 1 sees the deliverance as cause for repentance and change of heart. Only then will Jerusalem be called "the city of righteousness, the faithful city" (1:26). These two theological perspectives need not stand in opposition. But it is significant to note that the book opens, not with the visions of reunification and the limiting of Assyria, but with somber calls for repentance and obedience (1:20). Israel can refuse such calls, but with the same dire consequences as they experienced in the aftermath of the Syro-Ephraimite crisis.

It is on the basis of this somber introduction that chapters 2—4 have developed their own vision of pending judgment, "in that day." Here we may well have evidence of a later exilic (Babylonian) redaction that has adapted the penitential side of Isaiah's proclamation to the events of 587 B.C. and their aftermath. For then Zion was not just left as a booth in a vineyard; it was overrun completely. The vision of hope that chapters 1—4 finally embrace will take effect only after this later judgment and burning (4:2–6).

Theological Structure

30

The opening chapters (chaps. 1—4) certainly set the tone for what follows (chaps. 5—12). Visions of restoration and an end to Assyrian domination following the 701 deliverance can only be seen as provisional, now to be interpreted within the context of the vision of restoration found in these opening chapters. So too the historical experience of Israel, Judah, and Jerusalem during the Assyrian period—in terms both of judgment and of salvation—functions as a type for Israel's later experience in the Babylonian period. If the first royal oracle (9:1–7) has been presented in such a way as to point to Hezekiah and the deliverance accomplished in his day, the second oracle (11:1–9) looks even farther ahead. As such, it remains an eschatological statement in the book and functions together with visions such as are found in 2:1–5 to adumbrate the intention of God beyond the events of 701 and 587. Visions of restoration not fully fulfilled after 701 likewise retain an eschatological force.

If this is true, it is clear why the Book of Isaiah continued to call for new readings after the lifetime of the prophet. The visions of judgment and restoration remained so profound that they continued to call forth new interpretations in the light of later events. This must have been especially true of the latter. Israel continued to look for the fulfillment of Isaiah's vision of restoration, so eloquently stated in the presentation of chapters 1—12, long after Isaiah had himself passed from view. His message belonged not to himself but remained the "spiritual possession" both of God and of the generations who continued to look to him to fulfill this former vision of restoration and commonweal.

Isaiah 1:1–31
Like a Booth in a Vineyard

The opening superscription (1:1) makes clear that the Book of Isaiah will maintain a specific focus on Judah and Jerusalem, within the larger nation of Israel. So too the range of Isaiah's prophetic activity is stated with reference to Judah's kings. This perspective dominates the presentation that follows and is particularly germane in the opening chapter. Even where the larger book displays an interest in Israel and speaks of its wider reunification, these hopes are articulated with reference to Judah and Jerusalem. Another way of stating this is that Isaiah is fundamentally concerned with institutions, or theological

31

perspectives, that are rooted in the Southern Kingdom: namely, kingship and Zion.

Previous study has spoken of Zion theology and royal theology as the two central traditions that affect the prophetic activity of Isaiah. Whatever they may mean in the abstract, they are used in a specific and individual way by the prophet Isaiah. In both cases, the responsibilities—not the prerogatives—attending God's election of Zion and choice of David come to the fore in the prophet Isaiah's handling of these traditions. Zion and David are expected to fill certain roles that nurture and sustain the life of Israel. By the same token, Zion's righteous deportment remains the responsibility of the king and the people. It stands as a concrete symbol of God's presence. Yet if the citizens of Zion deal corruptly, that presence is transformed into a judging and cleansing fire. Election comes with a special cost, not just with a special benefaction. Nowhere is this theme stated more clearly than in the opening chapter.

One matter is made particularly clear in the opening chapter. A rebellion has already taken place (1:2); the nation is sinful and utterly estranged (1:4) even as the book opens. Moreover, they have already received punishment for their corrupt dealings. Verse 5 questions why the nation would choose yet more punishment and then describes the present condition as "bruises and sores and bleeding wounds" (1:6). In quite explicit terms the next verse depicts military invasion and desolation: cities are burned, aliens inhabit the land and devour it. Only Zion is left. It too might have been destroyed and become like Sodom and Gomorrah, had God not left a few survivors (1:8–9). This description follows so closely the events leading up to 701, when Assyria ravaged the Judahite countryside until only Jerusalem was left (36:1), that the logic of a setting in this period would seem clear. Whether we stand before or after Jerusalem's deliverance has been debated, much of the question hanging on the depiction of religious rites in the following verses (1:10–17). Some argue that the seemingly routinized nature of the worship points to a period of peace, others that such elaborate practices were relevant—even as they are condemned by Isaiah—precisely in times of crisis. It is not clear that this criterion alone can decide the issue.

One feature of the text, especially in verses 10–26, that is frequently overlooked involves those to whom the indictment is directed. In 1:2–9 the people of Israel in general are addressed. In 1:10, however, the "rulers of Sodom" are specifically addressed as one segment of the broader population. So too, 1:23 singles out the "princes" as rebels, as failing to defend the fatherless and the widow—an indictment that seemed more general in 1:16*d*–17: "cease to do evil, learn to do good; seek justice, rescue the oppressed, defend the orphan, plead for the widow." And finally, when God speaks of cleansing judgment in verses 24–26, he has in mind the restoration of just leadership: "I will restore your judges as at the first, and your counselors as at the beginning" (1:26). It is clear that within the broader indictment God takes a particular interest in the leadership: how it has failed to defend the powerless and replaced righteousness with murder (1:21); how the "silver" of the nation has become dross (1:22) that must be smelted away (1:25).

In attempting to understand the setting and the occasion of the indictment, which might properly be called a lawsuit on the basis of the opening summons to witnesses (1:2), one other feature of the text is frequently overlooked. Are there not linkages with the description of assault and deliverance now found in chapters 36—37? Most telling in this regard is the sign oracle given by Isaiah prior to the turning back of Sennacherib (37:30–32). There we hear of a "surviving remnant of the house of Judah" and a band of survivors from Jerusalem who shall "take root downward, and bear fruit upward" (37:31–32). This remnant shall go forth out of Mount Zion, for the "zeal of the LORD of hosts will do this." Isaiah 1:9 sounds like a confession linked to this promise: "If the LORD of hosts had not left us a few survivors, we would have been like Sodom, and become like Gomorrah." Precisely because it follows so hard on the heels of this confession, the sharpness of the next verse is doubly underscored: "Hear the word of the LORD, you rulers of Sodom!" The survivors of 701 B.C. were to have been a remnant that took root downward and looked back on the deliverance with thanksgiving and sobered wills. They were to have planted vineyards and eaten their fruit, a mere three years after the destruction of Judah (37:30). But now that promise must be predicated: "If you are willing and obedient, you shall eat the good of the land" (1:19). And more telling: "If you refuse and rebel, you shall be devoured by the sword" (1:20).

As to the indictment directed against the leadership, there are also hints of a link to the depiction of chapters 36—38. Verse 21 looks back on a "faithful city" in which righteousness once

33

lodged, that was once "full of justice." Are these just nostalgic reminiscenses of a bygone day, or can the references to righteousness, justice, and faith have a more specific intention, namely, to recall the correct deportment of King Hezekiah? Righteousness did once lodge in Jerusalem, in the person of King Hezekiah, whose prayer saved the city from disaster (37:21). In the highly parabolic passage that follows the account of Jerusalem's deliverance, accomplished "for my own sake and for the sake of my servant David" (37:35), Hezekiah falls deadly ill (38:1). Yet he prays again for deliverance, asking God to remember "how I have walked before you in faithfulness" (38:3). God hears the prayer of Hezekiah and reverses a sentence of death, for him and the city (38:6).

Where once there was righteousness, in the person of Hezekiah, now there are murderers (1:21). It is not necessary to press the historical argument in favor of a post-701 setting any further. We prefer instead to work with the clues provided in the text itself and with the larger literary context of the Book of Isaiah. But it should come as no surprise to learn from the Deuteronomistic History that the years following the death of Hezekiah proved to be the nadir of Judah's existence (II Kings 21). That such a swift movement from righteousness to murder, from justice to bribery, from silver to dross could have taken place so soon after the deliverance of 701 is staggering—but the record of Kings is clear. There we see the transition from a king who is regarded without equal for trust in God (II Kings 18:5) to one who is without equal for the evil he seduced Judah into committing, worse even than the nations (II Kings 21:9). In this regard, it is interesting to read the enumeration of crimes in Isaiah 1 against the witness of II Kings 21, where we hear of hands full of blood (Isa. 1:15; II Kings 21:6, 16), of futile offerings (Isa. 1:13; II Kings 21:5), and of murderers (Isa. 1:21; II Kings 21:16). Who knows but that Manasseh's name was chosen as an expression of hope for the return of the Northern Kingdom, a hope clearly articulated in Isaiah 11. If this was the case, those hopes were quickly dashed.

Following the long indictment in 1:2–23, Isaiah's sentence of judgment comes in 1:24–26. The wrath of God that was meant to protect Zion from all assaults (Ps. 2:5) is here turned against his own people (1:25): "I will turn my hand against you; I will smelt away your dross as with lye." Only then, afterward, will Zion again be called the faithful city. The sentence of judgment at II Kings 21:12–13 is similar in intensity, if not also in content: "I am bringing upon Jerusalem and Judah [note the pairing!] such evil that the ears of everyone who hears of it will tingle. . . . I will wipe Jerusalem as one wipes a dish, wiping it and turning it upside down." The Isaiah text goes on (1:27–31) to tell of the possibility of redemption for those who repent; but for those who forsake God, there will be eternal punishment "with no one to quench them" (1:31).

The Book of Isaiah ends on a similar note of warning (66:24). It is interesting that there the same language is used as that which appears when God destroys the Assyrians in 701: "And they shall go out and look at the dead bodies of the people who have rebelled against me" (cf. also Isa. 37:36). This is precisely the force of Isaiah's judgment oracle in the opening chapter: the punishment God had reserved for his foes he now unleashes against his own people (1:24–25). In the eyes of the Deuteronomistic Historian, Manasseh did more evil to Israel than the nations (II Kings 21:9), thus leading to the same final treatment for Judah and Jerusalem that Assyria had received in 701 B.C. During the reign of Manasseh, Judah became like the nations, and as a consequence God determined to treat it as such. The very Zion theology that had served to protect Israel was turned against them, so "utterly estranged" (1:4) had they become. The indictment opened with the image of rebellious children (1:2) and of a nation that no longer recognized its master (1:3). It ends with that nation becoming unrecognizable, one with the other nations, and receiving the treatment reserved for them. The only hope held out is for those who repent (1:27). Their righteousness will not be overlooked by the One who is righteousness itself.

At the beginning we spoke of Isaiah's use of Zion and royal theology. The former is evidenced in chapter 1. Yet the chapter also is interested in more than the restoration of Zion, narrowly defined. Murderers and dross are also to be replaced by righteous judges and counselors (1:26). If it is appropriate to read Isaiah 1 against the backdrop of II Kings 21 and the aftermath of 701 B.C., as is being proposed, then the chapter is clearly pressing for a proper understanding of royal theology as well. Are the leadership offices that are enumerated at 1:26 meant to be interpreted as a rejection of kingship and as a return to the judges and counselors of old, as in the days of Samuel? This is impossible to determine. The chapter does not single out the

35

king for special condemnation, however closely it is to be read against the backdrop of II Kings 21. The leadership in general is indicted ("rulers"; "princes"); so too in the language of restoration, more general terms occur ("judges"; "counselors"). Chapter 1 cannot be used to argue for a rejection of kingship, as such, in favor of another form of government. Something of the same ambivalence can be seen in the Deuteronomistic History, which depicts the end of Davidic kingship but never holds out for its absolute dissolution (see II Kings 25:27–30). Afterward Zion will be called the city of righteousness, the faithful city. Will a new David rule in it? The text does not say; only that those who repent will be redeemed. On this note of warning and foreboding, the opening chapter draws to a close.

A final word is in order concerning the present form of the superscription at 1:1. Chapter 1 has been interpreted against the historical backdrop of post-701 Judah and the abysmal reign of King Manasseh. Yet Isaiah's prophetic activity is clearly associated with the reigns of Uzziah, Jotham, Ahaz, and Hezekiah. How does this historical notice square with our interpretation of the setting of the opening chapter of Isaiah? Related to this question is a broader form-critical issue concerning how the superscription at 1:1 is to be related to other superscriptions in the book (2:1; 13:1) and whether 1:1 refers to the entire Book of Isaiah or to just chapter 1.

Also relevant in this matter is the specific language used in 1:1, which describes what follows as a vision *(ḥāzôn)* that the prophet saw. This terminology is somewhat rare in the prophetic corpus as referring to an entire book. Only the Book of Obadiah is called a *ḥāzôn,* and it consists of just one chapter, comprising a unified vision twenty-one verses in length. Nahum opens with the words: "An oracle concerning Nineveh" and the further "The book of the vision of Nahum." Again, however, the entire book is only three chapters in length and could be reasonably interpreted as a single vision, consisting of one long oracle against Nineveh. That an opening superscription can pertain only to the material that follows, not to the entire corpus, is demonstrated in the case of Habakkuk. "The oracle that the prophet Habakkuk saw" (1:1) extends to 2:20; a second superscription at 3:1 introduces what follows as "A prayer of the prophet Habakkuk according to Shigionoth." In this case, it would be wrong to subsume the entire book under the opening superscription.

36

For these reasons a strong case could be made for regarding Isa. 1:1 as the superscription for chapter 1 alone. At the same time, the historical notice is comprehensive enough to suggest that the superscription also pertains to the book at large, or at least to chapters 1—39, which take us to the end of Hezekiah's reign. Scholars have also noted that *ḥāzôn* frequently has a future character. This would explain why the vision of chapter 1 appears to suggest a setting in the post-701 period, during the reign of Manasseh. In sum, the superscription has a dual purpose: its historical notice serves to attach the prophet Isaiah to the material that follows in the larger book, where reference to these kings is made (6:1; 7:1; 36:1). At the same time, the term *ḥāzôn,* which generally means a single vision directed to the future, can apply to the contents of chapter 1 more narrowly, as a vision seen by the prophet Isaiah pertaining to coming days. In the course of time, 1:1 came naturally to be construed as the title of the Book of Isaiah, in something of the same way that the first words of books in the Pentateuch also came to function as titles (Genesis: "In the beginning"). But even in those books, the first words retained their primary function within the chapter they introduced. The situation in Isaiah is analogous.

The opening chapter of Isaiah presents a sober picture. The country lies in ruin. There is no one to press out the wounds, bind them up, or even soften them with oil. Israel's rulers are murderers, with no time to worry about the widow or the orphan. Yet will its survivors continue to be smitten?

The irony is that God's abiding promises to Zion were vindicated in the events of 701. While the Judahite countryside was ravaged by Assyrian forces, Assyria could only "shake his fist" at Zion, as Isaiah had promised (10:32). Jerusalem was dramatically delivered (37:36–38). Within the chapter we get only a brief glimpse at survivors who acknowledge their deliverance and give thanks for it (1:9). These voices are all but drowned out in the sustained indictment against a nation that has lost its bearings, against a leadership that ignores basic acts of justice and simple—not elaborate—acts of contrition and obedience (1:18).

Still, even within this picture Isaiah's particular view of Zion theology is vindicated. God has in mind a new faithful city with new faithful leaders. Those repentant ones in its midst will be redeemed by the same righteousness that saved the city in 701 (1:27). The Book of Isaiah presents the dark side of Zion

37

theology: what it means for God to treat Israel like the nations, whose assault on Zion was to be halted by God. Now the assault comes from within, and God must deal with it from within. This sober picture stands over all that follows, reminding the reader that Zion will be finally redeemed but those who forsake God will lose all protection Zion was to accord, until they finally stand outside the circle of God's grace (1:28–31).

Isaiah 2:1—4:6
In That Day

Zion and the Nations (2:1-5)

The superscription at 2:1 indicates that the following oracle is a word the prophet "saw" *(ḥāzāh)* concerning Judah and Jerusalem. That is, the same future perspective implied by the term "vision" at 1:1 *(ḥāzôn)* is carried over here. This is made explicit in the opening verse: "In days to come . . ." (2:2). Here Isaiah sees the destiny of Zion beyond his own days, beyond the cleansing judgment of 1:2–31. Because this future perspective can also be spotted in the following material, reinforced by the repetition of "in that day" and similar concepts (2:11, 12, 20; 3:7, 18; 4:1, 2), the opening oracle should be read in the context of chapters 2—4 rather than as a continuation of chapter 1. Chapters 2—4 clearly develop aspects of the opening vision in terms both of judgment and of salvation; yet they also go far beyond these.

In 2:1-5 the tone is set for what follows. Mount Zion shall be raised higher than any other mountain so that its prominence is clear to all—not just to Israel. The nations will then begin their pilgrimage to worship Israel's God and be taught his torah. A scene of judgment will be enacted and the God of Jacob will finally settle the divisions between the nations, bringing an end to warfare.

The oracle is remarkable in its own right, depicting a leveling, as it were, of national distinctions. What distinguishes Israel is God alone and his torah; like all the other nations, they must make their own way to Zion and be taught in God's ways. Indeed, the final verse (2:5) presents in direct speech the appeal to Israel to join these other nations: "O house of Jacob, come, let us walk in the light of the LORD." This decision can by no means be taken for granted. As the very next verse puts it: "For thou hast rejected thy people, the house of Jacob" (2:6, RSV).

Read in the light of the opening vision, where this rejection was depicted, our opening oracle makes complete sense. Israel did become like the nations and as such received the fury reserved for them (1:25). Here we see another remarkable transformation of Zion theology. On the other side of this judgment, in the latter days, Israel will join the nations to learn again God's ways and to be taught his torah once more. And in this scene of future exultation of Mount Zion, all the nations will be participants. With the explicit introduction of the nations, the reader is prepared for one of the more prominent themes in the book, elaborated in chapters 13—27 and elsewhere.

The opening chapter of the Book of Jeremiah describes Jeremiah as one appointed to be "a prophet to the nations" (Jer. 1:5). But in a very real sense Isaiah is the prophet with a specific task to nations beyond Israel's borders. The largest sustained section of the Book of Isaiah is concerned with establishing the God of Israel as God of all the nations (chaps. 13—27). Both there and here, it would be an oversimplification to talk of the prophet's pronouncements *against* the nations. In establishing himself as Lord over all peoples, Israel's God does not adopt a stance of judgment only; and where such a stance is adopted, Israel and the nations alike stand under a similar rule of universal justice. And as with images of restoration directed at Israel, so too God has a plan and a purpose involving every nation on earth.

While it may not be possible in every instance to attach oracles concerning the nations to the prophet Isaiah's own historical preaching, it is clear that such oracles have their roots in Isaiah's own conception of God's wider justice. We would argue that such roots are most evident in the prophet's handling of the nation of Assyria, "the rod of my anger" (10:5). Because the prophet sees in the military assaults of Assyria God's own righteous arm, and because he also identifies these assaults with God's activity *in a limited and subtle sense only* (10:15-19), the plans are laid for a conception of God's sovereignty over all the earth that finds fuller expression in chapters 13—27. We are given a glimpse of that fuller conception here. As such, at the very opening of the Book of Isaiah, appropriate prominence is

39

given to a theme that will hold center stage in conjunction with God's more specific attention to "Judah and Jerusalem" (1:1; 2:1) or even the vineyard of Israel more broadly conceived (5:1). That theme—of God's sovereignty over the nations of the earth, over Assyria and Babylon and finally Persia—extends beyond chapters 13—27 to take in the fuller presentation of chapters 40—55 and the Book of Isaiah as a whole. This is surely the other reason why the Book of Isaiah is so frequently cited in the New Testament: Isaiah is not just a prophet of salvation but a prophet who sees God's salvation affecting all nations and peoples.

At this juncture in the Book of Isaiah, 2:1-5 introduces the theme of God's attention to the nations beyond Israel. The fullest expression of this theme is now to be found in chapters 13—27. We will have more to say about the role of the nations in the Book of Isaiah at that point.

The Lord of Hosts Has a Day (2:6—4:6)

What follows is an extended section of heterogeneous material clustered around the theme of the coming day of the Lord. The point of the material is to stress the foregone rejection of Israel (2:6), thus clarifying the perspective of the opening unit (2:1-5), which depicts Israel as one with the nations. Here we find judgment oracles with extensive explanations for the punishment (2:6-11); descriptions of the day of Yahweh and its character (2:12-22); further descriptions of coming judgment (3:1-8, 9-15, 16—4:1). Catchwords and themes familiar from chapter 1 reappear here: "they proclaim their sin like Sodom" (3:9; 1:10); "Tell the innocent [i.e., righteous] how fortunate they are" (3:10; 1:27); "your leaders mislead you" (3:12; 1:23); "elders and princes of his people: It is you who have devoured the vineyard" (3:14; 1:8, 10, 23). This use of common themes and language argues for a close editorial relationship between the vision of judgment in chapter 1 and in chapters 2—3.

The reasons for the judgment given in 2:6 are supplied in the following verses (vv. 7-8). The rejection of the house of Jacob was strongly hinted at in chapter 1; now that rejection has been accomplished. The actual crimes remain somewhat obscure (striking hands with foreigners; soothsayers like the Philistines; land filled with silver and gold, with horses and chariots, with idols). We can only guess that the description is meant to imply that Judah has become like the nations. The sharpness of the language at 2:6 ("thou hast rejected thy people," RSV) is resumed at 2:9: "Do not forgive them!" Also striking is the way "the house of Jacob" is spoken of in the third person, as though the author of these denunciations wished to keep distance: Israel has become "foreign."

The next two sections (2:12–19, 20–22) continue to pursue the image of God's exaltation over all humanity. All that is high (cedars, oaks, mountains, towers, tall ships) will be brought low, so that God alone might be exalted. In that day all forms of idolatry will be revealed as nonsense, as moles and bats (2:20). Consistent with the image of Zion's exalted stature (2:1–5), God will himself rise in glorifying terror, relativizing all the grand schemes of humanity. The next section (3:1–5) also speaks of a reversal of rank: all honored and revered offices will be undone, as boys, and babes, and youth take charge, insolent and base to their "elders." Even those who are asked to be leaders in this time of distress (3:6–8) will refuse because of the extent of Judah's crime. This is a time when only God's glorious presence matters: nothing that is high in the human realm will remain so.

In 3:9–15 the crimes of the nation are repeated in a manner reminiscent of chapter 1 (sin like Sodom; leaders mislead you; you have devoured the vineyard; grinding the face of the poor). Then the final section (3:16—4:1) focuses on a new group: the haughty daughters of Zion. The final example of "high" behavior in the human realm involves similar reversals until all the finery is reduced to rottenness, and seven women must rely on one man—and then only to have their reproach removed (4:1)!

But as the final section reveals (4:2–6), all this judgment is more than a gratuitous display of God's own might and justice, over against the human realm. Rather, the judgment is to lead to a new day. In this sense, 4:2–6 and 2:1–5 function as bookends on an otherwise daunting scene of judgment over human pride and arrogance, in all forms. At the same time, it is important to note those features of 4:2–6 which differentiate it from the opening nations' pilgrimage scene (2:1–5).

First, the emphasis is clearly on Israel, not on the nations. Second, the exaltation of Mount Zion forms the conclusion of the unit, following the cleansing of Zion/Jerusalem. The "cloud by day" and "smoke and . . . a flaming fire by night" (4:5) recall of course the signs of God's presence from the exodus period, where they functioned as temporary guides and forms of protection until the entry into the Promised Land. Usually Zion

41

and exodus traditions are considered discrete; here they are brought together to emphasize God's permanent protection of Zion. A canopy and a pavilion are erected over the glory, affording protection even from nature's assaults.

Less clear is the opening image of "the branch of the LORD" (v. 2), which has certain messianic overtones (see 11:1, though a different word is used for branch; the Targum also adopts a messianic reading). On the other hand, if branch is paralleled by "fruit of the land," then the image would seem to point to the kind of bounty the "survivors of Israel" will enjoy (Clements, *Isaiah 1—39*, p. 54). The problem here is applying the term "branch of the LORD" to natural provision (for "branch" as a messianic term, see Jer. 23:5; 33:15; Zech. 3:8). Moreover, we know from 11:10 that the "root of Jesse" was to be sought out by the nations and that his dwelling was to be glorious; both images fall within the range of our passage. The term "survivors of Israel" is familiar to us from 1:8 and 37:32 (see discussion above); it also appears in 10:20–23, where "the survivors of the house of Jacob will no more lean on the one who struck them [Assyria], but will lean on the LORD, the Holy One of Israel, in truth."

It appears that our passage is presenting an exegesis of other passages in Isaiah (and elsewhere in the biblical record) that deal with the coming age. In that day the "survivors of Israel" will enjoy both the fruit of the land (see 1:19; 37:30) and the presence of the glorious Branch of the Lord. A spirit of judgment and burning will cleanse Jerusalem, so that it might again be the faithful city spoken of at 1:26. Those who were left in Zion before the cleansing will be called holy (4:3)—a notice that sounds remarkably unconditional. Yet they must have been "recorded for life," as the second half of the verse puts it (cf. Rev. 5:1). As in 1:27, the possibility is held out that righteous citizens might be found in the midst of Jerusalem and that these will be redeemed and set apart for the coming age.

Conclusion

Sweeney has described the contents of chapters 2—4 as concerned with "the cleansing and restoration of Jerusalem and Judah so that Zion can serve as YHWH's capital for ruling the entire world" (Sweeney, *Isaiah 1—4*, p. 134). This description captures nicely aspects of both the opening and closing scenes:

the focus on Zion and the people of Israel is maintained (4:2–6) even as Mount Zion becomes Yahweh's capital for all nations (2:1–4). The intervening material (2:6—4:1) speaks of the cleansing of Jerusalem and Judah as the necessary prerequisite for Israel's own pilgrimage to Zion (2:1–4) as well as the reestablishment of their king, their proper worship life, and their identity as a people.

What does it mean that the Book of Isaiah opens with this description of the coming days? Why is the presentation of the first four chapters ultimately concerned with the future—the future day of the Lord when all human pride must stand before the majesty and justice of God as well as the future day of restoration and glorification? In this respect, Ackroyd has spoken of "the prospect of the future . . . set out against the background of failure and doom" (Ackroyd, "Presentation," p. 45). The first chapters of the book certainly set us down in this sort of climate.

Historical reasons can be sought for this presentation. Isaiah 1, for example, is oriented around the failure of a people to take seriously the intention and purpose of their survival. The plausible historical backdrop is, in this instance, the 701 deliverance, during which time Judah was overrun and yet Jerusalem was wondrously delivered. It seemed as though a halt to Assyrian assaults—beginning with Israel and extending to Judah because of the refusal of Ahaz and the people to trust in God's promises—had finally come, as the prophet Isaiah had promised. Yet it is at exactly this denouement that the opening chapters pick up again. The end of the story becomes the beginning. Because of the failure of the people, and especially the leadership, to respond appropriately to this deliverance and because in fact they "continue to rebel," filling the capital with injustice, murder, elaborate but insincere worship, and pride in all forms, a yet greater "day of the LORD" awaits the people.

Here too historical information helps fill out the picture. In the course of world events, Assyria is replaced by Babylon and Isaiah's word of judgment is extended beyond his own historical period, to the time "in that day." Against a background of failure and doom, following Isaiah's own prophetic activity, there is to be a new judgment for Judah and Jerusalem that will properly cleanse it of pride and injustice and the many other crimes enumerated in chapters 1—4. Only then will Israel be restored. In this interpretation, then, the future day of judg-

43

ment is, for the reader, the past day of 587 destruction and desolation, when Judah and Jerusalem were finally overrun entirely and when all human pride and false worship came into confrontation with the day of the Lord.

For all this, a problem exists with a reading that is too narrowly historical. When additions are made that speak of the future ("in that day") it is quite possible that more is being said than that they were fulfilled in the lifetime and circumstances of the one who added them, in this instance, in the destruction of Jerusalem in 587 B.C.; after all, in the final form of the book, within its temporal presentation, they now refer to the future, beyond the point of standing of every generation of readers. This is all the more true in chapters 2—4, where the vision of future judgment exists alongside a vision of future restoration. For it would be very difficult—impossible—to argue that the vision of restoration found in 2:1–4 had been fulfilled in the lifetime and circumstances of a later editor. We still look for the time when nation shall not lift up sword against nation.

It may well have been the case that the oracles of judgment that use the motif "in that day" took form with an eye toward the destruction of Jerusalem in 587 B.C. But it is impossible to argue that this is their only point of reference, given the overwhelming future orientation of chapters 2—4. The "day of the Lord" and the day of restoration belong together in the presentation of these chapters: one follows hard upon the other. For readers that had experienced the 587 debacle, who were indeed survivors, these passages would still retain their future force, even as the period of judgment had already begun. It would be wrong to drive too sharp a wedge between "historical" and "eschatological" readings. The one requires the other. In the final presentation of chapters 2—4 a vision of judgment, one very reminiscent of 587 events and one that may have taken form because of these, still awaits its final denouement. Only then can one look for the fulfillment of oracles such as are now found at 2:1–5 and 4:2–6.

When Isa. 2:1–5 is read in the Christian church during the Advent season, the temptation is to connect the fulfillment of the passage with the events of Christmas—a different kind of "historical" interpretation that also sees the fulfillment as a past event. But such an interpretation is rendered problematic by the fact that "nations still learn war" despite the birth of Jesus Christ. Christians affirm that in Christ, God has redeemed the

44

righteous; but the church also lives "between the times," working toward and awaiting the fulfillment of all of God's promises as these have found expression in the Old Testament. A purely historical reading will not do; but neither will one that is purely eschatological.

There was a time in certain sections of the Christian church when Advent was the final season of the Christian year and where the promises of the Old Testament were largely connected with the Second Coming. That captures one aspect of the season, and it can still be seen in most lectionary schemes for the first Sundays of Advent. But then there are also promises that the church confesses were fulfilled in Jesus Christ, and these too form part of the Advent message. In this way we see that history and eschatology are aspects of the same mystery, and both require a proper appreciation if the full voice of the Old Testament witness is to be heard.

A careful reading is required to appreciate the subtle ways in which the world of the editors/shapers, the world of the text, and the world of the reader interact in the Book of Isaiah. Chapters 1—4 are not the only place where this interaction takes place. Precisely because Isaiah is a book that speaks so persistently to the future, by means of a complex appraisal of the past, the reader will invariably lean in one direction or the other. We must also be open to the possibility that certain passages that speak to the future are indeed fulfilled at later points in the Book of Isaiah. For example, does the first messianic oracle at 9:1–7 direct us to a future within the Isaiah presentation itself, to the figure of Hezekiah? Can the same be said for the second oracle at 11:1–9? Does the vision of cosmic judgment now found in chapters 24—27 likewise pertain to the Babylonian crisis or to some future debacle outside the Book of Isaiah itself, in the reader's own future? Each passage will have to be handled on its own terms, and it may be that two different readings will have to be held in tension.

Isaiah 5:1–30
My Beloved Had a Vineyard

Matters of Structure

There is little question that with chapter 5 we begin a new unit in Isaiah. Chapters 1—4 form their own collection, presenting us with an introduction not just to First Isaiah but to the entire Book of Isaiah. In chapter 5 we are introduced to the vineyard long before it has become nothing but a "shelter in a cucumber field" (1:8). Though the Song of the Vineyard (5:1–7) will speak of the final destruction of Israel, as of yet Israel is God's "pleasant planting" (5:7).

It is also clear that with chapter 6 we begin a separate tradition block, encompassing 6:1—9:6. Ironically, however, there is some question about the relationship of chapter 5 to material *after* this tradition block, in 9:8—10:34. The problem is that a chain of woe oracles beginning at 5:8 appears to continue at 10:1; also, the theme of the outstretched hand that appears in 9:8—10:4 (see too 14:24-27) can be seen at 5:25. The result is that 6:1—9:8 appears to have been set down in the middle of a relatively well connected section of text. What is the function of such a placement?

The editorial insertion of 6:1—9:8 "has had the effect of locating Yahweh's summoning of Assyria at the beginning of Isaiah's career" (Anderson, p. 239). In fact, as we pointed out above, it locates this summoning of Assyria even before the commissioning in chapter 6 (contra Anderson, p. 239). It also has the effect of situating Isaiah squarely in the midst of a sinful people, out of which he must be drawn to continue to exercise his prophetic ministry over against this people (Childs, *Introduction*, p. 331). In sum, every effort should be made to interpret chapter 5 in its present location and in its present arrangement. Explanations for this location can be found.

Rejecting the instinct to shift portions of chapter 5 to a "more suitable" location, we are left with the following structure. The chapter opens with the Song of the Vineyard (5:1–7); then we have a series of woe oracles (5:8–12; 5:18–23) with closing statements of judgment (5:13–17; 5:24–25). At the conclusion of the chapter there is a summoning of God's agent of judgment and a description of the terrifying power this "nation far away" wields (5:26–30).

The Song of the Vineyard (5:1–7)

An important debate has taken place about the genre of the song. If the song is a "love song" in the formal sense, one would expect the singer to be the bride or husband of the beloved, on whose behalf the song is sung. Yet the prophet is clearly the singer and Yahweh the beloved, and the song has more to do with the relationship between the "beloved" and his vineyard than between the prophet and God. The singer (prophet) is therefore better understood as the friend and advocate for his companion (God); he sings a song about the love of his companion for his vineyard.

Very quickly, then, the song turns into a prophetic indictment. The singer invites his listeners to hear about the careful attention his friend showered on the vineyard and of the disappointment he experienced when the vineyard yielded nothing but rank grapes. As in the case of Nathan's parable to King David (II Sam. 12:1–10), here too one expects the listeners to be beguiled by the straightforwardness of the tale. Moreover, the "song" format elicits the more "gossipy" side of their interest (Clements, *Isaiah 1—39*, p. 57); everyone has a perverse interest in love gone wrong. Without warning, the prophet-singer disappears in verse 3 as the owner of the vineyard speaks on his own behalf, inviting Judah-Jerusalem to pass judgment on the guilty party. Did God not do enough for his vineyard? Did he plant the wrong species of grape, perhaps? We expect the listeners to indict the vineyard when instead God himself speaks the harsh sentence of judgment (5:5). The vineyard's wall will be trampled down; it will become a waste, full of thorns and briers—an image pursued in more detail in a later chapter (7:23–25). Then the final verse includes the listeners again. They are the vineyard about to be destroyed! God looked for justice *(mišpāṭ)* but found bloodshed *(miśpāḥ);* for righteousness *(ṣĕdāqāh)* but instead of righteousness found a cry *(ṣĕʿāqāh)*. A similar contrast was set forth in chapter 1, where we heard of justice turned into harlotry and of righteousness into murder (1:21).

47

From time to time we have mentioned the problem raised by the location of Isaiah's call six chapters into the book and of the several attempts to explain this particular location. This problem is of one piece with the question of the location of chapter 5 and of its relationship to 6:1—9:7 and especially 9:8—10:34. Chapters 1—4, as we have seen, offer their own collective presentation. What, then, of chapter 5?

First, it is striking that the Song of the Vineyard is the first place in the Book of Isaiah where we see first-person speech of the prophet differentiated from divine speech, as such. In fact, the success of the "song" turns in part on the unexpected shift from prophetic persona ("Let me sing for my beloved") to divine persona, accomplished at verse 3. That is, the prophet begins by telling us he will sing a song for his best friend, but then the best friend (God) speaks on his own behalf: "judge between me and my vineyard" (5:3). Surely this appearance of the prophet as divine spokesman, in brief but explicit terms, has influenced the decision to designate the beginning of Isaiah's career *prior* to the death of Uzziah, as the superscription has recorded it (1:1), and not as starting for the first time in the "call" of the prophet during the reign of Ahaz (so chapter 6). That is, the book in its present form depicts Isaiah as active as prophetic speaker in chapter 5, under the cover of God's beloved, before the death of King Uzziah and the commissioning of chapter 6. Related to this is the observation of Duhm that the song must have been delivered early in the prophet's career, when the ploy of the prophet singing a song for his beloved would have still been effective. Duhm meant this of course as a *historical* observation. But it is also true in another, editorial sense, involving the logic of these opening chapters in the final arrangement of the book.

The difference between prophetic speech and divine speech cannot be overdrawn: God can only "speak" through the words of his prophets. The point of call narratives in prophetic books is to make this absolutely clear: God puts his words in the prophet's mouth (Jer. 1:9). The Song of the Vineyard, however, makes a similar point in the context of the Book of Isaiah. It introduces the prophet as singing a song on behalf of God (Isa. 5:1). This having been done, the song—quite effectively—shifts to direct divine address. In sum, the Song of the Vineyard functions in part to introduce the figure of the prophet as speaker on God's behalf. It is Isaiah's first clear pub-

48

lic act as God's prophet, even as this event has been overshadowed by the episode recorded in chapter 6.

The song also spells out the message of divine judgment (5:5–7). It is striking that the images of desolation in 5:6 resemble those uttered by the prophet to the house of David in chapter 7. Here God delivers the sentence personally to all Israel. Yahweh had done all he could for his beloved vineyard: selected the best location, painstakingly cleared away the stones, planted the best variety of vines, and even built a watchtower in it. But it did not yield grapes worth eating, much less grapes worthy of all this attention (5:2). Nothing more could have been done than was done (5:4).

In the Song of the Vineyard the prophet steps forward as spokesman for his good friend. In a sense his prophetic activity "begins" here. It would be wrong to think of the prophetic books as offering one fixed notion of the prophetic call. The Book of Jeremiah probably presents the most classic example of a call narrative (Jer. 1:4–19): it is positioned at the beginning of the book; it contains the initial address (Jer. 1:4–6), the prophetic objection (Jer. 1:6), the divine rejoinder (Jer. 1:7–8), cleansing (Jer. 1:9), and extended commission (Jer. 1:10–12, 13–19). Yet even it presents the beginning of Jeremiah's prophetic career at a point beyond the prophet's own comprehension: before he was born or even formed in the womb (Jer. 1:5). The Book of Isaiah begins with an extended vision of the future (Isaiah 1—4) in which all that is left of God's vineyard is a single booth (1:8). The prophet appears in chapter 5, only to recede from view, so that a decision for judgment might be made personally by God against a vineyard that was carefully tended but failed to bear fruit. The owner himself renders the judgment. What of the prophet's own fate in that vineyard? For the answer to that question we must wait until chapter 6 and a fuller unfolding of the prophet's call.

A Signal Is Raised (5:8–30)

Within this section we have a series of woe oracles (5:8, 11, 18, 20, 21, 22) interrupted by sentences of judgment (5:13–17; 5:24–25). Isaiah 5:25 introduces the theme of Yahweh's outstretched hand, which is pursued in chapters 9 and 10. The final unit (5:16–30) speaks of God's signaling "a nation far away" to execute the judgment.

49

What clues are given as to the addressees of the woe material? The crimes listed are at times quite specific (land appropriation; drunkenness, perhaps cultic; persistent iniquity; false regard for the purpose of God). Yet it is difficult to see how the leaders of Jerusalem and its citizenry have been singled out for rebuke. Indeed, the material seems similar in form and content to other prophetic indictments directed to the wider Israel, if not the Northern Kingdom more specifically. One thinks of the woe oracles of Amos (Amos 5—6) or the "lack of knowledge" theme (Isa. 5:13) in the prophet Hosea (Hos. 4:6; 5:4; 6:3, 6).

If we take our lead from the Song of the Vineyard, reference is made in the final verse to both "the house of Israel, and the people of Judah" (5:7). The terms are not in strict parallelism so that one term covers the other; rather, together they offer the most comprehensive designation for the nation. It is tempting to read the verse quite literally: Israel is the vineyard, while Judah is God's pleasant planting within the vineyard, one that has not produced fruit (so 5:2). In this case the wider Israel is still condemned, not just Judah or the Northern Kingdom alone (see also Hos. 10:1).

The extension of Isaiah's message to the wider Israel is not prominent in the opening chapters (chaps. 1—4), where the focus clearly remains on Judah-Jerusalem. We mentioned above the strong possibility that the wider Israel perspective is significant here in chapter 5. In the presentation of the Books of Kings, Assyria begins its work of judgment during the reign of Pekah, king of Israel (II Kings 15:29). At that time Tiglath-pileser captured significant portions of the Northern Kingdom, carrying their populations "captive to Assyria" (II Kings 15:29). The reference to exile at Isa. 5:13, together with the following images of Sheol consuming their "nobility," their "multitude," and their "throng," need not refer to the Babylonian exile. Instead, a very general indictment is directed against the entire nation, with initial signs of judgment seen first in the Northern Kingdom. Here we also find an explanation for the motif of the outstretched hand, and its repetition as far as 14:26–27. Yahweh stretches out his hand against his people, beginning with the Northern Kingdom. He raises a signal for a nation afar off: they growl, seize their prey, and carry it off (5:29). But his work is not completed with the punishment of the Northern Kingdom: "For all this his anger has not turned away, and his hand is stretched out still" (5:25). The nation summoned from afar will have a task vis-à-vis Israel, Judah, and Jerusalem.

50

Conclusion

We have discussed chapter 5 within the broader context of the emergence of the prophet Isaiah and the presentation of the beginning of his preaching activity. As such, the Song of the Vineyard represents a kind of opening address of the prophet Isaiah: "Let me sing for my beloved my love song concerning his vineyard." It is not surprising that the speech has to do not just with Judah and Jerusalem but also with the wider kingdom of Israel. There is no reason to assume that the remainder of the chapter departs from this wider perspective. Indeed, the chapter concludes with the calling of an unidentified nation whose task it is to wreak an awful desolation (5:26–30). God's anger is kindled against his people (5:25); he has already begun to smite them (5:25); his hand is stretched out still. First to be seized and carried off by this fierce lion was Israel, the Northern Kingdom.

Isaiah's message is remembered as having been primarily directed to Judah and Jerusalem, as concerned with the house of David and the traditions of Zion. Rooted in that message is a call for judgment at the hands of foreign nations and specifically at the hands of Assyria "the rod of my anger" (10:5). In large measure the house of David is viewed as responsible for the awful judgment meted out against Judah and Jerusalem because of the refusal of Ahaz to trust in Isaiah's word and in the promises to David (7:1–17). But he is not the only one to "melt in fear before" the coalition of Ephraim and Syria; "this people" also "refused the waters of Shiloah that flow gently" (8:5) and in so doing call down upon themselves the wrath of God in the agency of Assyria (8:7). King and people alike, in Judah and Jerusalem, refuse God's promises and signs of grace.

Within the core traditions of chapters 7—8, Israel, the Northern Kingdom, appears as a hostile force over against Judah, Jerusalem, Zion, and David. Israel is already in league with another nation, Syria, and has begun to wage war against its own onetime capital, Jerusalem (7:1). How did this come about? Chapter 5 answers this question in part by describing the wider deterioration of Israel, within which Judah-Jerusalem forms a distinct part (5:7). Assyria was summoned as a necessary agent of judgment against Israel before the Syro-Ephraimite crisis. Against this backdrop, "Ephraim" enters into intrigue with Syria in an attempt to escape God's punishment at the

51

hands of the Assyrians. The sad consequence is war against their own people (7:1).

We have also described Isaiah's call rather differently, based on our reading of chapter 5. Isaiah emerges as spokesman for Yahweh in the context of the Song of the Vineyard. In that same context we learn of the fate awaiting both Israel and Judah.

Isaiah 5:9 is another important text in this same respect. The sentence of judgment issued here is introduced with the words: "The LORD of hosts has sworn in my hearing." Clements notes that the language is appropriate to the divine council; that is, the prophet "overhears" a sentence of judgment issued by God within the context of his deliberations with the divine retinue (Clements, *Isaiah 1—39,* p. 63). Chapter 5 gives us clear intimations of the call of Isaiah, which then receives much fuller expression in chapter 6. At this juncture the prophet is given a sense of God's plan of judgment that reaches back even farther than the death of Uzziah (6:1) or the Syro-Ephraimite crisis, involving the summoning of an unidentified nation as agent of judgment against the vineyard Israel. Chapter 6 in turn gives a fuller statement of God's intentions, as the prophet actually enters the divine council, is set apart, and is personally commissioned for a specific task.

Isaiah 6:1–13
The Holy Seed Is Its Stump

Introduction

Chapter 6, the report of Isaiah's commissioning, is generally treated together with 7:1—9:6. The justification for this is the theory that 6:1—9:6, in its original form, represents a memoir of the prophet. This memoir was written by the prophet himself. It told of his experience in the Syro-Ephraimite crisis and gave a retrospective account of his call. Scholars disagree about the exact conclusion to the memoir, and there is debate about which portions constitute the original text and which form a secondary development.

How close a relationship does chapter 6 actually have to the following material? Most interpreters who hold to the theory of a memoir recognize that the material in its present form has been greatly overworked. If there was ever an original memoir, its first-person form has only erratically survived. If chapters 7—8 constitute an account of the Syro-Ephraimite crisis, they have been substantially expanded to deal with the later Assyrian period assaults, if not also those relevant to the Babylonian period. Suddenly we are at great remove from the basic conception of a memoir and are dealing with an editorially presented collection. The question then reappears: Why would a collection that has been secondarily interpreted maintain a difficult linkage between the prophet's call (chapter 6) and the events of the Syro-Ephraimite crisis? With all the other editorial interventions, why not simply move the call to the beginning of the book?

If we bracket out the notion of a memoir altogether, other reasons emerge for a connection between chapters 6 and the following material. There are definite links between the commission of Isaiah at 6:9–10 and its effect in chapters 7—8 (Steck). Isaiah's preaching does lead to "heavy ears and closed eyes" in the events of the Syro-Ephraimite war, in the person of Ahaz and in the wider population. If this motif is principally responsible for the placement of chapter 6 next to chapters 7—8, it does not follow that chapter 6 must be interpreted as a call narrative. Rather, as Steck has noted, the emphasis then shifts to the specific commission to make hearts fat—a commission that is carried out in the events of 734–732 B.C. Chapter 6 may have quite a different purpose than that of reporting an inaugural vision that constituted the prophet's call.

In sum, we view the relationship between chapter 6 and the following material as significant, though not for the reasons that were critical to most memoir theories. This in turn opens up the question about the form of chapter 6. Do we have a call narrative here? We have already begun to discuss this issue from the standpoint of chapter 5 and the broader presentation of Isaiah 1—5. In order not to prejudice the discussion, we will treat chapter 6 as a separate unit rather than as an integral part of a putative memoir extending to chapter 8 or 9. It may well be that the kind of linkages that can be detected between chapter 6 and chapters 7—8 are similar in kind to those which link chapter 5 and chapter 6.

Form (6:1–8)

Most interpreters distinguish two basic forms for call narratives in the Old Testament. One is dominated by the word of God (so Moses, Gideon, Jeremiah), the other by a theophany. Isaiah would belong to this second category and also II Kings 22:19–22. Isaiah 6 is a prophetic commissioning within the framework of throne scene. The constituent elements of this type of call account include the description of the vision, cry of distress, cleansing ritual, divine consultation, free declaration of fitness for the task, and commissioning.

It is fair to say that Isaiah 6 shares elements in common with II Kings 22:19–22, most especially the motif of the heavenly council. Yahweh is seated on a throne; the divine retinue flanks him; they call out to one another. Unfortunately, however, II Kings 22:19–22 is also a very distinctive text over against Isaiah 6 in that it involves the sending forth of a "lying spirit" who has put himself forward to entice Ahab. Micaiah ben Imlah witnesses the whole affair and reports it to the king. It could only with difficulty be termed a call narrative, and then a call narrative for false prophets!

Isaiah 6 opens with a throne scene (6:1–4) which partakes of elements heavenly and earthly. It is probably not a pure vision but takes place within the temple itself, even as it explodes the limitations of that sacred space: God is "high and lofty." The seraphim are probably not "above him" (NRSV) but flank him, guarding access to his throne. They cover their faces, in contrast to the prophet himself, who finds himself in unfamiliar environs. Their vocation, as it were, is to sing God's praises and announce him, which they do in such a way as to shake the very foundations of the temple itself. In four short verses we get a very good impression of the prophet's encounter.

The prophet's cry is found in 6:5. It is predicated on three basic facts: he is a man of unclean lips; he dwells among a people of unclean lips; and he has seen the King—not Ahaz or Uzziah but Yahweh of hosts. In the cleansing ceremony that follows (6:6–7), the first and third of these matters are dealt with: the guilt that is a consequence of these two realities is removed, and his sin is forgiven. Then the prophet hears God's voice, or rather overhears God speaking with his own retinue ("Who will go for us?"). At this juncture the prophet himself steps forward and offers his services, which God accepts without further ado (6:8–9*a*). The remainder of the account consists of the charge he is given to speak (6:9*b*–13).

On the basis of the information given, it is impossible to say whether this account speaks of the "call" of the prophet in the sense usually intended, namely, an inaugural episode setting the prophet apart for the first time for a prophetic task. The problem is the penetration of the heavenly realm into the prophet's experience. When the prophet cries out (6:5), he expresses spontaneously his sense of displacement within the most sacred realm: his eyes see the Lord of hosts! What prophet—even in "mid-career"—would fail to speak these words? Even when Isaiah refers to his unclean lips, it is in the context of the unclean lips of the entire nation. Surely the preceding chapter has established the rightness of that statement.

Steck has preferred to describe chapter 6 as "the conferring of a special commission within the heavenly assembly" (Steck, "Bemerkungen," p. 191), similar to what we find at II Kings 22:19–22. He rejects the call narrative interpretation that governs most readings. We agree with this formal designation and would add to it the considerations of context and placement already mentioned. The editors of the Book of Isaiah have dated his activity to the reigns of Uzziah, Jotham, Ahaz, and Hezekiah. Chapter 6 is clearly dated to "the year that King Uzziah died." Chapter 5 makes reference at two points to the prophet's own person and speech (5:1; 5:9). Yet the question might be raised: Just what is the prophet's specific task vis-à-vis the nation? What of his specific relationship to the owner of the vineyard, on whose behalf he has spoken?

Chapter 6 establishes the prophet as cleansed and set apart from a nation of unclean lips. His guilt is taken away and his sin forgiven. As such he is free to step forward and respond when God calls—something the nation is forbidden. He can hear and see; they can do neither.

The Commission (6:9–13)

That a commission to "make the mind dull" (6:10) is theologically problematic may already be true for the Greek text, where the imperatives of verse 10 have been changed to indicative forms. How could God charge Isaiah to so dull the hearts of his people that they could not turn and be healed? The answer to this question is not to be found in psychological explanations, however insightful these may be. That preaching can have the effect of exacerbating deafness is a truth not located in the Old Testament alone (Mark 4:12), nor is it lost on modern preachers and teachers. But the text does not give us an explanation for the charge at the level of general psychology. Despite the ongoing popularity of the retrospective interpretation (the prophet understood subsequently that his message had to fail), the text does not point in this direction.

It is to be noted that the text does make a distinction between the words the prophet is to speak to the people (6:9*b*) and the interpretation of this activity made by God to the prophet alone (6:10). Isaiah is to say to the people: "Keep listening, but do not comprehend; keep looking, but do not understand." This does capture a general truth about the prophet's preaching as this unfolds in chapters 7—8 and in the passages that follow. It is also consistent with an ironic tone that permeates Isaiah's message at several points (28:9–13).

The explicit charge to "make hearts fat" (RSV) so that the nation cannot turn and be healed—this charge is made to Isaiah in the privacy of the divine council. It cannot be so easily identified in passages that follow. In fact, the reverse seems to be true. Isaiah leaves the divine council preaching warning, exhortation, even salvation and divine presence (7:1–14). We prefer, therefore, to see its intent as pastoral, directed specifically at the figure of Isaiah and with due consideration for the prophetic office. Isaiah is not to interpret the refusal to hear, which comes as a result of his preaching, as a sign of his failure or as an indication of divine malfeasance. The prophet learns from God that he will make hearts fat with the effect that the people will not turn and be healed. God lets him know this at a critical moment in his career, as he is about to leave the divine council.

It is extremely important to keep this divine council perspective in mind in interpreting chapter 6 and its message. The chapter does not give us easy access to the mind of the prophet, nor does it provide clear guidelines for understanding the office of the prophet based on its depiction of the man Isaiah. Call narrative interpretations are prone to pursue these sorts of questions. It is interesting that the prophet does not object to this difficult commission; rather, he asks to see it in a larger temporal perspective ("How long, O LORD?"). See more on this below.

In chapter 6, God's decision in the divine council is revealed to Isaiah and to the reader. This people will not understand, nor will they turn and be healed. Isaiah's preaching will produce this effect. Chapter 6 makes clear that whatever else he may be, Isaiah is "no conventional preacher of a message of repentance" (Clements, *Isaiah 1—39,* p. 77). Nevertheless it will remain Isaiah's task to cry out, "Keep listening, keep looking." Unlike the Book of Jeremiah, the Book of Isaiah gives virtually no clue as to the prophet's reaction to this difficult task (cf. Jeremiah 11—20). Alternatively, the Book of Isaiah has chosen to emphasize that Isaiah the prophet actually entered the divine assembly, saw God, was cleansed, and received the sort of commission that required such unequivocal divine endorsement. That commission all but drowns out the figure of the prophet, about whose origins and final destiny we are left to know practically nothing.

Instead of responding, "How?" the prophet responds, "How long?" *How* the prophet is to translate this divine mandate into proclamation the following chapters will reveal. As we have said, Isaiah does not leave the divine assembly simply repeating what he heard there. Instead, we receive from him a complex message of judgment and salvation, at times paradoxically interwoven. The latter half of that paradoxical message is referenced by the prophet's own question to God, "How long?" and by the response he is given. Many interpreters wish to limit God's response to verse 11, seeing in verses 12–13 secondary additions reflecting later historical perspectives. Yet how convincing is this distinction?

First, it is clear that 6:11–12 pursues the same essential image: the divine mandate remains in effect until "the land is utterly desolate" (v. 11). The same image is repeated in verse 12*b:* "and vast is the emptiness in the midst of the land." It is the reference to deportation in 12*a* that influences the decision to regard verse 12 as secondary. Yet, as Wildberger points out, the reference to deportation makes historical sense during the lifetime of Isaiah, not just during the Babylonian exile; he relates the verse to the deportation of Israelites in 721 B.C. Even that may be too restrictive. We have a general reference to exile in 5:13 as one form of punishment following the woe oracle of 5:11–12. The verb form is quite general ("until the LORD sends far away"), maintaining the image of "distance" ("puts afar") familiar from 5:26, where Assyria is called "a na-

57

tion far away." The counterpart of utter desolation in the land
is the removal of its citizens. What is underscored is the total-
ity of the judgment.

The final verse (v. 13) is often eliminated because of its
"hopeful" character (v. 13c) and because it further nuances the
judgment oracle of the preceding verse: "Even if a tenth part
remain in it, it will be burned again, like a terebinth or an oak
whose stump remains standing when it is felled" (the verse is
difficult to translate; cf. NEB, e.g.). Clements puts it thus: "[The]
sense that, even after a period of fearful devastation, 'the land'
will thereafter be compelled to suffer a further period of destruction would appear to indicate the impact of Babylonian
imperialism after that of Assyria" (Clements, "Fall of Jerusalem," p. 426).

Against such an interpretation is the notion of graded judgment inherent in Isaiah's message. The best example of this is
the "outstretched hand" motif, which almost no one denies to
the prophet Isaiah (5:25; 9:12, 17, 21; 10:4; 14:26). God's anger
is kindled against his people and he smites them (5:25a), but for
all this his anger is not turned away, and his hand is stretched
out still. This image is quite close to the "tenth part remains and
is burned again" language at 6:13. In historical terms we know
that the assaults of Assyria were graded ones: first affected were
parts of the Northern Kingdom (II Kings 15:29), then Israel
itself (II Kings 17), then Judah (Isa. 36:1) and Jerusalem (36:2ff.).
A similar notion of graded judgment can be seen in chapters
7—8, which follow. Assyria will come against Ephraim and
bring an end to the "war against Jerusalem"; then Assyria will
come against Judah itself (7:18–25); yet the "waters of the
River" (8:7) will only "reach up to the neck" (8:8). It is difficult
to avoid the clear impression that Judah is the tenth burned
again and that what is left standing is Jerusalem or some portion
within it. Steck has observed the close connection between the
commission to make hearts fat and its effect in chapters 7—8.
Something of the same connection can be seen between the
images of desolation and further burning in verses 12–13 and
the descriptions provided in chapters 7—8.

We have spoken of the "dark side" of Zion theology in the
context of chapter 1. When Israel chooses to become like the
nations, and is finally indistinguishable from them, the fury of
Yahweh that was to protect Zion is turned against his own
people. But the positive side of Zion theology is that God has

an ultimate stake in Israel and will defend his presence among them, if only for his own sake (37:35). This theological position is rarely stated in such a blunt manner. Rather, we begin to see gradually in the proclamation of Isaiah a central conviction emerging: that beyond and because of a widespread devastation that God effects against his own sinful people, a stump "burned again" will yet remain. "In that day" we find those left to survive on curds and honey (7:22); we see people "pass through the land, greatly distressed and hungry" (8:21). Some are thrust into yet thicker darkness (8:22), while others emerge cleansed and renewed "by a spirit of burning" (4:4). They are a "holy seed"—the stump of a great tree that remains after much devastation, only to be burned again.

Some wish to attribute a comprehensive Zion theology to postexilic reflection; others see it taking mature form as the result of the deliverance of 701, when Zion was spared amidst widespread destruction. Ironically, the Book of Isaiah looks on the deliverance of 701 as a cause for penitence and sober reflection (chap. 1) more than as an occasion for theological elaboration. However one seeks to describe it, there is within the preaching of Isaiah a complex, paradoxical "remnant" theology that is interwoven with Zion theology and concerns over Zion's final destiny. We see it in chapters 7—8 in the context of Immanuel passages (7:14; 8:8, 10), as well as in chapters 28—32, where God rages against Zion and yet spares it and rescues it as well (31:5). It is impossible to pull these two dimensions apart, on literary-critical, historical, or theological grounds. There is to be a full devastation. There is to be a holy seed.

Most treatments of Isaiah's call focus on the hard commission to make hearts fat (6:9–10) rather than on the final divine response (6:11–13). The last word, "The holy seed is its stump," is overshadowed by either the preceding commission or the images of desolation. Alternatively, it is removed from the divine council on literary-critical grounds. Yet inherently the prophet's question "How long, O LORD?" points to a final positive word, since what proceeded was the sober command to close off all comprehension and possibility of repentance. How long will this go on? The answer is: until a widespread devastation is fully accomplished. Even that which remains must be burned again. But out of that burning will come a holy seed.

Here in crude form we can identify the source of any hopeful preaching to be found in Isaiah's proclamation. Like the command to dull hearts, it must be translated into proclamation that fits the occasion, and the same paradoxical character of the final salvation is frequently retained. This note from the divine council must be heard alongside the other chords sounded.

Isaiah 7:1—9:7
If You Do Not Stand Firm in Faith, You Shall Not Stand at All: Isaiah and the House of David

From the perspective of the New Testament, the Isaiah prophecy concerning Immanuel has fundamentally to do with the birth, life, and mission of Jesus of Nazareth. However, in the last two centuries critical interpretation has sought to determine the historical referent of Isaiah's Immanuel prophecy within the Old Testament period itself. But no clear consensus has emerged. In the section that follows we will look at the question of Immanuel's identity again, mindful of the role the larger Isaiah presentation plays in establishing the identity of this key figure.

EXCURSUS:
Who Is Immanuel?

The Problems

The section of text stretching from 7:1 to 9:7 is the most important sustained block of tradition in the presentation of Isaiah 1—12. The precise limits of this tradition block, and especially its conclusion in 9:1-7, will be discussed shortly. Given its central position and the significance of the subject it treats, here perhaps more than anywhere coherence in the final form of the material is to be desired. Yet at several points that coherence is failing, or it seems less than obvious. Consequently, commentaries and secondary literature disagree sharply over fundamental issues of interpretation. Not the least of these is the

60

identity of the Immanuel child (7:14; cf. 8:8, 10). One could mention as well many other only slightly less central matters: Are all three children the prophet's, or only the first and the third? Are the children to be interpreted as positive signs, negative signs, or both, depending on the recipient (Ahaz or some wider referent)? Is the "in that day" series at 7:18–25 comprised of negative or also positive images? What is the timetable for the end of the threat from Syria-Ephraim: sixty-five years (7:8), before the Immanuel child "knows how to refuse the evil and choose the good" (7:16), or before Maher-shalal-hash-baz "knows how to cry 'My father' or 'My mother' " (8:4, RSV)? Why is the name "Immanuel" (God with us) used again in 8:8 and 8:10? Is the royal oracle a birth or an accession oracle, and to whom does it refer—the child who was to be born (7:14; 9:6) or another candidate, historical or eschatological?

Taken together, these various problems of interpretation are substantial. When in addition one tries to relate the text as an integrated work to the "facts" of history, as these can be reconstructed from a variety of sources, yet greater problems emerge. Some of these have to do with the nature of our sources: we reconstruct much of our working chronology from the Books of Kings, and what we find there is frequently confusing. To take this particular historical period as an example: references in Kings locate the fall of Samaria eight years prior to the siege of Jerusalem (II Kings 18:10; 18:13), yet most modern reckonings place these events twenty years apart (the key dates are 721 and 701 B.C.). As to the Syro-Ephraimite crisis: the conspiracy of Pekah (Israel) and Rezin (Syria) against Jerusalem is said to have occurred during the reign of Ahaz according to Isaiah 7—8 (also II Kings 16:5). Yet King Pekah is also said to have been slain "in the twentieth year of Jotham" (II Kings 15:30), that is, *before* Ahaz took the throne. II Kings 15:37 concurs insofar as it states that "in those days"—in the days of Jotham—"the LORD began to send Rezin the king of Syria and Pekah the son of Remaliah against Judah" (RSV). Here is a clear instance where the various biblical notices resist coordination.

There is one further note from Kings that may figure into our interpretation of Isa. 7:1—9:7. Ahaz is said to have reigned just sixteen years as king (II Kings 16:1) after which he was replaced by his son Hezekiah, who was just twenty-five at the time (II Kings 18:1). According to this tally from Kings, Hezekiah was born nine years before Ahaz took the throne, making

61

his father Ahaz only eleven years old! (Ahaz became king at the age of twenty, according to II Kings 16:2.) In sum, there appears to be confusion in the Books of Kings over the precise length of reign for Uzziah, Jotham, and Ahaz. Interpretation of Isa. 7:1—9:7 falls squarely in this period and so does the problem of identifying the Immanuel child. We will return to this matter shortly.

One feature that is thought to provide coherence and unity in chapters 7—8 is the motif of the children, Shear-jashub (Remnant shall return), Immanuel (God with us), and Maher-shalal-hash-baz (Spoil speeds, prey hastes). They are evenly distributed throughout the text (7:3; 7:14; 8:1). The first is already born, the second about to be born, and the third not yet conceived (at least at 8:1). Most important, the summarizing note at 8:16–22 explicitly refers to the children as "signs and portents in Israel," thus giving the impression that in the foregoing they played a central role.

Shear-jashub and Maher-shalal-hash-baz are expressly children of Isaiah (7:3; 8:3). A certain symmetry might suggest that the second child, Immanuel, was also the prophet's son, a view held by such eminent scholars as Ibn Ezra and Rashi and a host of modern interpreters. Isaiah 8:18, "I and the children whom the LORD has given me," is frequently cited in support of such an interpretation. The mysterious woman at 7:14 (Heb. *hā 'almāh*, "the young woman"; cf. *bĕtûlāh*, "virgin") has even been linked to the office of cult prophetess, reinforcing the link to Isaiah. Yet others continue to see in the term *'almāh* royal associations. Obviously the Christian interpretation is based on such a royal association. One proponent of Immanuel as the prophet's own son has pointed out certain difficulties with the temporal staging implied by this interpretation, since two births (Immanuel and Maher-shalal-hash-baz) must be fitted within a fairly short three-year period. But this problem alone does not severely undercut the general theory.

While the three children hold much in common, there are also important differences between them. Shear-jashub is already grown. We know that his name means "Remnant shall return," but no formal interpretation of his name is linked to any situation in the text (cf. 8:1–4), nor is any significance attached to his presence as such (cf. 7:15–17). The third child's birth is the confirmation of a sign event made prior to the prophet's intercourse with "the prophetess" (8:3) and as such bears no analogy to the other two children and their births. More important, however, is the marked distinctiveness of the second child, whether he is the prophet's or someone else's child.

First, his birth is announced in specific connection with a sign to Ahaz, a sign that comes in the context of impatience and exasperation at the house of David. Second, interest in the child goes beyond his birth: it also involves his growth and a timetable related to his maturation. Third, the child's birth portends good things insofar as the Syro-Ephraimite threat is halted (7:16) but also bad things for Ahaz and his father's house (7:17), again suggesting a close connection between Immanuel and the destiny of Ahaz and the royal house. Indeed, while some have tried to interpret 7:17 positively (a return to days when the kingdom was united), the more obvious sense of the verse is that a severance such as the one that took place in the royal house at the split of Israel from Judah is about to take place again. The king of Assyria will play a key role in the dark days that lie ahead for Ahaz and his father's house. Fourth, and finally, Immanuel is the only name that is specifically used in a new and distinct context, namely, at 8:8 and 8:10. "Immanuel" has something to do with the halting of Assyria (8:8) and the general halting of the nations (8:9–10), such as we hear in the psalms (see, among others, Psalms 2; 21; 46—48; 68; 76). If Immanuel is the prophet's son, he plays a unique role among the three children.

One further feature that must be taken into account in interpreting the Immanuel passages is the final oracle at 9:2–7. Clements, who argues for an original interpretation of Immanuel as the prophet's son, and an original disjunction between the royal oracle (9:2–7) and the memoir material, nevertheless concludes that a conscious editorial decision was made to link the two passages, thereby bringing about "a significant reinterpretation of the Immanuel prophecy of Isaiah 7:10–17" (Clements, "Immanuel," p. 238). Clements continues: "We can also see why this prophecy subsequently became obscure in its complexity. It originally referred to a child shortly expected to be born to the prophet's wife and stands second in the sequence of three such names which formed a major core of the Isaiah memoir. However, once Isaiah's prophecies came to be edited with a view to presenting a very favorable picture of Hezekiah, and more significantly still a favorable picture of the outcome of the events in 701 B.C., then we have a key to understanding

63

why this prophecy has undergone such a major reinterpretation" (p. 238). Clements regards the royal oracle at 9:2–7 as associated with King Hezekiah.

Clements's remarks point to yet another feature that must be taken into account in the interpretation of Isaiah 7:1—9:7, namely, the close association of this tradition complex with that found at the end of First Isaiah, in chapters 36—39. The features held in common are distinctive and suggest a deliberate and conscious shaping meant to draw out the contrast between Ahaz and his successor Hezekiah (Ackroyd, "Structure and Function"). In both instances we have an assault on Jerusalem (7:1, 6; 36:1–2). The critical encounter takes place at the fateful "conduit of the upper pool on the highway to the Fuller's Field" (7:3; 36:3). A sign comes for Ahaz even though he refuses one, and it is a negative one in the context of that refusal (7:14–17); Hezekiah repeatedly receives signs (37:30–32; 38:7) which come as a consequence of his obedient deportment (37:14–21; 38:3–6) or following upon proper requests (38:22). Ahaz does not believe and Assyria is unleashed on his foes and on himself; Hezekiah prays for God's deliverance so that God's name might be vindicated (37:20), and Assyria is halted. Here it is King Sennacherib who is dramatically "not established," slain by his own sons while worshiping his "no god." If we interpret the royal oracle at 9:2–7 in connection with the figure of Hezekiah, the contrast with Ahaz is set up already in the context of 7:1—9:7 (so Clements, "Immanuel"). What the "zeal of the LORD of hosts" promises to do at 9:7, namely, to uphold the Davidic king on his throne, the "zeal of the LORD of hosts" in fact accomplishes during the 701 Assyrian assault on Jerusalem (37:32). Hezekiah is defended by God "for my own sake and for the sake of my servant David" (37:35).

The Immanuel name has been reused on two occasions beyond the original birth notice at 7:14–17. It appears at the conclusion of the divine oracle to Isaiah in 8:5–8. Because of the refusal of the people to believe, God will bring against them the king of Assyria, who will sweep into Judah, "even to the neck." In the final clause Immanuel appears to be addressed, though a vocative form ("O Immanuel") must be implied: "its outspread wings will fill the breadth of your land, O Immanuel." The name appears again in the very next unit (8:9–10), where the positive image of the nations being finally halted is repeated, "for God is with us." Because of the suit-

64

ability of both of these oracles to the situation of Jerusalem's deliverance in 701, it would make sense to interpret Immanuel as none other than Hezekiah. The contrast that exists between Ahaz and Hezekiah in the two large narrative sections of Isaiah (chaps. 7—8; 36—39) would then also appear within the first section alone, by virtue of the royal oracle now juxtaposed at 9:2–7 and also by virtue of passages such as that found at 8:5–10. We are suddenly quite close to another logical juxtaposition, now established at 7:10–17, between Ahaz and the Immanuel child. Ahaz was warned in 7:9: "If you do not stand firm in faith, you shall not stand at all." His refusal to ask for a sign is clearly interpreted by the prophet as wearying God, if not an outright refusal to believe. The sign is given in this context, and as such we might expect it to be a sign that "dis-establishes" (Gese). The only way for Ahaz to be unequivocally judged is if Immanuel is a royal figure. This too allows Immanuel to function positively for the nation (7:16) but negatively for the king (7:17).

What, then, is to prevent the identification of Immanuel as Hezekiah, the actual historical successor of Ahaz? Everything points to a contrast between Ahaz and Hezekiah: within the memoir itself; due to the juxtaposition of the royal oracle at 9:2–7; and further enhanced by the contrast between the deportment of the house of David during the Syro-Ephraimite crisis and that which obtained during the Assyrian invasion in 701 B.C. The problem is chronological. According to Kings, Hezekiah had already been born nine years before Ahaz took the throne. Isaiah clearly speaks of the birth of Immanuel at 7:14. This chronological factor has proven decisive for the rejection of Hezekiah as the Immanuel child. The witness of the chronology of Kings has meant that Immanuel, if he is a royal figure, must be either a scion who never takes the throne (Laato) or a scion who becomes Hezekiah by secondary adjustment (Clements). Attempts to read the birth of Immanuel as a general reference to the name all young women will give their children in the age of weal to come (Kaiser) remain unconvincing. There is a specific intention to pronounce judgment on Ahaz and his house that is left to the side in such a reading. For this and other reasons we reject the interpretation of Immanuel as the prophet's son and incline toward a reading that points forward to the figure of Hezekiah, faithful king and obedient counterpoint to Ahaz.

65

History and Interpretation

The standard procedure for using historical information to illuminate the exegetical task is to coordinate all the available sources, having determined their genre and relative standing, in order to produce as coherent a total picture of historical events as is possible. Then the biblical account is interpreted against this historical backdrop. The Syro-Ephraimite crisis is reconstructed and the biblical account is then placed into this historical framework.

This method has its drawbacks, however. It may well be that certain sources are in irreducible tension or that we simply do not have the necessary source material to produce a coherent larger picture. Moreover, the unique features of each source presentation can be lost in deference to the task of producing an objective historical picture. What if we simply cannot solve certain chronological problems or discrepancies in the final text of II Kings, for example? Perhaps there are tensions in the text that a reader in antiquity was prepared to accept; precisely these tensions, however, frustrate the task of the modern historian. It might be better to try to appreciate the distinctive, subjective character of the source we have before us rather than trying to make it fit into some larger historical nexus, coordinated with other sources that themselves reflect a variety of genre and origin.

Several features of the Isaiah text are striking and bear further consideration in this context. First, while almost all historical reconstructions presuppose that the background of the Syro-Ephraimite assault involves the attempt to throw off Assyrian overlordship, our text makes no mention of this. The opening notice describes the assault as simple hostility: Pekah and Rezin "came up to Jerusalem to wage war against it, but they could not conquer it" (RSV). The background is not revealed to us. It is interesting that II Kings 15:37 describes the Pekah-Rezin assaults as divinely ordained: "In those days the LORD began to send King Rezin of Aram and Pekah son of Remaliah against Judah." When Isaiah interprets the hostility at 7:5 he says that Syria and Ephraim "have plotted evil" against Ahaz: "Let us go up against Judah and cut off Jerusalem and conquer it for ourselves and make the son of Tabeel king in it" (7:6). Here the particulars of the plot are revealed: Rezin and Pekah wish to conquer Jerusalem and put the son of Tabeel on

66

the throne. Perhaps the broader context is an anti-Assyrian intrigue. The point is that our text does not choose to focus on this. Rather, the hostility involves the house of David and the question of who will rule in Jerusalem. Unfortunately we do not know who the son of Tabeel is: Davidic, non-Davidic, "pliant Aramean," or a Tobiad out of Gilead—all have been suggested. But the emphasis up to this point is on the fate of the house of David. This is the reason for the hostility from Pekah and Rezin.

Incidentally, it may be wrong to overemphasize the situation of "siege" in the formal sense. Here there is a contrast with the narratives at Isaiah 36—39. Those narratives clearly depict war machinery, the presence of a "great army," and the concrete particulars of an assault, coming on the heels of widespread destruction in Judah proper. In the context of events in this earlier period, it is II Kings 16:5 that speaks of a siege—a siege of Ahaz. While we hear in Isaiah of war being waged, this matter remains in the background. Ahaz is the target of the hostility. There is a plot to devise evil against him. It is against this primary backdrop that the speech of the prophet unfolds.

Isaiah's response to this threat is enigmatic. The prophet gives an answer: it shall not stand, that is, the plot against Ahaz (7:7). What follows is open to interpretation (7:8–9). Syria is headed by Damascus which is headed by Rezin; Ephraim is headed by Samaria which is headed by Pekah. Country; capital; ruler. Many assume that what the prophet is hinting at is that these countries are ruled by mere men, and their plans will therefore fail. On analogy, Judah is headed by Jerusalem, which is headed, not by Ahaz, but by the Lord. Therefore Judah will not fall. Another interpretation would keep the emphasis firmly on Ahaz. Rezin heads up Syria-Damascus; Pekah heads up Ephraim-Samaria. A question is then implied, "Who heads up Judah-Jerusalem?" in the form of an ominous statement, "If you do not stand firm in faith, you shall not stand at all." The third link in the analogy is: Ahaz heads up Judah-Jerusalem—but only if he stands firm.

Then the prophet offers Ahaz a sign to confirm what he says. By refusing the sign, Ahaz hands over his right to head up Judah-Jerusalem. He does not believe and is not established. The sign that is given anyway is a sign of judgment, for it points to his eventual replacement: Immanuel. The king of Assyria will come in judgment to bring an end to the rule of Ahaz and his father's house, and by this act the whole land will become briers and thorns, as the Song of the Vineyard had promised (5:6; 7:23–25). Those who are left in the land in that day will eat curds and honey (7:22). Among them will be Immanuel (7:15). Before this time comes, Syria-Ephraim will become a desolation. Yet finally Immanuel will stand as a sign of God's presence, when the waters of the mighty river are halted at Jerusalem's neck (8:7–8). If this interpretation is correct, it explains why we hear absolutely nothing further from Ahaz after the sign is given. It is the prophet's last word to him. From then on he is overshadowed by the Assyrian judgment, on the one hand, and the emerging figure of Immanuel, on the other. The next we hear of Ahaz is at 14:28: an oracle is given on the year of his death.

Several other features in the depiction of Ahaz are striking. First, he is never referred to by Isaiah as "King Ahaz." In the context of chapter 7, Ahaz is consistently referred to under the broader rubric "the house of David" (7:2, 13). On two occasions, Ahaz is referred to together with "his people" (7:2, 17). In the latter instance, we hear of judgment "on you and on your people and on your ancestral house." This final reference is curious: why is Ahaz's ancestral house condemned for the recalcitrance of Ahaz? Who are Ahaz's "people"—does the prophet mean the larger population? Or is some smaller support group intended?

These questions are relevant for a number of reasons. If the opening verse (7:1) summarizing matters were missing, would it be at all clear that Ahaz was already king, and not just one of "the house of David" in line to rule after his father Jotham? We know of co-regencies during the long reign of Jotham's father, Uzziah. Was this a period of upheaval in the capital? Did the Syro-Ephraimite coalition wish to exploit this and place a rival claimant on the throne, Davidic or otherwise? We know from Kings that there is some disagreement regarding the timing of the Syro-Ephraimite threat. In II Kings 15, Pekah is slain during Jotham's last year as king, that is, before Ahaz ever took the throne (v. 30), and verse 37 reports Rezin-Pekah assaults against Judah during the reign of Jotham. II Kings 16 contradicts this by having a Pekah-Rezin siege of Ahaz. Can these two sources be coordinated, or are they finally in irreducible tension?

The opening verse (Isa. 7:1), theoretically drawn up on the basis of Kings, is also curious. Why give the names of all three kings: Ahaz, son of Jotham, son of Uzziah, king of Judah? Presumably the final "king of Judah" refers to Ahaz, the first in the list. Why the link to Uzziah—in order to pick up the reference in chapter 6 to "the year that King Uzziah died"? Did the final "king of Judah" always refer to Ahaz, or perhaps also to Uzziah or Jotham?

Unfortunately no clear answers to these questions are to be found in any of our sources. It is possible to consider a scenario whereby a period of transition in the Davidic house was made worse because of the long illness of Uzziah and the resultant co-regencies of Jotham and Ahaz (Kings has a two-year gap following the rule of Uzziah—cf. II Kings 15:27 and 15:32). Were Jotham and Ahaz considered co-regents at any point, or were their reigns otherwise felt to be somewhat connected? Hence the condemnation of "you . . . and your ancestral house" at 7:17. Hence the reference to Ahaz and "his people"—that is, the supporters of his kingship. Hence the attack on Jerusalem: in order to plot evil against Ahaz and place another ruler on the throne.

Into this situation of transition and external challenge, the prophet Isaiah steps forward, with his son Shear-jashub, to strengthen the royal house against the challenges of Rezin and Pekah. As A. Schoors puts it, he appears as "minister of royal anointment" (Schoors, p. 85). If Ahaz will stand firm, he will be worthy to rule as king. He refuses to accept this prophetic word and "is not established" in the final sense. He will continue to rule but with the specter of the king of Assyria overshadowing his kingship. The prophet turns to "the woman" and announces that she is pregnant and will give birth. As J. J. M. Roberts recognizes, "Either Isaiah was referring to a wife of Ahaz or to his own wife" (Roberts, p. 198). The former should not be ruled out. She will give birth to a son and she will call his name Immanuel. As he grows to maturity, he will usher in a period of peace that will stand in contrast to the fate in store for Ahaz and his father's house.

The single fact standing in the way of an identification of Immanuel with Hezekiah is the regnal year tallies of Kings. Yet as we have seen, Kings disagrees over the Pekah-Rezin assault and sets forth an incredible birth for Hezekiah when his father Ahaz was only eleven years old. If we are dealing with a young Ahaz in danger of retaining the throne, perhaps in his twenties if II Kings 16:1 is to be trusted, this would be a far more logical time for him to father sons.

All interpretation of the Immanuel texts, and the broader framework in which they are now found, has labored under this

69

"historical" data from Kings, which made an identification of Immanuel as Hezekiah impossible. We have put forward a hypothetical scenario that can be confirmed in none of our sources, though it might explain some of the tensions and contradictions that now exist in the final form of II Kings, at this particular historical period. But we are not so much interested in setting forth the "objective facts" as in trying to interpret Isa. 7:1—9:6 in a connected fashion. Immanuel appears to be a royal son who will grow to replace Ahaz. His birth is announced in connection with Ahaz's refusal to ask for a sign from the prophet which was to confirm the divine word uttered at 7:9: "If you do not stand firm in faith, you shall not stand at all." The prophet's promise that the plot against Ahaz would fail (7:7) is fulfilled, but the king is done in by his own refusal to believe and thereby be established.

The Book of Isaiah has clearly developed the contrast between Ahaz and his son Hezekiah in the present form of the text. The two main narrative sections (chaps. 7—8; 36—39) show a king who fails to trust replaced by one whose obedience and faithful deportment save a city. The birth of Hezekiah prior to Ahaz becoming a teenager strains the imagination. This chronological problem in Kings should not, however, be allowed to stand in the way of the more significant identification of Immanuel as a royal figure: Hezekiah.

The presentation of Kings is clear in its evaluation of Hezekiah (II Kings 18:1–8). He did what was right in accordance with all that his father David—not Ahaz—did (II Kings 18:3). He trusted in the Lord the God of Israel, unlike his father Ahaz, *"so that there was no one like him among all the kings of Judah after him, or among those who were before him"* (II Kings 18:5). It is difficult to improve on that evaluation. The best that can be done is to repeat it for the later Josiah, at the end of his reign (II Kings 23:25), to mitigate the harsh decision that follows (II Kings 25:26–27). It is probably no accident that as the encomium for Hezekiah continues, the Historian states: "The LORD was with him" (II Kings 18:7). The promise made by Isaiah in Ahaz's day is fulfilled in the child Immanuel. Because of his presence and obedient deportment during the Assyrian invasion, the people could truly say, "God is with us" as the prophet Isaiah had promised. So the Deuteronomistic Historian also says in turn of Hezekiah, "The LORD was with him."

The linkage of Immanuel to Hezekiah is not made in re-

70

verse (Clements) but is forward effecting. As he grows to maturity and succeeds his father, Hezekiah becomes Immanuel—not the reverse. Isaiah appeared before the house of David and presented it with a stark choice. Because the house of David refuses to believe and stand firm on the original promises to David—similar promises to "be with" the king (II Sam. 7:9; II Kings 1:37; Ps. 89:21–25)—Isaiah announces the birth of a child who will reign in faithful contrast to his father. His mother shall call his name Immanuel. While it may be possible to detect reverse influence from the narratives of Jerusalem's deliverance in chapters 7—8, there can be little doubt that the promise of Immanuel belonged to the period in question. It was a time of decision. Isaiah's promise of a faithful ruler was not forgotten. It comes as no surprise that as the Isaiah traditions developed and took form, the contrast between Ahaz and Hezekiah was yet further strengthened. Jerusalem's deliverance in 701 B.C. was a powerful confirmation of the prophet's Immanuel promises.

Royal Theology and Christian Interpretation

We have spoken of Isaiah's specific interest in Zion and in proper leadership for Israel. Older biographical studies of Isaiah frequently presented the prophet as a man of the court, urbane, sophisticated, with access to the king as well as the common folk—a man to be contrasted with Amos, for example. Such a reading was grounded in an appraisal of the prophet's "lofty speech" and his ironic, often enigmatic language and metaphor selection. But clearly the most influential force behind such a reading is revealed in the material under discussion (7:1—9:6). Isaiah confronts the house of David without a hint of reserve. He is acquainted with the royal traditions and he uses them to argue for a certain kind of king of Judah. He is not anti-royal in any simple sense, even as he takes a stand against Ahaz and his father's house. The prophet does not propose a different form of government, one under the control of priest, or wise man, or prophet (his own son Immanuel!). Nor does he propose a return to an earlier model, where the nation was governed by judges. Isaiah is not concerned with the form of government but with the substance of Israel's governors. If Ahaz will not stand firm on the promises to David, he shall not stand at all. Isaiah is not anti-king, he is anti-Ahaz. He is pro-Immanuel.

Zion theology and royal theology are frequently thought to

71

be more unconditional in terms of divine endorsement than, say, the traditions of exodus and wilderness and promised land. A whole generation died in the wilderness because they refused to believe in the promises of God. Their entry into the promised land was conditioned on their belief and willingness to stand firm. Jeremiah can use these same traditions to remind Israel that the way of life and death stands before them. God will not unconditionally preserve them before the Babylonian forces. The temple is not an unconditionally endorsed place of sanctuary. God can cast off another entire generation of unfaithful people, and in fact does so.

We have seen how carefully Isaiah handles the traditions of Zion. We have yet to see how subtly and mysteriously he treats these same traditions in chapters 28—32, where God's work with Zion is termed "strange" and "alien" (28:21). Isaiah can speak of Zion in terms familiar from the Psalter, where God wreaks havoc on nations that plot against him and assault his holy hill (29:5–8; 31:4–31; also 8:9–10). Yet God also can fight against his own people, in these same familiar terms (28:21–22; 29:1–4), as we have indeed seen in chapters 1—4. Precisely because of his "unconditional" endorsement of Zion, God may have to take up arms against his own people. If Israel becomes so disenfranchised as a people, unrecognizable from the nations, God will—must "unconditionally"—treat them as such. Israel becomes a threat to Zion, as it were, like the nations who "set themselves" and "take counsel together" (Ps. 2:2). The ironic twist in the Book of Isaiah is that the nations finally turn and seek Zion (2:1–3), leaving the house of Jacob to follow their lead (2:5). Such is Isaiah's employment of Zion theology and its "unconditional" aspects. God is unconditionally committed to Zion and for this reason must judge his own people Israel unconditionally.

Royal theology is handled similarly by the prophet. The Book of Isaiah displays an interest in the Davidic house without real analogy in the prophetic corpus. One thinks here of the two royal oracles within Isaiah 1—12 (9:2–7 and 11:1–9) and also the Immanuel texts. Isaiah 32:1–8 is a powerful statement about what can happen when a righteous king reigns—eyes will not be closed and ears will not be shut. That is: Isaiah's prophetic commission can be turned to good. The king can even reverse a prophetic sentence of judgment, thus saving both himself and the city (38:1–6). Such is the divine endorsement of the royal house, rooted in the promises first made to David (II Samuel 7; Isa. 37:35). The nations that rage against Zion also take counsel "against the LORD and his anointed" (Ps. 2:2). God will defend both Zion and the king he has placed there, "on Zion, my holy hill" (Ps. 2:6).

But when Israel's king becomes like other kings, like "the kings of the earth" (Ps. 2:2), God's "unconditional" endorsement of kingship will turn to necessary judgment, for the sake of the office and for the sake of the one to whom the promises were first made. In the context of those promises, we learned what kind of "unconditional" devotion God had to kingship—it was a devotion that would necessitate punishment of individual kings, for the sake of the office of kingship itself: "When he commits iniquity, I will punish him with a rod such as mortals use, with blows inflicted by human beings. But I will not take my steadfast love from him, as I took it from Saul, whom I put away from before you" (II Sam. 7:14–15). Ahaz is not removed from being king, like Saul before him, on account of his disbelief and refusal to trust in God's promises. But he is chastised by the prophet, who speaks of his eventual downfall at the hands of the Assyrians and his final replacement by Immanuel.

It is accurate to speak of the prophet Isaiah as standing in the traditions of Zion and David, if by that is meant that Isaiah takes a specific interest in the royal house and in God's choice of Zion and David. But it would be wrong to understand those traditions as more inherently "unconditional" than the traditions of exodus, wilderness, and occupation. Isaiah has a clear sense of the importance of kingship for Israel, and for that very reason he denounces Ahaz in his unbelief and calls for a king who will rule with justice and righteousness (32:1). We will have more to say about this in the comment on 9:2–7; 11:1–9; and 32:1–8. Equally important for its portrait of proper kingship is the narrative complex in chapters 36—39, which focuses on the figure of Hezekiah.

One question remains. If the logical interpretation of the Immanuel child leans in the direction of King Hezekiah, why did later interpreters not see this? To be sure, one prominent strain in Jewish exegesis has identified the Immanuel child with Hezekiah; the same is true of the royal oracle at 9:2–7. But what of the Christian interpretation of Immanuel as Jesus Christ and of the "young woman" as Mary? More generally, how did the many Isaiah texts that speak of kingship become texts con-

73

cerned with a *future* ruler, not a historical figure, whether Hezekiah or someone else? How did an allegedly historical referent become an eschatological referent? We saw above that the relationship between history and eschatology in Isaiah is often unclear: is the vision of judgment found in chapters 2—4 fulfilled in the context of the larger book, in the events of 587 perhaps, or is that vision primarily directed to a future outside the book's own presentation?

Whatever one may think of the Immanuel child in chapters 7—8 (prophet's son; royal figure; symbol; Hezekiah), one's reading of the Immanuel passages is now affected by the larger context, specifically the royal oracle in 9:2–7. Isaiah 7:14 spoke of a child to be born; 9:6 states, as if in response: "For to us a child is born." Isaiah 7:16 speaks of the Syro-Ephraimite threat coming to an end; 9:5 tells of the broken rod of the oppressor. The child would be called "God is with us"; "and he is named 'Wonderful Counselor, Mighty God' " (9:6). It is virtually impossible to read the Immanuel passages in the light of 9:2–7 and not catch the clear connections that exist as a consequence of the present organization of the material.

We have argued that within this present organization the clear referent for Immanuel is Hezekiah. This conclusion is reached in part by the appeal to an even broader context, namely, one that closes with the narratives of Isaiah 36—39. Yet even this meaningful context, with its rich and detailed focus on the figure of Hezekiah, has itself been reinterpreted within the present shape of the book. We saw that the book opened with an interest in the aftermath of 701 B.C. and with the future that stretched out beyond the events recorded in chapters 36—39, beyond even the 587 B.C. debacle. An episode from the past is used to speak to the future. That future involved Israel's leadership: righteous counselors and judges as at first (1:26); the glorious branch of the Lord (4:2). Isaiah traditions have developed with a distinct interest in the figure of Hezekiah, as a model for proper kingship in Israel.

But this interest is not primarily nostalgic or memorializing in nature. What Hezekiah is as king, how he conducts himself, becomes a type for later kings to follow. This is made clear through the addition of 11:1–9 to the present context of Isaiah 1—12. Beyond the closed circle of Immanuel and "the child born unto us," represented by the traditions in 7:1—9:6, Isaiah also looks ahead to a new kind of kingship (11:1–9). Picking up much of the same imagery of Isa. 2:1–5 and 4:2–6, this "shoot from the stump of Jesse" will rule in days to come, in a period of peace and justice, as king over all nations (11:10–11).

We will have more to say below about these several passages. Because of the conjunction of the royal Immanuel traditions with this vision of future messianic rule, the former has been reinterpreted by the latter—but not so severely that the original historical referent is lost. The future ruler finds his point of departure based on the figure of Immanuel and King Hezekiah. What kingship shall become in Israel, and for the nations, it becomes with reference to the Immanuel child and the historical rule of King Hezekiah. Out of that historical matrix a model for kingship emerges that is filled full in the person of Jesus of Nazareth, King of the Jews, Messiah of the nations.

The larger context of Isaiah 1—12 has affected our interpretation of the core material in 7:1—9:6. Just as it is impossible to read the Immanuel texts in isolation from the royal oracle at 9:2–7, so too the royal oracle at 11:1–9 tends to affect our comprehensive vision of kingship as found in chapters 1—12. But the messianic role that Jesus fulfills is not an eternal "type" with no earthly referent. The church confesses that out of the messiness of earthly government, specifically rooted in the house of David, God prepares a place for his son to rule as King. That Jesus explodes all mundane aspects of kingship is itself not unprecedented. Israel's own vision of kingship, and from time to time its own historical kings, prepared the church to see in Jesus a king like no other, yet like what Israel longed for and at times experienced a foretaste of in kings like Hezekiah.

Isaiah's Word to Ahaz: It Shall Not Stand (7:1–9)

The encounter between prophet and king is the focal point of these verses. The challenge from Syria-Ephraim is specifically directed at Ahaz. He is the target of a coup that seeks to replace him with "the son of Tabeel." The opening verse is related to II Kings 16:5, but they go very different ways in their respective contexts. Kings offers a summary of events, such as those reported in Isaiah. In Isaiah, the verse may in fact be wrongly interpreted as a summary of events that unfold. It states that the military attack against Jerusalem failed. Consequently, the coalition pursues another line of attack: the terrorizing of Jerusalem, with the intent of setting up another king "in

75

it" (7:6). As such, 7:1 is not a summary of events that follow but only stage one in a plot against Judah-Jerusalem-Ahaz.

It is also to be noted that the verse is not dated. We know that it is quite possible for the Deuteronomistic Historian to supply dates, which he does more often than not; the 701 assault of Sennacherib, for example, comes in the fourteenth year of Hezekiah (II Kings 18:13; Isa. 36:1). We have seen that there are clear problems with the dating of the Pekah-Rezin assault(s) in Kings. Our text avoids these by speaking of an attack "in the days of Ahaz son of Jotham son of Uzziah." Ahaz may be king, but we do not know how long he has ruled, nor how long he will yet rule. We know that when the "house of David" is told about a Syro-Ephraimite coalition, Ahaz and his supporters are terrified (7:2). It is interesting that the term "Israel" is not used but rather "Ephraim." The Northern Kingdom has already begun to experience the gradual loss of territory at the hands of the "nation far away" (5:26; II Kings 15:29). The wall of the vineyard is broken (5:5). Now Ephraim in desperation turns against his brother to the south, aligned with a non-brother to the northeast. Israel is slowly becoming one of "the nations."

Into this situation of hostile alignment against Ahaz, God dispatches Isaiah and his son Remnant Shall Return (Shearjashub). The son appears without any explanation of his origin. We saw that many wished to regard the final verses of Isaiah's commission (6:12–13) as secondary, since they spoke of a remnant that would remain and be burned again. The son, however, might well be construed as an embodiment of precisely that dimension of Isaiah's commission: there is to be a final remnant beyond the vision of total deafness and destruction. This is not a secondary but a primary dimension of the prophet's ministry. The king is confronted by the prophet and by the concrete symbol of God's final preservation of Israel: Remnant Shall Return. As it turns out, by rejecting the prophetic word, the king rejects the son as well. An end will come to his house and the house of his father. The Remnant will be handed over to Immanuel.

The counsel of Isaiah, "Take heed, be quiet, do not fear, and do not let your heart be faint" (7:4), may sound like the kind of unrealistic advice that religious people constantly give in the face of concrete hostility. But consider the context more carefully. An assault on Jerusalem has failed, according to 7:1. Ahaz and his supporters fear the coalition and its intent to replace the king (7:2, 6). Isaiah's words are directed to this precise fear. The coalition will not succeed; the "son of Tabeel" shall not rule; Ahaz is the head of Judah-Jerusalem. But if he does not believe, he will not be established.

We know from Kings that the form which Ahaz's "disbelief" took was the decision to call for help from the king of Assyria and to become his servant rather than the servant of the Lord, the Lord's son (Ps. 2:7): "I am your servant and your son. Come up, and rescue me from the hand of the king of Aram and from the hand of the king of Israel, who are attacking me" (II Kings 16:7). The counsel of Isaiah to "take heed, be quiet, do not fear" means at a minimum that Ahaz must stand firm in the promises to David and not denounce his sonship, his servanthood. Ahaz is king only because Yahweh has chosen him. If he chooses to become the servant and son of another, then he must expect his overlord to demand payment. This means for Judah vast desolation and the transformation of the remnant-vineyard into a place of briers and thorns.

Isaiah prophesies instead that the coalition will fall of its own accord. Assyria will see to the destruction of Ephraim without Ahaz having to lift a hand, and the same holds true for the other "smoldering stump of firebrand," Rezin the king of Syria. Isaiah does not explicitly mention Assyria until after the refusal of Ahaz, and then in the context of judgment against him, not on his behalf. But he makes it clear that the coalition against him will not stand (7:7). The nation from afar will bring an end to Ephraim and this vain assault "against the LORD and his anointed," as God promises in Psalm 2. By joining with Syria, Ephraim has become like the nations that "conspire" and "plot in vain" (Ps. 2:1). In this context it is to be recalled that Psalm 2 ends with a solemn warning to the "kings" and "rulers of the earth" (Ps. 2:10): the warning is presumably to kings who set themselves against Yahweh's anointed. But Yahweh's anointed must also take care to "serve the LORD with fear" (Ps. 2:11) "or he will be angry, and you will perish in the way" (Ps. 2:12).

While some have assumed that the notice of Ephraim's demise within sixty-five years (Isa. 7:8*b*) stems from a later hand (e.g., Clements, *Isaiah 1—36,* p. 85), it is possible to understand it as originally part of the context. The prophet announces that Ephraim will fall within sixty-five years and then states that the head of Ephraim is Pekah, the son of Remaliah. Not only will it fall, it "will be shattered." This is as positive an oracle of

77

salvation to the house of David as the prophet could give. But he must believe or he will not be established. He refuses to believe, and the prophet follows with an oracle of judgment against him and his father's house. Following a long string of judgment oracles (7:18–25), the prophet receives another word from God, concerning the birth of Maher-shalal-hash-baz. The birth of the child, Spoil-Speeds-Prey-Hastes, is interpreted to mean that hastily, speedily, the spoil of Samaria will be carried away by the king of Assyria—before the child knows how to cry out "My father" or "My mother" (8:4).

We either have two oracles concerning the demise of Samaria-Ephraim, the second more accurate historically (8:4) and the first a curiously inaccurate gloss (7:8b); or the two concern different aspects of Samaria's demise (the first would still be curious in its timing); or the second is given to revise the first, based on a new word from Yahweh to prophet, concerning the birth of this curiously named child. That is, a sixty-five-year prediction concerning Ephraim's demise, which was to function positively for the house of David, is ironically shortened to a much more imminent demise after the king's refusal to believe. The timetable of Ephraim's demise is to be discussed in the next unit also.

Isaiah's Word to Ahaz: You Shall Not Stand (7:10–25)

Having announced God's sure protection of Judah against hostile assaults from the north, the prophet now moves to offer Ahaz some concrete sign of God's intentions. The provision of a sign that is meant to confirm the divine promise is a theme that appears in another, later encounter between prophet and royal figure: on the occasion of Hezekiah's sickness unto death (37:7). There as here, the point of the sign is to underscore God's intention to do as he has promised. The question the text poses is, How will the sign be received—gratefully or with caution? Ahaz responds one way, Hezekiah another. Therein lies at least part of the difference between them, as these two pivotal figures have been presented to us in the final form of the Book of Isaiah.

Most assume that this unit (7:10–25), which opens with a fresh word from prophet to king, has received much secondary enrichment. Verses 15 and 16 are considered partly overlapping; the "king of Assyria" reference at the end of verse 17 seems tacked on; the string of oracles beginning with "in that day" (vv. 18–25) contains material that is principally judgmental, but some oracles are arguably positive in tone (vv. 21–22). On the assumption that even secondary additions would be made to produce a coherent final text, we will try to interpret the material as it stands.

As discussed in detail above, we interpret the provision of the sign in the context of the king's refusal to ask—especially when offered in such expansive terms (7:11)—as inherently indicting of the house of David. This interpretation is confirmed in most readings where Immanuel is a royal figure. The prophet addresses a specific figure who is known by him and the king, namely, "the young woman" *(hā 'almāh)*. We take this specificity to mean that the young woman is one of the king's own consorts, who is known by him. She has already conceived and she will soon bear a son. The Hebrew text indicates that it is the mother who will call the child's name Immanuel, not the king. Only later will others call him Immanuel as well (8:8, 10).

If the context is a royal one, the reference to choosing good and refusing evil in verses 15 and 16 may pertain specifically to the age at which Immanuel is fit to rule as king. Before this time, the Syro-Ephraimite threat will be vanquished and their land— Ephraim and Syria are considered a single land—will be deserted. In this context, then, the sixty-five-year period (7:8*b*) has already shrunk considerably; the threat against Ahaz will not outlast the child's age of maturity. (Isaiah 8:4 will shrink the period yet further.) We hear, then, of the child reaching an age where he is fit to rule, while for Ahaz and his people and his father's house there are other days ahead, days worse even than the time when the nation was first divided. The final "king of Assyria" (7:17*c*) simply stipulates the agent of this judgment. The same king of Assyria who brings an end to the Syro-Ephraimite threat (7:16) brings dark days for Ahaz, his people, and his ancestral house.

It might well be that 7:15 has been secondarily interpolated into this otherwise coherent sequence of events as a gloss on verse 16, as many have assumed. On the other hand, the reference to eating curds and honey at the age of maturity may be linked to the same image at 7:21–22. This is the one image in the series of "in that day" oracles that seems somewhat positive.

Yet even it presupposes a disaster, after which a remnant is left, both of animals and of humankind. In that day, the surviving remnant will eat curds and honey. In their midst—so 7:15 suggests—will be the Immanuel child, now having reached the age when he might rule over this remnant left in the land. The mixture of positive and negative images in 7:18–25 simply maintains the same ironic stance of 7:10–17: good news for the remnant and for Immanuel is bad news for Ahaz and his people and his ancestral house. "In that day" the land will be thoroughly occupied by Assyrian—and Egyptian—forces. The Assyrian razor will shave clean (7:20). But a remnant will return (7:21–22), as the divine commission revealed (6:13) and as the prophet's elder son attests. The final verses (7:23–25) speak of expensive vines which become thorns and briers, in fulfillment of the judgment oracle of the Song of the Vineyard (5:6). King Ahaz, by his refusal to trust in the prophetic word and the promises made to David, forfeits his right to divine protection and opens himself and his people to the assault of the king of Assyria—all in the name of avoiding an assault from the Syro-Ephraimite coalition, which Isaiah promised would fall of its own accord.

Immanuel Stands Firm (8:1–10)

Isaiah 8:1–4 reports that a second child is born to the prophet. Shear-jashub appeared with Isaiah as a concrete symbol of God's concern to raise up a remnant within Israel, beyond the judgment and desolation the prophet was to announce. Here we hear of the birth of a second son. The prophet is given the command to write on a tablet: belonging to Spoil-Speeds-Prey-Hastes. No explanation is given as to the meaning of the command. Isaiah does as he is told, and even gets witnesses to attest to his having written the strange words "Maher-shalal-hash-baz" on a large tablet. What spoil speeds, what prey hastes? Following upon the previous chapter, is this yet a further vision of judgment against Judah and the house of Ahaz? No explanation is given.

Now it is the prophet's turn to father a son. He goes to "the prophetess" and she conceives. The prophet acts on no command. He has been informed only of a name. Perhaps in the climate of auspicious naming, he realizes that a child will be born, to him and the prophetess, with an equally auspicious

80

future yet to be revealed. And so Maher-shalal-hash-baz is born. God interprets the name to the prophet. Even before Immanuel can refuse the evil and choose the good, before Maher-shalal-hash-baz can say "daddy" or "mommy," the king of Assyria will turn back the Syro-Ephraimite threat.

The transition to the following unit (8:5–10) is somewhat abrupt. We hear of a salvation oracle, brokered through the prophet's son, in the opening unit (8:1–4). Suddenly, however, the tone shifts. A similar sequencing was attested in chapter 7, where an oracle of salvation was followed hard upon by an oracle of judgment against the royal house. Here there is no explanation, however, for the shift in tone. In this context, the object of the indictment is not the royal house but "this people."

Clements and others have argued that the original conclusion to 8:1–4 is now found at 8:16–18. The original referent for "testimony" and "teaching" (8:16) was the Maher-shalal-hash-baz tablet, while the "disciples" were the witnesses Uriah and Zechariah (8:2). This leaves 8:5–15 as an intrusive unit whose addition is meant to extend the meaning of "testimony" to the entire preceding memoir. It is clear, however, that both 8:5–15 and 8:16–22 maintain a focus on the broader population as hostile to the message of the prophet. "This people" are spoken of at 8:5, 11, 12; the same people are intended by the more general "they" at 8:15, 19, 21, 22 and "a people" at 8:19. In sum, chapter 8 shifts the focus from the house of David to a wider referent. Not only was the house of David hostile to the message of the prophet, so too were "this people." Moreover, a certain symmetry is achieved in respect of the prophet's children. The house of David is confronted by Shear-jashub; "this people" are confronted by Maher-shalal-hash-baz. Two children carrying names portending salvation are each rejected in their own way, thus transferring the significance of the names to another day and for another generation (8:18).

Within the unit 8:5–10 the initial contrast is between the waters of Shiloah and the waters of the River. The people reject the first, which symbolize indigenous sustenance, and are therefore given the second, which symbolize external power and might. Here a direct analogy is made to the decision of the house of David in chapter 7. Ahaz rejects the promises that pertain to him and as a consequence receives the judgment of the king of Assyria. So too this people reject their own waters, steady and gentle, and receive instead mighty and powerful

81

waters. Instead of saving them, they overflow and reach to the neck (8:8). Only then, at the last moment, are they halted before Immanuel. The portion of text at 8:9–10 looks as though it could have been taken directly from the Psalms of Zion: the nations set themselves against the Lord and against his anointed. But their plans are thwarted, because of Immanuel (God with us). Judgment for Ahaz and "this people" for rejecting indigenous promises and receiving foreign aid is then finally turned back only because of the Immanuel promise and only after much desolation ("even to the neck"). The 701 B.C. situation stands very near to this depiction.

The Teaching Stands Firm (8:11–22)

What follows in 8:11–15 is a private oracle of warning to the prophet. With Kaiser, we regard the primary context to be that represented by the term "conspiracy" used at 8:12. The prophet has denounced the house of David and spoken of a new replacement in the figure of Immanuel. But the final working out of Immanuel's reign, his maturing that brings with it a halt to the Assyrian threat—these events still lie in the future. In the meanwhile, the prophet has pronounced judgment over the royal house and is likely to be considered a conspirator by many. For the prophet and those who learn from his teaching (8:16), it will be a time of hardship and patient waiting. The prophet is not to regard the charge of conspiracy as accurate; he is not to fear the Syro-Ephraimite threat, as do others. He is to fear God alone. It will be a time when the Holy God, his word to the prophet and royal house, will be a snare and a stumbling block (8:14–15). Like the nations that gather against Zion, many will fall because of the prophet's word.

But 8:14 also spoke of the Lord of hosts as a sanctuary. In 8:16–22 we see the concrete form that sanctuary will take. The prophet's testimony and teaching in this troubled time will be bound up and sealed, and deposited among the prophet's disciples (literally, "those who are taught," so Isa. 50:4). We heard of Ahaz and "his people" (7:2, 17); the prophet also has "his people" (8:16), though they are few. As further witnesses, the prophet has "the children whom the Lord has given me" (8:18), who are "signs and portents" from God. And he has the teaching and the testimony (8:16, 20). In the troubled times that lie ahead—times of conspiracy charges, of Assyrian assault, of wa-

82

ters reaching to the neck—when questions finally arise about the will of God, Isaiah and his children and his disciples can take their stand on the divine word vouchsafed to the prophet during this crisis. Here the notion of a memoir is not far wrong: the contents of chapters 7—8 were to serve as a memoir against which could be tested contrary claims of divine revelation (8:19–20).

The theory that the testimony of Maher-shalal-hash-baz (8:1–4) should be connected more directly to the testimony sealed up among the prophet's disciples (8:16) is right in one respect. In 8:1–4 a testimony is given (vv. 1–2) whose meaning and purpose is then established by God (v. 4). The prophet must only wait the nine months of the prophetess's pregnancy to see the testimony established: immediately—before the child can even utter his first words—the spoil of Samaria and the wealth of Damascus will be whisked away by the king of Assyria. The prophet learns that what appears obscure by God's command is nevertheless to be trusted. The same lesson is relevant at the close of the memoir.

The prophet must wait for the Lord. The truth of the teaching and testimony regarding the Syro-Ephraimite threat, the king of Assyria, but especially Immanuel, will take time to be established. In the meantime, God leaves the prophet with concrete signs of the faithfulness of his word, in the form of his two children and in the teaching he has given the prophet concerning Immanuel, just as before the prophet had his large tablet that was a witness to the Lord's command: Maher-shalal-hash-baz.

The memoir closes on a very ominous note (vv. 21–22). The period of hardship is already beginning. People will pass through "it," presumably the land (not Jerusalem more narrowly), and will be enraged. They will curse their king—presumably Ahaz—and their God, for they are estranged from him. They will be thrust into thick darkness. What is finally established is neither the house of David (Ahaz) nor "this people" but only the word of God as a testimony and a teaching. For Isaiah, his children, and his disciples the teaching will be a sanctuary in the troubled times ahead, until Immanuel reigns and the Assyrian threat is finally halted at Zion's neck.

A Child Is Born (9:1–7)

It should come as no surprise that one of the best-known passages in Isaiah is also one that has received a variety of interpretations in the modern period. While it has often been placed in the postexilic period, there are features of the oracle that suggest it belongs in the preexilic period, when the monarchy was still in existence. It is not possible, however, to wrest from the oracle too much historical precision. On the one hand, the correct translation of 9:1 is by no means clear. The NRSV contrasts a former time of contempt with a latter time of glory, when in fact both verb forms render a past tense, and the second form could just as easily be translated "made severe." Also, the opening verse in its entirety—not just the first phrase—appears to be secondarily related to the oracle as such (9:2–7). It is not an integral part of the oracle, even as it clearly attempts to situate the oracle at some point in time. Finally, when one moves toward seeing the oracle as a traditional piece, the temporal location of the oracle, on the basis of historical reconstruction, becomes more and more difficult.

By the same token, we have seen that clues are provided in the larger context of the memoir that strongly urge a reading related to the Immanuel child of 7:14. Attention to the yet larger context of chapters 36—39 further strengthens an interpretation related to King Hezekiah. Whether the insistence upon accession rather than birth is justified, a closer reading of the oracle itself will determine. The larger context, with its interest in the birth of the Immanuel child, may play a role here as well. In the present form of the memoir, with this royal oracle forming a new conclusion, traditional material related to royal accession may have been adapted in this instance to speak of Hezekiah's birth. More on this will be discussed below.

Apart from the question of accession or birth, the royal oracle is fairly straightforward. Unfortunately the same cannot be said of the opening verse. The first phrase appears to reverse the image of gloom found in the previous verse (8:22). An exception is being made, though the referent is not clear. If the following phrase telling of a former and a latter time means to hold these periods in contrast (so NRSV), then one might expect the referent to be "the way of the sea, the land beyond the Jordan, Galilee of the nations"—territories annexed by Tiglath-pileser from Israel in 733 B.C. (see II Kings 15:29).

Those who hold that both temporal references refer to Assyrian hegemony (i.e., "in the latter time he treated harshly the way of the sea") must seek the exception to the gloom-anguish elsewhere. So Clements sees the contrast between the "disastrous fate of Israel at the hands of Assyria, which came as a consequence of the disunity between Ephraim and Judah, [and] the salvation which could come if they were reunited under a single Davidic ruler" (Clements, *Isaiah 1—39*, pp. 104–105). Since the attempt has been made to link the royal oracle to the preceding memoir itself, through the agency of an unfortunately confusing verse, one would expect to get some clue from this larger context. Clements's reading has in its favor the clear sense of impending judgment that was to be visited upon the Northern Kingdom, through the agency of the Assyrians (7:8*b*, 15; 8:4). Judah too was to be visited with anguish and doom, as a consequence of Ahaz's disbelief (8:21–22). However, consistent with the image of an Assyria finally restrained (8:8–10), this opening verse speaks of an end to gloom for the one in anguish. God thoroughly judged the Northern Kingdom (9:1*bc*), but for the people who walked in darkness in Judah, "on them light has shined" (9:2). As in the memoir, the contrast is between those who are punished by the Assyrian waters—most obviously the Northern Kingdom—and those who are able to say, finally, "Be broken . . . for God is with us" (8:9–10, RSV).

It may be important to keep the timetable of chapters 7—8 clear. The land of the Syro-Ephraimite coalition was to be deserted before the Immanuel child had matured, before even Maher-shalal-hash-baz could speak his first words. Isaiah 9:1 confirms that, for all intents and purposes, the coalition has indeed fallen to Assyria. At the same time, the following royal oracle confirms that for the people who walk in darkness a time of light has come. The main question is whether the broken rod of the oppressor is the rod of the Syro-Ephraimite coalition or the rod of Assyria itself. Yet this question turns on the degree to which the royal oracle has a fixed historical location in its present context. Here the matter of accession or birth plays an important role.

It is clear that the opening verses (9:3–5) depict the end of military oppression. Verse 4 speaks as though the defeat of the oppressor is an accomplished fact: "the rod of their oppressor you have broken as on the day of Midian." In historical terms, it would be possible to link the defeat of the Syro-Ephraimite coalition with the accession of Hezekiah. Yet the oracle strains

85

at an even grander depiction, and for this reason most have assumed that the defeated foe is Assyria. Clearly, however, Assyria was neither on the verge of defeat nor even threatened with such defeat at the accession of Hezekiah. It is for these reasons of mundane historical accuracy that Josiah has been put forward as a candidate who better fits the scenario of possible Assyrian defeat.

When one treats the oracle as a traditional accession piece, however, the language of military defeat need not conform so closely to historical facts. The cause for joy is not so much pending military victory but the "birth" of a new ruler, in whose wake such victory will come in due course. The king is given throne names appropriate to the hopes his rule engenders: Wonderful Counselor, Mighty God, Everlasting Father, Prince of Peace (9:6).

Most regard the references to birth and the language "child" and "son" at verse 6 as referring to the king's accession rather than to his actual birth, in line with the imagery of Ps. 2:7 ("You are my son; today I have begotten you") and common Near Eastern practices. Whether or not this is so in the strict historical sense, the reference to birth is surely meant to pick up the language of 7:14: "a young woman shall conceive and bear a son" (RSV). On chronological grounds, a royal accession oracle is out of place at this juncture in the presentation. Hezekiah's mature reign still lies ahead, as is made clear by the material following (9:8—10:34), where the Assyrian foe is still gainfully occupied in the role of "rod of my [Yahweh's] anger" (10:5). Therefore one is already dealing with a decision to place the royal oracle at this juncture secondarily, whatever its original historical circumstances. If a link has been established intentionally between the "birth" of 9:6 and the promise of Immanuel at 7:14–16, then the effect is to focus the royal oracle on the birth rather than on the accession of Immanuel. The birth then *portends great things* and in that sense is analogous to children of the prophet, who are "signs and portents in Israel from the LORD of hosts" (8:18).

This may be a further reason for the decision to place the oracle at this juncture, following the memoir proper. Isaiah's first son appeared at 7:3. The second son was born within the brief compass of 8:1–4: the prophet received a name; the child was conceived; he was born; his name was interpreted. The birth served as a concrete fulfillment of a previous word given

86

to the prophet. At 7:14–16 we hear of a similar provision of a name (Immanuel) and promises associated with it. The name reechos at 8:8 and 8:10 in visions of the future. But we hear nothing about the birth as such, as a concrete fulfillment of the word spoken to the prophet, which was to be a sign for the house of David. The royal oracle at 9:1–7 provides that concrete fulfillment: "For a child has been born for us." With us, for us (9:6), is Mighty God. The repetition of *lānû* ("for us, to us") at 9:6 evokes the promise of the name *ʾimmānû* ("with us"), just as *ʾēl gibbôr* ("mighty God") evokes *ʾēl* ("God"). The promise of the son is fulfilled. The promises related to his maturation await their fulfillment, even as the oracle closes with a vision of his reign: "His authority shall grow continually, and there shall be endless peace." Where the Davidic throne was threatened by the rule of Ahaz and his house, it will be established and upheld in the person of Immanuel. "The zeal of the LORD of hosts will do this"—the oracle concludes.

In sum, there are good grounds for interpreting the closing royal oracle as an integral part of the much wider tradition complex, now located at 7:1—9:7. It is fitting that the final oracle speaks of the birth of the child who was only promised at 7:14, yet whose maturation and reign were to figure in such important ways in the days to come. Yet next to that vision of just and righteous government stands the stark and sober portrait of a prophet under siege, of a God who is sanctuary for some but a snare and stumbling block for many. Before we encounter a people who see a great light, we must first encounter a people thrust into thick darkness. The memoir represented by this complex stands as a testimony and teaching for a generation to come, a memorial to God's provision of Immanuel, but also a testimony to the refusal of Ahaz and "this people" to trust in the promises to David and Zion, preferring the waters of the great River to the waters of Shiloah. The next unit, Isaiah 9:8—10:34, places us firmly in the midst of those waters.

Isaiah 9:8—10:34
The Rise and Fall of a Great Forest

Introduction

The opening material in 9:8–21 is organized around the refrain, "For all this his anger has not turned away; his hand is stretched out still" (9:12, 17, 21), and for this reason it has frequently been treated in the context of 5:25–30. We have attempted to interpret the organization of the material in the form in which it has been presented to us on the theory that secondary editors have sought to produce an intelligible text as well as one that reflects their appraisal of the prophet and the word of God. The theme of the outstretched hand and the calling of Assyria (5:25, 26–30) has been introduced prior to the Syro-Ephraimite debacle in order to underscore that God had already begun to wreak judgment on the vineyard before the specific events of 734–732 B.C. took place. Israel had already experienced judgment from the nation afar off, and in desperation and pride it turns against Judah and the house of David, aligned with a foreign nation.

A variety of prophetic material has been organized in 9:8—10:34 around the theme of God's razing of great forests. At 9:10 Israel boasts that it will replace the sycamores cut down with majestic cedars; at 9:18 the thickets of the forest are burned up by Yahweh's wrath; 10:15 speaks of Assyria as an ax (cf. 10:5) or saw wielded against wood; 10:17–19 tells of the destruction of Assyria, from thorns and briers all the way up to the glory of the forest; finally, the section concludes with Yahweh hewing down everything that is great in height (10:33–34). It is not surprising that some commentators have seen a link between the final scene of deforestation and the initial image in the following royal oracle: "A shoot shall come out from the stump of Jesse" (11:1). Such a reading might imply that the final deforestation was visited upon Judah and the royal house. We will look at this matter in more detail below. It should be mentioned in passing that the image of thorns and briers familiar from the Song of the Vineyard (5:6) and scenes of destruction

88

in the previous section is also to be found here (9:18; 10:17). However, while the image was used to stress the severity of God's judgment in the prior cases, so that all that was left were briers and thorns, here even they are burned up! Deforestation extends from the highest trees to the underbrush itself.

Keyed to this theme of deforestation is the punishing role of Assyria, rod or ax of Yahweh's fury. In the opening scenes (9:8–12, 13–17, 18–21), no mention is made of Assyria. Instead, the judgment is directly the consequence of Yahweh's outstretched hand. Yet we know from the introduction of this theme in chapter 5 that the two are linked: God's anger is not turned back, so he raises a signal for a nation afar off (5:25–26). The linkage is made explicit in this section at 10:5–11. Here, however, a new theme is introduced: the hubris of Assyria that results in its overreaching the role God had given it. As a consequence, it too must be judged (10:15–19).

The final verse at 10:19, which speaks of the tiny remnant of Assyria, has triggered a discussion about the remnant of Israel, now found at 10:20–27. Here explicit reference is made to the "burden" and "yoke" of the oppressor and the day of Midian—images rooted in the royal oracle just discussed (9:4). The phrase "a remnant will return" at 10:21 is obviously connected to the prophet's son Shear-jashub. This section is best understood as a piece of inner-biblical exegesis, where images and themes from other sections of the book are interpreted within a new literary context in the light of new circumstances. This piece means to emphasize that while a full end has been decreed concerning Judah, God's indignation will shortly end— but not before Assyria is itself destroyed (10:25).

We then have a short piece of text (10:27c–32) containing a military itinerary that has occasioned much historical discussion. While the final image seems to suggest the 701 deliverance of Zion, the military expedition follows an unusual route. The scene closes with Yahweh bringing down the "great in height" (10:33–34, RSV).

His Hand Is Stretched Out Still (9:8–21)

Isaiah 9:8–21 is clearly organized around the theme of the outstretched hand (9:12, 17, 21). The primary referent in these verses is Israel, the Northern Kingdom. This is made clear at several points by the explicit mention of Israel (9:8, 11, 14),

89

Ephraim (9:9, 21), Samaria (9:9), and Manasseh (9:21). Were there any further doubt, the final verse establishes the clear distinction between Judah and Israel (9:21), the latter taking out its hostility on the former.

In the first unit (9:8–12) we pick up in the middle of things. The anger of the Lord was already directed against Israel in 5:25–30. This is now made clear at verse 10, which speaks of bricks having fallen already. The people boast that they will replace the bricks with a better grade of stone. The replacement of sycamores with cedars may be a veiled reference to the coup that brought down Pekah, co-conspirator with Rezin: II Kings 15:30 reports that Pekah was slain by Hoshea, himself in conspiracy against the royal house. The final days of the Northern Kingdom were messy ones, with new "cedars" replacing old "sycamores" in one coup after another. The Hebrew at 9:11 even has the adversaries of Rezin aligned against the Northern Kingdom, devouring Israel "with open mouth" (9:12). For all this, there is still more devastation to come.

As we argued above, the theme of the hand stretched out still is meant to emphasize the gradual but steady way in which Yahweh's judgment is effected through the agency of Assyria against the sinful vineyard. That judgment has its starting point in the Northern Kingdom, before it moves on to Judah, this people, and the house of David.

The next unit (9:13–17) shifts the attention to Israel's leaders: prophet, elder, and honored man. They had the responsibility of warning Israel and directing Israel away from disaster. But just as in chapter 1, where the survivors should have taken care to inculcate righteousness and justice in Jerusalem, so too Israel's leaders fail to learn from the preceding episodes of judgment visited upon the Northern Kingdom: "the people did not turn to him who struck them, or seek the LORD of hosts" (9:13). So extensive is Israel's refusal to turn that God has no compassion even on those normally deserving of mercy: the orphans and the widows (9:17). Everyone—even the orphan and the widow—is godless.

The final unit (9:18–21) reveals the consequences of this extensive evil: wickedness consumes like a burning fire, so that even the briers and thorns are not left after the conflagration. The Song of the Vineyard (chap. 5) had spoken of God's trampling down the wall and of the decision to allow the vineyard to become a waste, full of briers and thorns where once there had been expensive vines (also 7:23–25). Even these are consumed, however, by God's anger directed at Israel's wickedness. As a result of this judging fire, Ephraim turns against Manasseh and Manasseh against Ephraim. Finally, these join together against their own brother to the south, Judah. Through these descriptive prophetic oracles, the final dark days before Israel's demise are sketched in graphic detail. We see the background of the Syro-Ephraimite debacle as well as the fall of Israel not long thereafter.

Perhaps one might have expected Yahweh's anger to have abated at this juncture, with the destruction of the Northern Kingdom. But the final verse rings out with the same refrain: his anger is not turned back and his hand is stretched out still. For this reason, we regard the following unit (10:1–4) to be directed against the remnant of Judah. We argued that the chief addressant of the woe oracles in chapter 5 (5:8–23) was the Northern Kingdom. But here the woes are extended to include Judah more specifically.

Assyria, Rod of My Anger (10:1–34)

The preceding memoir (7:1—9:7) made it clear that Judah would receive its own share of the judgment meted out by the king of Assyria after the collapse of the Syro-Ephraimite coalition. Assyria would reach "even to the neck" before being stopped by Immanuel and God's final concern for Zion. The woe oracle at 10:1–4 singles out Judah's leaders for special indictment. Certainly the cause of justice for the needy, the poor, the widow, and the orphan was finally in the hands of the king, however he may have delegated such responsibility. The memoir spoke of Ahaz and "his people" on two occasions (7:2, 17). While it is impossible to link this woe oracle specifically to the royal court, such a reading would make sense, given the larger context of especially chapter 7. In any event, in the storm that is approaching, the wealth accumulated by these unjust leaders will matter little. The defeat of Judah is envisioned here. All that will remain for them to do is to take their place among the many prisoners, if they are so lucky, or to fall with those who are slain. Within the larger depiction of gradual assaults on the vineyard, the widespread destruction of Judah in 701 B.C. is probably intended here (Isa. 36:1).

Yet Yahweh's anger is not yet stopped (10:4). The next oracle makes it clear that the final target of Assyria, the rod of God's anger, is Jerusalem itself (10:11). From northern sections of Israel, to Ephraim, to Judah, and now even to Jerusalem is the nation afar off sent. The initial oracle (5:26–30) emphasized Assyria's efficiency as a war machine: "None of them is weary, none stumbles, none slumbers or sleeps, not a loincloth is loose, not a sandal-thong broken" (5:27). It should come as no surprise that now Jerusalem finds them on its doorstep. The nation afar off is suddenly at the neck.

The opening "Ah" (10:1, NRSV) is the same Hebrew word consistently translated "Woe" (RSV) at 5:8, 11, 18, 20, 21, 22 and at 10:1, in the unit just discussed. Assyria is God's instrument of judgment. But this does not exempt them from standards of justice that God requires of his own people. The woes now extend to it as well. Its injustice is pointed to by the charge at 10:7: Assyria was to wreak an awful judgment on God's own people, but it has in mind total annihilation. Incidentally, this woe oracle against Assyria makes it clear that whatever else is meant by thorough judgment in the preaching of Isaiah, a line is also drawn by God; the final word from the divine council concerned a tenth burned again and a holy seed. God decrees a full end, as 10:23 puts it, but there is also to be a surviving remnant, however small (10:21). Assyria seeks to cut off nations, entirely. Its crime is hubris, as 10:13 points out. But from the perspective of the prophet's broader proclamation, its crime is also that it threatens God's remnant promises. It boasts that it will eliminate Jerusalem as it eliminated Samaria.

Verse 11 may point to a yet more serious crime as well. Assyria boasts that all nations are alike before it (10:9). On the other hand, it has destroyed nations whose storehouse of idols was greater than Samaria's. Jerusalem and Samaria are "kingdoms of the idols" (10:10) whose one distinguishing feature is that, compared with other nations, their idols are not very numerous. Assyria implies that if Samaria and Jerusalem had more idols, they would be more difficult to defeat (10:10a). This is a charge that could only be considered the most blatant form of blasphemy: I defeated Jerusalem because it did not have sufficient idols.

The Rabshakeh's speech (36:4–10) contains similar blasphemous logic: Hezekiah has destroyed all the high places, therefore Jerusalem will fall (36:7); the gods of Hamath, Arpad, Sepharvaim, and Samaria could not save when confronted by the power of Assyria and its gods (37:19), so how could Jerusalem's god save? Israel may become like the nations and call God's judgment down upon it. But Yahweh remains the Lord of Israel and the Lord over all nations (37:20), not just another god or graven image to be counted as part of a war chest. Hezekiah prays that "all the kingdoms of the earth may know that you alone are the LORD" (37:20). Assyria's boasting includes the charge that Yahweh, Lord over all nations, is just a god, and a puny one at that. As we shall see in Isaiah 36—37, God cannot let such a charge go unpunished. After a military defeat at the "neck" of Jerusalem (so 8:8), Sennacherib is slain by his own sons while worshiping in the house of Nisroch, his no-god (37:38).

Verse 12, which may be a prose addition (so NRSV), makes the link to events of 701 B.C. and Isaiah 36—37 clearer. God has a work to do on Mount Zion. What is this work? On the one hand, God's agent of judgment will destroy widespread portions of Judah, as Isa. 36:1 has it: "all the fortified cities of Judah" (the Annals of Sennacherib speak of "46 walled towns and fortifications"). This "work" of God is a "work" of cleansing judgment, which comes as a consequence of the disobedience of Ahaz and "this people" during the Syro-Ephraimite crisis. But God has another work to do. The blasphemy and arrogance of Assyria must be revealed for what it is so that "all the kingdoms of the earth may know" (37:20) that Yahweh is God alone. Assyria's king was acting only under God's authority, not of his own accord, nor of the accord of Nisroch "his god" (37:38).

The oracle at 10:13–14 permits Assyria to condemn itself out of its own mouth. With deep irony Isaiah reveals that Assyria fulfills God's purposes, on the one hand, by swiftly gathering the wealth of the nations (Spoil-Speeds-Prey-Hastes) but then condemns itself in the process by arrogating to itself great strength and independence of action. The judgment against Assyria is issued at 10:15–19. Through blasphemy and arrogance, the rod of God's fury has sought to wield its own strength against the one who hewed it in the first place. As God's agent, Assyria was to reduce the vineyard Israel to briers and thorns. Now even its briers and thorns will be consumed by the righteous anger of the Lord, all at once and not in stages (10:17).

While some have sought to connect these oracles against Assyria to Sargon's incursions into Judah around 713–711 B.C., they are more likely related to the 701 invasion of Sennacherib.

93

The references to a "wasting sickness among his stout warriors" at 10:16 and the sick man who "wastes away" at 10:18 certainly appear related to the punishment finally visited on the Assyrian forces outside Jerusalem in 701 B.C. (37:36). Within the presentation of Isaiah, the 701 deliverance remains the dramatic instance of God's final punishment of the arrogant pride of Assyria. The Great Forest is felled, not by the vaunted ax, but by the one who dispatched it in the first place.

The reference to Assyria's insubstantial remnant at 10:19 has triggered a section of text concerned with the remnant of Israel (10:20–27). With the destruction of Assyria envisioned, proclamation regarding Israel's remnant is given brief expression. We mentioned above that this unit appears to have been developed literarily, on the basis of other tradition found in the broader context of Isaiah 1—12. So we hear of Israel not leaning "on the one who struck them." In this context, the reference is to not leaning on Assyria and making alliances with it (10:20). At 10:13, Israel did not turn to "the one who struck them," namely, the Lord. "On that day" Israel will reject alliances with Assyria and will instead lean on the Holy One of Israel in fulfillment of 9:13. Isaiah 10:21 explicitly picks up the hope of a remnant returning, based on the name of the prophet's son Shear-jashub. The return is to the "Mighty God" (so 9:6). The decree of full judgment "in all the earth" (10:23) recalls the prophet's commission at 6:12: "And vast is the emptiness in the midst of the earth."

The oracle in 10:20–27 confirms that with the coming assault of Assyria against Jerusalem the "full end" decreed by God will be accomplished. Those who dwell in Zion are not to fear. God's hand is stretched out still—this time not against God's own people but against Assyria (so too 14:24–27). The defeat will not be gradual, as was the case with Israel's punishment, but sudden and final, as on the day of Midian (another clear allusion to the previous royal oracle at 9:4). Yahweh's rod will be "over the sea" as when he granted victory over Egypt at the Red Sea; now it is the "mighty flood waters of the River" (8:7) that are halted. The final verse speaks of the fulfillment of the royal oracle: "For the yoke of their burden, and the bar across their shoulders, the rod of their oppressor, you have broken as on the day of Midian" (9:4), as the burden departs from Israel's shoulder and the yoke on Israel's neck is destroyed once and for all. The promises associated with the reign of Immanuel are to

94

come true "on that day." The clear historical point of reference for these hopes is the deliverance of Zion in 701, when Assyria was halted at Zion's neck. Jerusalem is saved "for my own sake and for the sake of my servant David" (37:35). Hezekiah's request for vindication against the hubris and blasphemy of Assyria is granted (37:21). Assyria's arrogance "has come to my ears" (37:29), Yahweh proclaims, and so the Great Forest is felled.

The unit 10:27*c*–32 consists of a military itinerary depicting the advance of hostile forces. The larger context strongly suggests that these verses are related to the 701 Assyrian assault. Everything in the scenario represented by 9:8—10:34 points to a culmination at Zion's neck, where the Assyrian foe is finally defeated.

The argument from context pertains as well to the final unit at 10:33–34. Because of the following royal oracle which speaks of "the stump of Jesse," some have interpreted 10:33–34 as an oracle of judgment against Judah. Yet such a scene of judgment would be out of place here where the emphasis remains firmly on Assyria and its pending demise. The itinerary has brought us to the mount of the daughter of Zion (10:32). In a context where the concern is to depict the fulfillment of Isaiah's earlier proclamation regarding the halting of Assyria, it would be curious if this final act of judgment were not explicitly mentioned, leaving Assyria shaking its fist at Jerusalem. The final two verses dramatically show the zeal of the Lord of hosts accomplishing the act of swift judgment against the Great Forest. The ax is now in God's own hands, and he wields it against the former "rod of God's fury," the ax that claimed it had no equal.

Isaiah 11:1–16
The Vineyard Restored

Introduction

The material in Isaiah 11 is organized around the theme of Israel's restoration. An opening oracle concerning the royal house (11:1–9) is followed by a brief prose piece where the "root of Jesse" image is extended into a scene of international weal

95

(11:10) and national restoration (11:11). The final poetic oracle extends the image of ensign yet again into a scene of the gathering of the dispersed (11:12) and a description of the peaceful fellowship Israel will again enjoy (11:13). Anticipating the long nations section that follows (chaps. 13—23), the final verses depict a reversal of fortune for Israel, as it now stands strong against its once hostile neighbors Philistia, Edom, Moab, and Ammon. True to another theme developed in the nations section, a highway is established by God from Assyria to Israel (19:23). The image also anticipates the charge from the divine council at the opening of Second Isaiah chapters: "Make straight in the desert a highway for our God" (40:3).

Before turning to the specific exposition of the units in this chapter, two matters need to be addressed in order to understand them properly. One is the meaning and reference of the "shoot . . . from the stump of Jesse," and the other is the extent to which Isaiah is to be understood as a prophet of salvation. This second matter is of special concern because Israel's prophets are generally conceived of as critical (and for the most part negatively so) appraisers of Israel's destiny, especially when this involves the king. Is Isaiah an exception to this popular conception? How, and if so, why?

A Shoot from the Stump of Jesse

The royal oracle in 11:1–9 is frequently associated with the prior royal oracle in 9:2–7. Even more important in the larger context, however, is the intervening material, that is, the section just discussed in 9:8—10:34 that leads into this description of a new king and a new age. That section was concerned to describe the rise and fall of the Great Forest Assyria. We noted at the outset the controlling image of forest, from "the lofty" (10:33), "Lebanon with its majestic trees" (10:34), "the glory of his forest" (10:18); to "thickets" (9:18) and "briers and thorns" (9:18; 10:17). Assyria was to be an ax in God's hand reducing Israel to "briers and thorns"; the forest was to be burned "through the wrath of the LORD of hosts" (9:19). In the end, it is the Assyrian ax that is broken or, better, returned to him who hewed it; the final scene is one of Assyria reduced to "thorns and briers in one day" (10:17), its "thickets" cleared away by the ax of the Lord (10:34).

Some have, quite logically, seen a link between the stump

image at 11:1 and the preceding deforestation scene at 10:33–34. Yet 10:33–34 does not speak of the deforestation of Israel but of Assyria. The final scene of "the tallest trees . . . cut down" is the culmination of hopes related to Assyria's downfall as these found expression in the memoir (8:8–10), but more directly from 10:5 onward. At the same time, 9:8—10:4 does indeed speak of the deforestation of Israel. The turning point comes at 10:5–11, where for reasons of hubris, blasphemy, and loyalty to a surviving remnant, the ax is taken away from Assyria and Yahweh's anger—not abated—turns against the rod of his fury. Because the remainder of the chapter is occupied with this theme, and with the theme of Israel as remnant (10:20–27*b*), the stump image at 11:1 may seem out of place. Many regard it as a harsh sign that the monarchy has fallen, either into disrepair or altogether.

Another interpretation can be put forward that finds support in the larger context of Isaiah 5—12. The "stump of Jesse" refers to the reduced kingdom of Jerusalem and those portions of Judah left after the Assyrian assault of 701. The preceding section spoke of the end of Assyrian might, but it also spoke of the gradual desolation of the vineyard, until "overgrown with briers and thorns" (5:6—see also 9:18). The same image of briers and thorns is extended into the memoir itself (7:23–25), repeated three times for emphasis. The divine commission had closed with reference to a tenth burned again (Judah) and "a terebinth or an oak whose stump remains standing when it is felled" (6:13). Though a different word for "stump" appears at 11:1, the controlling image remains the same. Amidst the "briers and thorns" there stands a stump left of a great tree. The Davidic kingdom is nothing but a stump. Was the watchtower that was built "in the midst of" the vineyard pulled down along with its wall? What of the promise of "a young cow and two sheep" (7:21) and of curds and honey for everyone left in the land (7:21)?

Later sections of the Book of Isaiah (chaps. 36—38) verify that one important aspect of the prophet's proclamation was fulfilled—Assyria was turned back after gradual assaults that reached right up to the neck. Zion was spared by the prayer of the king and the prophetic word. At the same time, the vineyard was all but destroyed. One might imagine a paradoxical sense of thanksgiving. Yet here the prophet gives voice to his hopes for a new day following the defeat of Assyria, the sparing

97

of Zion, and the pious deportment of Hezekiah. A shoot will come forth from this remaining stump. What God did once with Immanuel he will do again. But now the king will not just stand as a final bulwark against Israel's sin and God's judgment at the hands of Assyria. A new age of royal government and international peace is envisioned.

The important point to make is that the stump image is perfectly at home in the larger context of Isaiah 5—12. There has been a fairly consistent employment of metaphors, even as vineyard and forest are distinctive forms of natural growth, and as Mighty River, Great Forest, and roaring lion (5:29) capture separate aspects of Assyria's role vis-à-vis Israel. A shoot goes forth from the stump, and a branch from the roots of a great tree fallen and burned again. But the stump is also a holy seed (6:13). Here too the separate metaphors do not always come together to form a unitary picture. Is the holy seed a remnant people, the royal seed alone, some other referent now lost to us because of historical factors? This is hard to say. But that the stump image could be restricted to just one period, that is, a period presupposing the fall of the monarchy, cannot be sustained, given the larger context in which metaphors of forest, vineyard, and great trees are governing ones, deeply rooted (so to speak) in the traditions. That a secondary editor would also employ the same images rooted in the traditions before him is not to be doubted. But stump need not imply that the monarchy has fallen entirely, as was the case in the aftermath of 587 B.C. It is an important concept within Isaiah 6, and its usage there does not imply total destruction (as in 587) but a standing remnant. It is in that same sense that the image is employed in this royal oracle.

Isaiah, Prophet of Salvation

There is another aspect to the problem of interpretation here in 11:1–9 and elsewhere within Isaiah 1—12. Does the prophet's message contain elements of hope, for the present and for the future, or is the message of Isaiah primarily one of judgment? This question hovers over much of the literary-critical task. Are passages that speak of a remnant, of restoration, of support for the Davidic house or Zion—are these integral to the prophet's historical preaching or have they been secondarily interpolated in the light of later concerns? The answer to this question need not be simply one or the other. But it is clearly the case that one's larger conceptual image of Isaiah as prophet of judgment or salvation will affect the exegesis of individual passages.

Another aspect to this question involves the larger growth of the Book of Isaiah. Why did the traditions of Isaiah develop beyond their eighth-century setting into the present sixty-six-chapter book? What was it in Isaiah's message that triggered this massive growth, and why have similar developments not occurred within the Book of the Twelve? These two questions—Is Isaiah a prophet of salvation? Why did the book grow as it did?—are not unrelated.

We have seen that within the memoir material (6:1—9:7) Isaiah takes a firm stand against the royal house, denouncing Ahaz and calling for an end to his line and that of his father's house. Over against this proclamation we hear of the birth of Immanuel. Whether Immanuel is prophet's son or royal son, his birth is a hopeful sign, a promise that the Syro-Ephraimite threat will not stand, if not also that the later Assyrian assaults will finally be halted. Virtually no one regards this Immanuel proclamation as secondarily interpolated into the prophet's preaching. In many respects it forms the core of traditions attributed to him. At the same time, because there is disagreement over Immanuel as a royal figure, there is also disagreement about the prophet's ultimate regard for the royal house and the traditions of David. It is not surprising that those who regard Immanuel as a nonroyal figure (or even a secondarily construed royal figure) tend to see the prophet's larger appraisal of the royal house as rather negative, perhaps grudgingly tolerant. This in turn leads to the judgment that royal oracles expressing positive regard for the Davidic line are either secondary additions or oracles that are finally disappointed in their hopes.

The problem is somewhat more complicated depending on whether 9:2–7 or 11:1–9 is under discussion. Many regard the first oracle as Isaianic, directed to the figure of Hezekiah. Yet they also see the final evaluation of Hezekiah as decidedly negative, and as a consequence the prophet is dashed in his hopes for the royal house. That is the end of the matter. The oracle at 11:1–9 has therefore no place in the prophet's preaching and has been supplied after the fact, by an editor and an age more willing to be sanguine about God's intentions for the monarchy.

Alternatively, 11:1–9 is treated as Isaianic, but, as in the previous interpretation, it too has developed on the basis of disappointments in both Ahaz and Hezekiah. The prophet looked to the future for fulfillment of hopes dashed in the present, when God would raise up an ideal ruler from the stump of Jesse. That is to say, the constitutive core of traditions regarding the royal house in Isaiah's own day remains negative in its appraisal. The prophet could only look to the future when such a verdict could be finally and permanently reversed.

It is at this point that the question of the book's larger growth becomes more relevant. Why did the preaching of Isaiah give rise to such extensive supplementation, especially when much of the prophet's proclamation was not fulfilled as he hoped in his own lifetime? Many regard the answer to the question already given in the question itself: the book grew precisely because what the prophet longed for would have to be directed to another day, another Israel, another David.

We have oversimplified the matter in order to isolate certain aspects of this description that are true and others that need reformulation. An explanation that relies too strongly on the "cognitive dissonance" argument (i.e., the message of Isaiah is extended to account for its nonfulfillment) begins to encroach on a theological position regarding authentic prophecy articulated in Deuteronomy:

> You may say to yourself, "How can we recognize a word that the LORD has not spoken?" If a prophet speaks in the name of the LORD but the thing does not take place or prove true, it is a word that the LORD has not spoken. The prophet has spoken it presumptuously; do not be frightened by it (Deut. 18:21–22).

If Isaiah's proclamation concerning Immanuel essentially never "took place or proved true" (so Laato and others), why was it not regarded as presumptuous speech? Why has the Book of Isaiah chosen instead to *emphasize* that a record regarding Immanuel and other preaching of the Syro-Ephraimite period was solemnly sealed and deposited among disciples, if not because the prophet's preaching did in fact come to pass and come true? One buries presumptuous speech or lets the ages relegate it to the shadows of past history.

This is particularly true of salvation proclamation, which has a way of proving embarrassingly inaccurate under the test of time. The Old Testament is frank that judgment prophecy has on its side the testimony of the past. Another relevant passage in this regard is to be found in Jeremiah, where the salvation prophet Hananiah is confronted by the yoke-bearing prophet:

> The prophets who preceded you and me from ancient times prophesied war, famine, and pestilence against many countries and great kingdoms. As for the prophet who prophesies peace, when the word of that prophet comes true, then it will be known that the LORD has truly sent the prophet (Jer. 28:8–9).

The burden of proof lies with the prophet who prophesies peace. Why preserve the prophecies of Isaiah concerning Immanuel and the Davidic line—prophecies of peace (7:16), endless peace (9:7), an end to war (8:10), and a coming righteous king (9:6)—much less *extend* them into a larger prophetic book? Why not regard Isaiah as a crackpot or a dreamer, misguided, or relevant, if at all, only to some age to come? The problem is particularly acute in the case of Isaiah because it appears that alongside his message of judgment against the vineyard, the royal house, and "this people," the prophet also spoke of a righteous king and an end to Assyrian hostility. The problem is that one cannot isolate Isaiah's judgment prophecies from his salvation prophecies, such that the fulfillment of one could be regarded as the warrant for preserving the other. They are too interconnected: the end of Ahaz marks the beginning of Immanuel; the end of Syria-Ephraim marks the beginning of Assyria; the end of Assyria marks the beginning of a remnant.

This complex message of judgment and salvation posterity concluded had been fulfilled, and it is for that reason that Isaiah's prophecies were preserved. Immanuel does take the throne; Assyria is stopped by his piety and steadfastness; the vineyard is destroyed, with only a burned remnant remaining. Both the message of judgment, which placed Isaiah in good company as far as the witness of the past was concerned, and also his message of peace were confirmed. A special burden lay with the latter, as the prophet Jeremiah reminded Hananiah; false prophecies of judgment meant the community could ignore the prophet (Deut. 18:23), but false prophecies of peace brought with them a more severe reprimand: "In that same year, in the seventh month, the prophet Hananiah died" (Jer. 28:17).

101

It is in this context that the prophecies of chapter 11 must be interpreted. For not just the royal oracle at 11:1–9 but the remainder of the chapter as well gives voice to hopes regarding a new king, a new age, the reunification of Israel, the return of the diaspora, and a period of natural harmony and peace without analogy. It is difficult to see how these prophecies could be regarded as fulfilled in any even modest sense. This would be an even more acute problem were the prophecies of Isaiah regarding Immanuel and a Davidic ruler so disappointingly off the mark, as von Rad and others finally conclude. Given the strictures regarding authentic prophecy, why not preserve the clear judgment tradition from Isaiah and let the other fall into the background? Yet precisely this cannot be done because the two are fundamentally related. And precisely the opposite move has taken place: the final chapters of this presentation of Isaiah (chaps. 11—12) let the last word be one of salvation. Moreover, chapters 11—12 do not arrive without warning, the disconnected voice of a later day giving expression to hopes not contained in Isaiah's own discourse. Rather, they flow quite naturally from the presentation that precedes, beginning with a vineyard under judgment and ending with a halted judge and an emerging remnant.

If we reject the move to interpret chapter 11 as secondary interpolation (which solves the problem of prophecies of peace, but at the cost of detaching the message from core Isaiah traditions), how is one to regard the proclamation in the light of the concern with authentic prophecy? Our thesis is that precisely because Isaiah's salvation preaching was vindicated in the course of history—with Assyria stopped at Jerusalem's neck, with Immanuel establishing and upholding the throne of David, with a remnant returning—so too his wider salvation proclamation was preserved, even when it spoke of a day that was yet to come, that had not yet taken place or proved true. Isaiah's core salvation proclamation was vindicated in the events of 701 B.C., as chapters 36—38 make clear and as 10:5–34 anticipates. Isaiah remains for his own day and for posterity that rare example of a prophet who prophesied peace and had his word verified over time within the course of his own prophetic career. For this reason we are given the opportunity to hear that message of salvation at its widest and most celebrative sweep. Isaiah is a prophet of salvation that came to pass but also finally a prophet of *salvation that has not yet come.* Yet he is a true

102

prophet and no misguided dreamer. He is that rarest of examples of a prophet who prophesied peace, whom posterity knew the Lord had truly sent (Jer. 28:9). That is why his total message of salvation is now heard, not just those portions pertaining to Immanuel and his own day.

Prophets who prophesy judgment have the witness of the past to back them up. Prophets who prophesy peace must also have a "track record" if their visions are to command an audience willing to hear God's intentions for the future and not just the yearnings of their own hearts or longed-for reversals of the present age. There are two royal oracles in the opening presentation of the Book of Isaiah. There is little indication that the second intends to modify or comment on the first, as though such modification were necessary, given disappointments that arose with Hezekiah's reign. Actually, the opposite appears to be true: both are equal in their expectations and their descriptions of the coming reign. What distinguishes them is the clear martial setting of the first: the reign of Immanuel comes to put an end to actual Assyrian and Syro-Ephraimite aggression (9:3–5). The following section confirms that the rod of God's fury has been relieved of duty and has been smitten "as on the day of Midian" (9:4—10:26). In the context of this present defeat—not one longed for or promised—the second royal oracle goes forth. Israel has been judged, Immanuel has stood firm against Assyria, a remnant has returned. The question now shifts: What of the days to come, following this fulfillment of promises? The second royal oracle is not introduced by "on that day"; rather, the opening verse states indicatively: A shoot shall come forth from the stump of Jesse (11:1). The reign of this righteous branch stands close on the horizon.

In sum, it is on the basis of hopes fulfilled in Immanuel that a second royal oracle is issued. The question then arises: Whom did the prophet, or those associated with him, have in mind—a second Immanuel, perhaps, but one for the days that lay ahead, one with special endowments meant to ensure just government in the coming reign of peace, the Assyrian foe having been vanquished? Here is the place where the question of "cognitive dissonance" might more properly be raised. According to II Kings 18:2, Hezekiah succeeded Ahaz when he was twenty-five and then reigned for twenty-nine years. He was fifty-five years old, then, when replaced by his son Manasseh, who was himself just twelve years old at the time.

We do not know whether Hezekiah had other sons, though one might expect that by the time he fathered Manasseh, at age forty-three, he had also fathered other sons. But this is pure speculation. There is no hard-and-fast rule of primogeniture in Israel (Solomon is a good example), so we cannot know whether Manasseh was the eldest son. What we do know is that Manasseh took the throne as a young boy, perhaps over other choices, and reigned longer than any of his predecessors (fifty-five years), longer even than his great-grandfather Uzziah. The choice of name for him is striking: Manasseh was of course a northern tribe. While it is only speculation, many have wondered whether his name was chosen to reflect hopes for the reunification of Israel, hopes that find clear expression in chapter 11 of Isaiah (11:12–14).

We know two things about the reign of Manasseh. First, it is judged the worse reign in the history of Judahite kingship. Manasseh is held responsible for the fall of Judah at II Kings 21:10–15 and II Kings 23:6. In the commentary to Isaiah 1 we noted the links between Manasseh's reign and the denunciations of false leaders especially at 1:10–17. Second, we know that Esar-haddon ruled in place of his repulsed and slain father Sennacherib (II Kings 19:27), and Assyrian influence in the region, rather than diminishing, actually increased. The Assyrian foe is not finally turned back; moreover, he is very quickly replaced by a new neo-Babylonian nation afar off.

If the shoot from the stump of Jesse of which the prophet spoke never arose, but instead Manasseh took the throne in the blunt course of historical events, then this is arguably one of the more outstanding examples of a prophecy that went unfulfilled. We raised the question in the context of chapter 1 whether the deliverance of Zion in 701 B.C., rather than giving rise to sobered wills and righteous leadership, instead was followed by a period of worse injustice and callous disregard for the destruction already visited upon the vineyard (1:4–8), in which only a booth remained. Isaiah's prophecy regarding the righteous shoot was certainly not fulfilled in the figure of Manasseh. Yet Isaiah was a prophet whose previous word of judgment and salvation had been fulfilled. The oracles of chapter 11 rightly close off this presentation of his word and activity. They remain visions for a future day, based on the experience of the past fulfillment of the prophet's word.

One of the consequences of canonical shaping is that our

104

interpretation of the final presentation of the material is not directly dependent upon the accuracy—or inaccuracy!—of historical reconstruction. That pertains to the reconstruction set forth above. We would argue that our interpretation of the royal oracle at 11:1–9 is consistent with certain features of both the historical and canonical dimensions of the text. But it also remains the case that the shoot from the stump of Jesse is never identified in the final presentation of the material, and this stands in some contrast, we would argue, to the Immanuel texts and the first royal oracle at 9:1–7. Rather, Isa. 11:1–9 and the material following it remain salvation proclamation that is never entirely fulfilled within the full presentation of the Book of Isaiah. The proclamation of chapter 11 speaks of an age yet to come, when a king shall rule with a "spirit of wisdom and understanding" (11:2), when "the wolf shall live with the lamb" (11:6), and when the dispersed of Israel are finally gathered (11:12). It is in precisely this spirit that both church and synagogue have looked to Isaiah as the prophet who spoke a word of salvation to the future. In sum, the royal oracle at 11:1–9 is not "prophecy that failed" but prophecy that remained to be fulfilled, precisely because Isaiah was a prophet whom posterity knew the Lord had truly sent.

His Delight Shall Be in the Fear of the Lord (11:1–9)

As mentioned above, the royal oracle divides into two sections (vv. 1–5 and vv. 6–9). The first section deals explicitly with the character of the king and his reign. The fourfold repetition of spirit in verse 2 is striking: the king will be properly endowed with God's spirit, for tasks requiring wisdom, the exercise of authority, and reverent discernment. The last spiritual gift ("fear of the LORD") is repeated twice, as if to prepare us for the quality of his justice, which depends not on external testimony or "hearsay" but true discernment. We heard in chapter 1 of leaders who failed to judge the fatherless and the widow, to correct oppression when it surfaced (1:17–18). This king will with full authority and full attention correctly stand on behalf of the oppressed, clothing himself in vestments of righteousness and faithfulness.

The second section (11:6–9) describes an almost mythologi-

105

cal scene of natural harmony that is apparently to attend the rule of the king. The emphasis is on natural predators who are able to coexist peacefully and thrive with their prey: wolf-lamb; leopard-kid; calf-lion; cow-bear; lion-ox. In addition, the figure of a little child has worked its way into the scene (vv. 6, 8); this is the only human figure in the picture. A small lad has charge of the first group: wolf, leopard, lion together with lamb, kid, calf, and fatling. Verse 8 then speaks of a baby ("sucking child," RSV) who plays beside the asp's dwelling, while the child just weaned places his hand on the adder's den. The final verse provides the title for the depiction: "They will not hurt or destroy on all my holy mountain." Isaiah had heard of God's glory filling the whole earth (6:3); now the earth is full of the knowledge of God "as the waters cover the sea" (11:9).

One problem of interpretation involves the relationship between the two sections (vv. 1–5 and vv. 6–9). For all its clear idealism and nobility of depiction, the first section remains fully in a nonmythological mode. The spiritual endowments are extensive, but they are not of another age. They are required precisely because the poor, the meek, the wicked, and the unjust still exist and still prey on one another—hence the need for a king whose garments are faithfulness and righteousness. How does this scene fit together with a holy mountain, with babies playing with poisonous snakes, and a little child leading a curious assembly of animals? To say that the second section employs traditional mythological motifs begs the question: why are they employed in this context, where a shoot from the stump of Jesse is given real gifts for real tasks ahead? It does not sound as though this holy mountain is in need of royal government or a king who will slay the wicked with the breath of his lips!

It could be argued that the two sections are to be understood sequentially: the king's just reign gives rise to the period of peace when all know the Lord (11:9). On the other hand, the second section might be better interpreted in a symbolic sense (cf. here Daniel 7—8). The predator animals are symbols of nations in their devouring capacities. We heard of Assyria that "their roaring is like a lion . . . ; they growl and seize their prey, they carry it off, and no one can rescue" (5:29); the Syrians on the east and Philistia on the west "devoured Israel with open mouth" (9:12); Manasseh Ephraim against Ephraim Manasseh, and both against Judah: "they gorged on the right, but still were hungry, and they devoured on the left, but were not satisfied;

106

they devoured the flesh of their own kindred" (9:20–21); the Assyrian hand reaches out, finds a nest, and then gathers all its contents (10:14). In place of this we hear of predators living at peace with their prey; of food enough for both cow and bear; of a hand that reaches out and is not destroyed. Instead of Assyrian waters rising and overflowing in hostile judgment (8:7), the earth is full of the knowledge of the Lord "as the waters cover the sea" (11:9). The chief burden of the section is that hostility *directed at Israel* will cease. The hostile powers will be neutralized, such that a little child can lead them.

In this state where international forces are no longer directed against Israel (11:6–9), the king can take up his charge to rule Israel and the nations with justice and righteousness (11:1–5). Isaiah 11:13 pursues a similar image: "The jealousy of Ephraim shall depart, the hostility of Judah shall be cut off." At the same time, this picture of international peace has its point of origin and its specific authorization at the holy mountain, where God's righteous king rules with justice, smiting the earth with the rod of his mouth, and slaying the wicked with the breath of his lips. For those nations who seek the justice of Israel's God and God's anointed king, it might be appropriate to speak of "international peace." But justice cannot exclude force and might, as 11:4 makes clear. The images of 11:9 ("they will not hurt or destroy on all my holy mountain") and 11:4 ("he shall strike the earth with the rod of his mouth") must be held in tension and not played off against each other. The final section at 11:12–16 makes clear that in the age of righteous kingship to come, justice does not exclude Israel sweeping down on the Philistines in the west and plundering the people of the east (11:14)—thus reversing the scene at 9:12. Indeed, in many ways chapter 11 in its entirety provides a fitting introduction to the nations section which follows in chapters 13—23, where the theme of God's righteous governance of the nations is dealt with in more detail.

In sum, the royal oracle provides a unitary picture of God's governance of Israel and the nations under the authority of the "shoot of Jesse" following an end to the hostility that had been directed at the vineyard. As such, 11:1–9 flows naturally out of the preceding section, where the Assyrian lion was finally halted and caged. In the reign of the shoot of Jesse he will lie down with the calf and fatling (11:7). Moreover, Israel will not lose its special status vis-à-vis the nations, nor will God give up

107

on Davidic kingship as the chosen form of government. Following the widespread desolation of the vineyard, he goes to the
root itself and selects a new pleasant planting (5:7) for a new
vineyard.

The Root of Jesse (11:10–11)

What follows is a brief unit spelling out certain implications
set forth in the royal oracle itself. The "on that day" opening
phrase may well indicate that the royal oracle has begun to be
interpreted more eschatologically, that is, loosened from whatever concrete historical moorings it had in the prophet's own
day and directed to a future expectation. Yet the picture these
verses portray is a consistent development of features inherent
in the royal oracle itself.

At the close of chapter 5, God raised a signal for a nation far
away to begin a work of judgment against the vineyard (5:26).
Now the role of ensign is handed over to the root of Jesse.
Rather than being assigned a task of judgment, the root of Jesse
is to stand as an ensign of justice for the nations. The next verse
indicates that "on that day" God will extend his hand "yet a
second time." The point of reference for the oracle is again to
be found in chapter 5 and the scene of God's commissioning of
Assyria. There God's hand was stretched out as a consequence
of his anger, and it remained stretched out still until the vineyard was a place of briers and thorns. Now his hand is stretched
out to repopulate and reestablish the vineyard. The "remnant
that is left of his people" (11:11) picks up the theme of the
prophet's son (Remnant Shall Return) as well as the divine
council promise that a tenth would remain (see also 10:20–27).
The list of nations was probably expanded in the period in
which Isaiah traditions were being transmitted to account for
the widest possible diaspora; the reference to "coastlands of the
sea" is familiar from Second Isaiah and may represent the final
frontier for Israel's promised gathering.

An Ensign for the Nations (11:12–16)

The original picture of gathering and return is to be found
in this closing unit. As pointed out in the discussion above, the
conceptual framework of the unit is consistent with the royal
oracle's depiction of justice and national reunification. The

focus remains on Ephraim and Judah. The theme of nonharassment (11:13) reverses the picture found at 10:21. The theme of sovereignty over "the Philistines in the west" and "the people of the east" reverses the picture found at 9:12. The "sea of Egypt" and "the River" (11:15) pick up images from the memoir (7:18; 8:7); once hostile, they are now neutralized. A highway is even established for the return of exiles from Assyria.

This final unit fits firmly into Isaiah's own historical period. The emphasis on exiles in Assyria is certainly within the historical range of Isaiah's own activity. Moreover, this rather simple picture of a highway from Assyria has formed the basis for more elaborate depictions, such as those found at 19:19–25. There the highway extends from Egypt to Assyria; Egypt and Assyria are considered God's own people; the Lord has an altar in Egypt where the Egyptians offer sacrifice and worship him. Clearly this more elaborate depiction has taken its point of departure from the more modest portrait of return found here. When 40:3 speaks of a "highway" it is as much a highway for God's return as it is for the return of his people: "Make straight in the desert a highway for our God." Here again, the foundational image is rooted in our text at 11:16; Second Isaiah has developed it in new and important ways.

We regard it as highly likely that this passage, which speaks of return from the nations, justice among the nations, and Israel's final restoration, has stimulated the growth of much of the tradition now located in the nations section to follow (chaps. 13—23). The final concern of the presentation of Isaiah 1—12 is with Israel's restoration and place among the nations. It is not surprising that this concern also forms the central theme of the nations section as well.

Chapter 11 presents a unified picture of Isaiah's hopes for the vineyard beyond the deliverance of 701 B.C. and the halting of the Assyrian lion. A new king will rule in the form of his father Immanuel, but with special endowments for a new day of justice and an end to international hostility toward Israel. The promised remnant will not be formed only from within Zion but will include those survivors exiled beyond Israel's borders as well. The Lord will initiate a return from exile reminiscent of the exodus from Egypt. This very brief statement of the "second exodus" theme will form the basis of much more extensive elaboration within chapters 40—55, which may in turn have influenced the small "on that day" addition now found at

11:10–11. The hopes of chapter 11 are now related to a broader picture of restoration and reunification, one that takes us to the very end of the Book of Isaiah's historical range.

Many feel that in Isaiah 40—55 the restoration of the monarchy belongs to the past hopes of a nation. Instead, the promises to David are transferred to the people as a whole. Such is the interpretation of Isa. 55:3: "I will make with you an everlasting covenant, my steadfast, sure love for David." Or, somewhat related, Cyrus the Persian is God's anointed one (45:1). The Davidic monarchy is transmuted to account for new concerns in a new day.

Ironically, it is during this same period that, other scholars argue, hopes arise for the restoration of the monarchy, such as those found in 11:1–9. Against this view of the origins of the royal oracle, for example, as a postexilic addition to the presentation of Isaiah 1—12, we have argued that 11:1–9 belongs to the final vision of the prophet himself, as he looked beyond the days of Immanuel and a defeated Assyria to days of restoration, proper Davidic rule, and an end to international aggression. As such, Second Isaiah chapters are silent on the matter of restored Davidic kingship, not because Cyrus fills this role or the promises of David have been handed over to the wider populace, but because Isaiah's prophecy remains in force. In other words, the lack of fulfillment of 11:1–9 within the larger presentation of the developing Book of Isaiah ensured that it remained God's final will and intention, requiring no further comment or expansion. A view of Second Isaiah that overemphasizes the independence of chapters 40—55 from First Isaiah traditions is partly responsible for such a concept of the monarchy in the exilic and postexilic period. Second Isaiah is silent, not because he has nothing to say, but because Isaiah has already spoken in the context of the Book of Isaiah, and his word has not been fulfilled. And as we have emphasized, this final vision of Isaiah was bequeathed to posterity precisely because the prophet was considered a true prophet whom the Lord had sent and whose vision could be trusted, even when it went unfulfilled in his own day—and in later days as well. The royal oracle at 11:1–9, and the depiction of Israel's restoration found in chapter 11, remain normative statements of Isaiah's expectations for the new vineyard.

Isaiah 12:1–6
A Final Hymn of Praise

With chapter 11 the proclamation of Isaiah reaches its point of culmination. Chapters 5—11 trace the fate of the vineyard, the royal house within it, the rise and fall of Assyria as agent of judgment, and the future for God's new vineyard among the nations. The disobedience of Ahaz and "this people" gives rise both to judgment at the hands of the Assyrian lion and also the possibility for a new remnant to return, under the leadership of Immanuel, and the future reign of the shoot from the stump of Jesse. A natural conclusion is therefore reached at the end of chapter 11, as the prophet describes the highway that will be built to ensure that the entire remnant returns.

Nothing is left to add to this picture of Israel's restoration. What is lacking, however, is the proper response to it. We saw in chapter 5 that the "inhabitants of Jerusalem and people of Judah" (5:3) could not speak on behalf of the vineyard. Instead, God spoke directly on his own behalf and in judgment of the vineyard. So too in chapter 7 the prophet offers the king a sign that God will do as he has promised, namely, destroy the attempt to thrust him from power. But Ahaz refuses a sign and is therefore mute before the one that is given him. It is a sign of judgment for him, while for others it is a sign of hope and the possibility of new life beyond the coming judgment. But there can be no proper response in such times of hardship and conspiracy and stumbling. The sign of Immanuel is one for whose fulfillment the prophet and those with him must wait. Even when the birth of the king is proclaimed in chapter 9, it is with the knowledge that until he matures and takes the throne, the Assyrian "rod of God's fury" will remain stretched out against the people. The final victory can only be sketched out by the prophet, as the Assyrian is left to shake his fist at Zion before he is felled by Yahweh's ax.

The entire destiny of the vineyard is portrayed in this presentation, but the remainder of the book will provide the details of that destiny. Chapters 13—23 will explore Israel's fate among the nations; chapters 24—27, Israel's fate in the cosmic judg-

111

ment; chapters 28—35, Israel during times of conspiracy and stumbling, with further hopes for the days to come. Not until chapters 36—39 do we actually see the Assyrian defeated, Immanuel standing strong, and the prophetic word of promise fulfilled. Even then a pall hangs over the final chapter, as the Assyrian is replaced by a new Babylonian foe bent on terror and destruction.

Yet the opening presentation of Isaiah, word and prophet, is brought to a fitting close at this juncture with a psalm of response to the vision of salvation Isaiah has set forth in chapter 11. Israel must be given a chance to speak, finally and properly, and to respond to the word of salvation vouchsafed to the prophet. God's anger has been turned back, and now God turns to Israel in comfort (12:1). Instead of fear and shaking hearts (7:2), the unknown voice says boldly, "I will trust, and will not be afraid" (12:2). At 12:3 the commanding voice again tells Israel (now the plural "you") what they are to say "in that day." This time, however, there is no shift to the first-person voice, as the commanding voice continues, calling for thanksgiving, the proclaiming of Yahweh's great deeds among the nations at large, and songs of praise for what God has done. In the final verse the addressant is revealed simply as "inhabitant of Zion" (RSV).

Some interpreters have noted that while the Hebrew word for "salvation" appears rather infrequently in First Isaiah (primarily in chaps. 25; 26; 33), and not at all in this opening presentation, the root *yš'* appears three times in this brief psalm (vv. 2–3). They further note the link between the term for salvation (*yĕšû'āh*) and the prophet's own name (*yĕša'yāhû*), Isaiah, "The LORD is salvation." It is striking that here at this moment of culmination, when the vision provided in chapter 11 is responded to by a commanding voice and an unknown respondent, the prophet's name is alluded to three times. The significance of names and naming is indisputable in this opening presentation: Remnant Shall Return; God with Us; Spoil-Speeds-Prey-Hastes. Moreover, all of these names are provided with a distinct interpretation. Shear-jashub is reused at 10:21 in the depiction of the remnant of Jacob; Immanuel is referenced at 8:8 and 8:10, if not also at 9:6; Maher-shalal-hash-baz is interpreted immediately at his birth (8:4). This is consistent with the fact that the children of the prophet were to be "signs and portents in Israel from the LORD of hosts" (8:18); that the royal

112

child Immanuel was to be a sign belongs to the very logic of the narrative: "Therefore the Lord himself will give you a sign" (7:14).

But a closer look at the prophet's own words at 8:18 reveals that it was not just his two sons who were to serve as signs in Israel: *"I* and the children whom the LORD has given me are signs." Where is the interpretation of Isaiah's name to be found in this opening presentation—do we not see that interpretation here, in the final chapter? The people's proclamation in response to Isaiah's vision invokes the prophet's own name: "Surely God is my salvation; I will trust, and will not be afraid, for the LORD GOD is my strength and my might; he has become my salvation" (12:2). To this the commanding voice then responds in affirmation: "With joy you will draw water from the wells of salvation" (v. 3). The voice of thanksgiving alludes to the prophet's name, and then as if in final acknowledgment, the prophet picks up the allusion and reapplies it. Nowhere else in chapters 1—12 does the term appear on the prophet's lips. Here it appears three times: Isaiah is, in his own word and person, a sign and portent in Israel from the Lord of hosts. That sign is finally one of salvation. At the conclusion of this presentation of Isaiah, word and prophet, it is fitting that the subtle but unmistakable signature of the prophet appears: Isaiah, "the LORD is salvation."

PART TWO

God of Israel, God of the Nations

ISAIAH 13—27

Overview

It would be wrong to imply that the Book of Isaiah's presentation of Yahweh's relationship to the nations is located only in the middle section of the book (chaps. 13—23). As we have seen, this theme plays a prominent role in chapters 1—12. In chapters 1—4, Israel threatens to become like the nations, leading to a massive scene of judgment, which in turn gives way to the worship of the nations at large, Israel now forming but one part (2:1–5). Especially fundamental to the presentation of chapters 5—12 is the role of Assyria as agent of judgment. A wider grouping of nations is explicitly referred to at the end of this presentation, including Philistia, Syria, Edom, Moab, Ammon, Assyria, and Egypt (11:14–16); they are mentioned in the context of descriptions of Israel's return and reunification (11:10–11). The final hymn expressly charges Israel to "make known his deeds among the nations" (12:3). The praise of God is to be known "in all the earth" (12:5). Clearly the final two chapters form a transition to the section that follows, where more exclusive attention is paid to foreign nations. For all this, it would be fair to conclude that the theme of God's relationship to the nations is only introduced in chapters 1—12, while in chapters 13—27 it forms the true center of attention.

Literary Structure

As in chapters 1—12, we are interested in the larger context and structure of chapters 13—27 as an important guide to the exegesis of individual passages. Form is closely related to function. Have these chapters been arranged in such a way as to present a specific theological message within the larger context of the Book of Isaiah? What was the intention of those who shaped the material into its present form? Why move from a scene of reunification and praise (chaps. 11—12) to a scene of massive judgment directed to nations beyond Israel's borders? Is there any coherence or order to the material found in this section, or do the nations oracles appear somewhat randomly?

Scope

Before we can attempt to answer these and other questions, the scope of the section must be discussed. We have made frequent reference to the fact that the nations section is generally taken to consist of chapters 13—23. Bernhard Duhm, for example, argued that the larger Book of Isaiah was comprised of several smaller "booklets." He regarded the smaller sections at chapters 24—27 and 34—35 to be independent booklets, composed under the influence of apocalyptic thought in the centuries just before the Christian era. That is, Duhm and others have generally argued for a division between the nations material as such (chaps. 13—23) and an independent apocalyptic collection (chaps. 24—27). Similar conclusions were reached about the distinction between chapters 28—33 and chapters 34—35.

There is no doubt that with chapter 13 a new beginning is intended. The final hymnic unit in chapter 12 marks a clear conclusion for the preceding section, which appears to have been shaped as a relatively independent section of the larger book. In these opening chapters, a distinct focus is maintained on the prophet Isaiah before, during, and after the Syro-Ephraimite crisis (chaps. 5—10). The section concludes with a glimpse of the future beyond the period of Assyrian hegemony (chaps. 11—12).

The superscription to chapter 13 is reminiscent of similar superscriptions at 1:1 and 2:1. Isaiah's full name is given ("Isaiah son of Amoz"). The familiar verb form ("that he saw") is also used here. But instead of "vision" (1:1) or "word" (2:1), here the material is classified as an "oracle" *(maśśā')*, a term that is frequently though not exclusively used in the context of oracles against foreign nations (Numbers 22—24). The fact that the term is frequently repeated within the chapters that follow

116

(13:1; 14:28; 15:1; 19:1; 21:1; 21:11; 21:13; 22:1; 23:1) has led most to conclude that here we have an editorial signal that a larger comprehensive section is intended, with a distinct beginning and end. The term is not used in chapters 24—27, nor in the material that follows (chaps. 28—35).

On the other hand, we do not find in chapters 13—23 an orderly progression of oracles against foreign nations and nothing else. Nations are referred to without the designation *massā'* ("oracle, burden"), including the Medes (13:17), Assyria (14:24-27), Ethiopia (18:1), and Elam/Kir (22:6). Other material of a mixed nature is also found here, including salvation oracles (14:1-4), "on that day" oracles (17:7-9; 19:16-24; 22:8*b*-14), explanatory notes (23:13-14), a "sign and portent" oracle against Egypt and Ethiopia (22:1-6), and a curious oracle against Shebna the steward (22:15-25). In several oracles introduced with the term *massā'*, it is not entirely clear what nation is intended ("the wilderness of the sea," 21:1; "the valley of vision," 22:1). It appears, then, that an original collection of nations oracles has been filled out and editorially shaped in a variety of ways.

Also unclear is the upshot of these oracles vis-à-vis Israel. Are oracles against foreign nations derivatively or primarily oracles of salvation for Israel (Hayes, "Foreign Nations")? Not all of the oracles are clearly *against* the nation to whom they are addressed. Clements has argued, for example, that the opening oracle concerning Babylon is in the first instance an oracle commissioning Babylon for a task of judgment—it is not an oracle *against* Babylon. Only at 13:17, where the Medes are mentioned, does the force of the oracle shift toward judgment against Babylon. Initially, the Babylonians are God's "consecrated ones" called for a task of judgment against Israel. We will have occasion to look more closely at this important opening oracle below. A reverse movement can be seen in the oracle concerning Egypt: following an unequivocal scene of judgment (19:1-17), the oracle shifts to a remarkable scene of Egyptian restoration, in which Egypt's citizens offer sacrifice and worship the God of Israel (19:19-22), finally becoming God's own people together with Israel and Assyria! In conclusion, it may well be the case that a characterization of chapters 13—23 as oracles for or against foreign nations misses some larger purpose at work within this presentation. We will return to this question below.

But to return to the question of scope, are there clear

117

grounds for a division between chapters 13—23, on the one hand, and chapters 24—27, on the other? There is little doubt that a new section appears with chapter 28. Both this chapter and the five chapters that follow (chaps. 29—33) are introduced with the Hebrew word *hôy* (32:1, *hēn*). This section (chaps. 28—35) returns to the historical period of the prophet Isaiah when the Assyrian threat, and the challenge from Egyptian rapprochement, were still very lively issues. To what extent are chapters 24—27 to be considered an independent section, both of what precedes and of what follows?

First, it is clear that the climate of historical reconstruction has changed dramatically since the time of Duhm, and this is probably nowhere more true than in reconstructions of Israelite apocalyptic thought. As such, a designation "apocalyptic," even if fitting, need not automatically locate chapters 24—27 in a late historical period and in a literary and sociological provenance distinct from chapters 13—23. Second, on literary and form-critical grounds it is by no means clear that the subject of chapters 24—27 can be neatly distinguished from themes found in chapters 13—23. Dan Johnson has recently rejected the late apocalyptic interpretation in favor of a reading closely linked to the events of 587 B.C. and the fall of Jerusalem. The city to be desolated in chapter 24 (vv. 10, 12) is none other than Babylon, and the widespread destruction of the earth spoken of there is tied to Babylonian incursions and the ultimate desolation of Babylon itself. These chapters are a kind of "tale of two cities"— Babylon the destroyed and Jerusalem the protected (chaps. 25—26). The final chapter includes a hymn to be sung on behalf of God's new restored vineyard, which God will protect against all assaults (27:2–6).

What is striking is how close the descriptions of "cosmic judgment" found in chapters 24—27 resemble those of the opening chapter 13. In both places the text describes a desolation of the whole earth and then a final judgment over the agent of desolation. More generally, chapters 13—23 and 24—27 are united in their depiction of God's widespread judgment over all human pride and national military pretension. In contrast to human arrogance and folly, God has in mind a pleasant vineyard and a scene of national reunion and the obedient worship of diverse peoples. From both a literary and historical perspective, chapters 13—27 are framed by a concern with the destiny of Babylon, both as agent of judgment and as final symbol of national arrogance and blind disregard for the ways of Israel's God and his chosen people Israel.

There is one final argument in favor of an interpretation of the larger tradition complex extending from chapter 12 through chapter 27. We noted the clear structure of chapters 1—12, which culminated in a brief hymn of praise, evoking the name of the prophet and looking forward to a time when, after the Assyrian was halted and a new ruler had taken the throne, Israel would rightly sing God's praises. So too chapters 24—27 describe the final defeat of "the fortified city" (25:2), giving way to descriptions of "that day" yet to come (25:6–9). What follows, then, are two hymns of praise (26:1–6; 27:1–5) that function on analogy with chapter 12, directing our gaze beyond the preceding judgment scene ahead to a new day when a faithful city and a faithful vineyard will emerge.

Internal Arrangement

Certainly some aspects of the peculiar internal arrangement of this section are to be explained as due to the tradition-historical development of the material. Several things, however, are striking about the list of "original oracles" set out above. Explicit reference is made in chapter 11 to nations that will be judged by Israel's God, including Philistia, the people of the east (Syria, see 9:12), Edom, Moab, Ammon, Egypt, and Assyria. It is plausible to assume that at one time a section of nations oracles existed that dealt with these nations. It is striking that from 14:24 on, the following nations are treated in order: Assyria, Philistia, Moab, Syria-Damascus, and Ethiopia-Egypt. A final oracle at 20:1–6 makes it clear that Assyria is the agent of judgment, as was the case in chapters 5—10. At the same time, just as in chapters 5—10, it is also clear that following upon its activity of judgment, Assyria will in turn be destroyed. Hermann Barth and Ronald Clements have persuasively argued for an original connection between 14:24–27 and the preceding theme of the outstretched arm, such as we saw in chapters 5—10. This very important oracle makes clear that Yahweh's hand is stretched out, not just against his own people, but against Assyria and the whole earth: "This is the plan that is planned concerning the whole earth; and this is the hand that is stretched out over all the nations" (14:26). Indeed, it would

119

come as no surprise if this exact oracle is responsible for the development of a separate nations section in the Book of Isaiah. There will be further discussion on this below.

If an original literary connection existed between Isa. 14:24–27 and the material in Isaiah 1—12, that connection has been broken in the final shaping of the book. So too, if the oracle at 14:24–27 functioned to introduce an original series of oracles against nations, that series has now been recast under a much broader historical and theological perspective. Whatever its primary historical origin, the opening material in 13:1—14:23 concerning Babylon now functions to subsume an original depiction of Assyria as "agent of judgment judged" under the broader perspective of later Babylonian hegemony, a new and more ferocious "agent of judgment judged." So too at the conclusion of the nations material the judgment of the several nations in Isaiah's day is placed within the broader perspective of God's activity through the agency of Babylon (chaps. 21—27), itself then later destroyed. The note at 23:13 makes the "replacement" of Assyria by Babylon explicit: "Look at the land of the Chaldeans! This is the people; it was not Assyria." This "replacement" motif is handled more subtly at the beginning of the nations material. Indeed, one wonders whether the exchange of Babylon for Assyria caused much less historical "friction" in antiquity than in the modern period. In sum, we would not want to rule out the possibility that the prophet Isaiah spoke a word of judgment against the Babylon of his day (so Hayes; see also Isaiah 39). At the same time, it is also clear that the Babylon of Isaiah 13—27 has been depicted under the influence of the events of 587 B.C., the fall of Jerusalem, and the final defeat of Babylon itself (21:9). This raises the important theological question of how and why the events of 587 and the defeat of Babylon have found their way into the presentation of the Book of Isaiah at this particular juncture. It is to that topic that we now turn.

Function and Theological Intention

In the presentation of chapters 1—12 we learned of a timetable in which Assyria would gradually ravage God's vineyard, Ahaz would be replaced by Immanuel, Assyria would then suddenly be halted, and a new king and a new Israel would arise. The presentation reached a sort of crescendo in chapters 11—12. At the same time, we also learned in chapter 7 that times

120

of trial and hardship awaited the prophet and those who stood firm with him before the final defeat of Assyria. However, relatively little space is devoted to a description of these days within the presentation of chapters 1—12. More will be said about this in our treatment of chapters 28—39 below.

The question remains: Why does the nations section now follow hard upon the crescendo represented by the conclusion of chapters 1—12? In chapters 28—35 we clearly return to the period of the Assyrian domination, prior to the deliverance accomplished in 701 B.C. Yet in chapters 13—27 we are presented with a scene of cosmic judgment plausibly modeled on events that took place much later, involving the Babylonian empire and the fall of Jerusalem. One answer to this question of larger coherence was mentioned in the Introduction: however we understand the larger movement of the Book of Isaiah, that movement is not straightforwardly chronological. Or, put in another way, we may be able to spot some chronological organization within individual sections (chaps. 1—12; 13—27; 28—39), but taken as a whole, strict chronological movement occasionally defers to thematic arrangement.

We mentioned above several possibilities for the existence of a nations section at this juncture in the book. The final chapters of 1—12 make mention of nations who will be judged by Israel's Lord; the oracle of the hand outstretched against Assyria at 14:24-27 may have at one time been more directly connected to material within chapters 1—12; in turn, it may also once have served to introduce a longer series of oracles against nations (Assyria, Philistia, Moab, Syria-Damascus, Ethiopia-Egypt). These are literary-critical observations. Are there also reasons of content and theological concern that have stimulated the development of this large nations presentation? It is worth remembering that this nations section (chaps. 13—27) forms the central panel of the larger First Isaiah presentation, overshadowing both the preceding section (chaps. 1—12) and the diverse material to follow (chaps. 28—39) in terms of length and breadth of historical treatment.

In our judgment, the answer to these questions is to be sought in the framing material in which Babylon plays the decisive role (chaps. 13—14; 21—27). Whatever the original series of oracles against nations may have meant for the larger theological presentation of First Isaiah, that series has now been placed in a new framework. It appears that in the original series

121

the chief crime for which the nations are held accountable is pride (Hamborg). That is, *the oracles against foreign nations are not primarily oracles of salvation for Israel; rather, they make clear that God's sovereignty over human pride and arrogance reaches to every nation on earth.* Just as God judged Israel for human pride and blind disregard for his glorious presence (chaps. 2—4), so God takes his indictment beyond Israel's borders to include all nations with a grandiose claim to independence and self-determination. The root of this theological conception is to be found in Isaiah's treatment of Assyria.

We saw that Isaiah's teaching on the role of Assyria was complex and multileveled. On the one hand, he introduces the rather outrageous notion that Israel's God will utilize a foreign nation to wreak his judgment on his own people. Such a conception cannot be taken for granted. It is outrageous from Israel's perspective precisely at the point where the claims of Assyria must be taken into consideration. For Assyria does not claim to act on behalf of Israel's God but on behalf of its own gods, *who are stronger than the "idols" of Israel* (10:8–11). It is a risky business for the prophet to claim that Assyria is a rod of Yahweh's anger (10:5). It threatens to backfire when Assyria boasts of its self-determination, the power of its gods, and the impotence of the God of Israel. As we shall see in the treatment of Isaiah 36—37, another option remains open for the manipulation by Assyria of the prophet Isaiah's teaching: Assyria is free to claim that it has come to destroy Jerusalem *precisely at the command of Israel's God:* "Moreover, is it without the LORD that I have come up against this land to destroy it? The LORD said to me, Go up against this land, and destroy it" (36:10). Like all good propaganda, the claim is accurate but not in this context and not in the mouth of an Assyrian bent on national and military self-aggrandizement. Hezekiah recognizes it for what it is: blasphemy plain and simple, a mocking of the living God (37:17).

It is in the context of this theological debate that the nations section forms its point of origin and secondary development. Isaiah counters the claims of Assyria and reveals the complexity of his own theological position by stating that the God of Israel is the Lord of all nations. Israel's God commissioned Assyria; Israel's God can decommission Assyria. All national theological claims are parochial and mistaken, especially when they are used to further arrogant human goals. Israel's God stands against all forms of human pride and self-indulgence, wherever they are found. He uses the mighty to execute judgment against a people who refuse to acknowledge his saving presence. At the same time he judges his own agent of judgment on the same grounds. Such is the complex theological position of Isaiah regarding necessary judgment over an agent of judgment.

It is at this point that the "Babylonian framework" of the nations section comes into play. In the final shaping of the Book of Isaiah, Babylon is clearly seen to function on analogy with Assyria, with several important differences. That is, as Assyria was commissioned as agent of judgment against Israel and then itself hewn down, so too Babylon functioned as agent of judgment at a later day: "Look at the land of the Chaldeans! This is the people; it was not Assyria" (23:13). The final hewing down of Babylon is depicted at several points, both in chapters 13—14 and 24—27 and at other points as well: "Fallen, fallen is Babylon; and all the images of her gods lie shattered on the ground" (21:9).

There are important ways, however, in which the depiction of Babylon as "agent of judgment judged" differs from the depiction of Assyria, on which it is ostensibly based. As we shall see in the commentary to chapters 13—14, interpreters have disagreed over the identity of "my consecrated ones" at 13:3. Some argue that the oracle is *against* Babylon; therefore the "consecrated ones" are the Persians-Medes sent to destroy Babylon (13:17). Others argue that the "consecrated ones" are the Babylonians; that is, first Babylon is sent on a mission of judgment, described as a "day of the LORD" (13:9), and only then, after the judgment, does the Lord stir up "the Medes against them" (13:17). Still others argue that the oracle originally spoke of Assyria and was only secondarily applied to Babylon (Erlandsson).

One can see that there is a measure of truth in all three interpretations. Babylon is depicted on analogy to Assyria, though attempts to argue for an original referent to Assyria in chapter 13 may ironically undercut the force of the analogy. Babylon is itself judged in the context of chapters 13—14, though its role as judge is also clearly envisioned, both here and within chapters 24—27. What the depiction of Babylon within the nations section accomplishes is rather subtle and goes beyond the staging conception of Assyria: first judge, then judged. Babylon's role as judge goes well beyond that envi-

123

sioned for Assyria. Now the entire earth is to be affected (13:5), if not the cosmos itself (24:4–5). Babylon in its might and military power wreaks a judgment so awesome that all earth's citizens are obliged to recognize a show of strength without real analogy, going well beyond the judgment wreaked by Assyria.

But precisely in that show of strength the pride and arrogance of national powers is revealed for what it is, a power that corrupts the one wielding it. What the nations section reveals is a massive, worldwide *implosion*. The "proudly exulting ones" (13:3) are dispatched with the consequence that all the world is affected. The most egregious example of human pride is allowed to work its will, and in so doing, it and all it comes into contact with is destroyed. The nations show their strength. The result is cosmic judgment. The scene of judgment depicted in chapters 2—4 is enacted as "the haughty eyes of people shall be brought low, and the pride of everyone shall be humbled" (2:11).

The nations section makes clear that all military strength and political stratagem—no matter how shrewd or how carefully wrought—is nothing before the wisdom and counsel of Israel's God. Whatever nation presumes to act by its own accord and with its own final destiny is mistaken. Israel's God rules the destinies of nations and their kings and wise counselors. There can be no judgment of Israel unless Yahweh wills it, acting through the agency of foreign nations. So too there is no display of human pride or military strength that stands outside God's final sovereignty. As Second Isaiah, reflecting on the same reality, puts it: "Even the nations are like a drop from a bucket, and are accounted as dust on the scales" (40:15).

What is the final intention of this depiction of the nations in the Book of Isaiah? First of all, we learn that what was true for Assyria in Isaiah's day will be true for Babylon at a later day: God may will the destruction of his own people in order to remove all vestiges of human pride and idolatrous schemes. But what holds true for the judged holds true for the judge as well, and for all nations on earth. Second, by showing us that a yet greater scene of judgment awaits the vineyard after the defeat of Assyria, the reader is prepared to regard the deliverance of Jerusalem in 701, as this is described in chapters 36—38, not as the final denouement of God's plans, but only as a rare example of what singular royal obedience and trust can accomplish in the midst of a sinful people. God can save a city and its people

124

on the strength of the king's trust. No plan of final cleansing judgment is immune to modification and transformation when the proper circumstances are fulfilled, as they are in Hezekiah's day. At the same time, Hezekiah can only retard a yet greater judgment and, like Josiah after him (II Kings 22:20), can only enjoy peace and security in his own days, being spared an eyewitness experience of the judgment yet to come.

One further purpose is accomplished by the placement of the nations section at this particular juncture of the book. The section that follows (chaps. 28—39) is especially concerned with the possibility that Israel might be spared Assyrian judgment by dint of clever foreign alliance. Isaiah rejects such scheming wholly and completely as nothing but a lack of trust in God and as an affront to God's sovereignty. The nations section makes absolutely clear that any foreign alliance is doomed to failure from the start. Foreign alliances derive their logic from the notion that nations act outside the will and purpose of Yahweh and could therefore be enlisted as agents of support simply by virtue of their military strength. The nations section reveals the folly of all political scheming when it takes place independently of trust in the one God of all nations. "The Egyptians are human, and not God; their horses are flesh, and not spirit" (31:3). Isaiah reveals that trust in foreign alliances very quickly turns into a form of idolatry, a belief that some force in the human realm of activity can be better trusted than the God who sets up nations and brings them down.

In the Book of Isaiah, Israel's God is not in a contest to prove his superiority over the gods of other nations: Israel's God is the one God of all nations. Here we see the roots of the conviction uttered so bluntly in Second Isaiah, who regards it as an "old truth": "Who told this long ago? Who declared it of old? Was it not I, the LORD? There is no other god besides me, a righteous God and a Savior; there is no one besides me" (45:21). Hezekiah also gives utterance to a similar conviction in his prayer during the Assyrian invasion: "Truly, O LORD, the kings of Assyria have laid waste all the nations and their lands. . . . So now, O LORD our God, save us from his hand, so that all the kingdoms of the earth may know that you alone are the LORD" (37:18–20). What Hezekiah expresses in the context of his petition, the nations section makes clear in extended form. The God of Israel is God of the nations.   125

As mentioned above, the oracles against nations in chapters

13—27 do not function in the first instance as oracles of salvation for Israel. They are concerned with establishing Israel's God as God of all peoples and as judge over all forms of human pride and idolatry. As such, it is not surprising to see within the nations section oracles that speak of the final worship of Israel's God by foreign nations. Most striking in this regard is the series of "on that day" oracles attached to the material that deals with Egypt (19:18–24). A similar oracle telling of the tribute of the Ethiopians can be seen at the end of chapter 18. In the former instance, we also hear of the incorporation of Assyria together with Egypt as part of God's people (19:24–25). The oracle takes its cue from the preceding unit (19:23) where a highway running from Egypt to Assyria is spoken of; this may well be an instance where a later oracle has developed on the basis of original Isaiah tradition. We heard of such a highway at Isa. 11:16, though there it was a highway for the remnant of Israel returning from Assyria. Clearly the passage at 19:18–25 goes well beyond this, as it envisions the worship of Israel's God by both the Assyrians and the Egyptians.

At the same time, it would be wrong to consider the treatment of this theme in the nations section as a form of universalism (Davies; Van Winkle). As in the sections of Second Isaiah that deal with the tribute of the nations, sections based in our view on the depiction of the nations in Isaiah 13—27, the prophet clearly understands that the nations are converted to the worship of Israel's God. What we have here is not some enlightened form of religious generosity, whereby Yahweh discloses that he has revealed himself under the cover of other gods and other religions. When in Isa. 45:14–17 the Egyptians, Ethiopians, and Sabeans acknowledge Israel's God, this excludes devotion to any other deity; precisely at this juncture Yahweh's exclusivity is underscored: "They will make supplication to you, saying, 'God is with you alone, and there is no other; there is no god besides him'" (45:14). Again this is consistent with the force of the nations presentation, whereby Israel's God reveals himself as God of the nations—not only in judgment but also in conversion and restoration.

Finally, it should also be emphasized that in the nations section a hopeful note is sounded for God's own people Israel. As all forms of idolatry, military pride, and mighty fortification come to nought, "strong peoples will glorify you; cities of ruthless nations will fear you" (25:3). During this time of cosmic judgment and the reversal of fortunes, God remains a refuge and sanctuary for the poor and needy. In distinction to the fortified city that is brought low, Jerusalem will emerge as a new and stronger city (26:1) where the righteous nation may enter in. In the meantime, as Israel awaits this cosmic judgment, God remains attentive to his people, who are counseled to "enter your chambers, and shut your doors behind you; hide yourselves for a little while until the wrath is past" (26:20). For then, as when the Assyrian was defeated (12:1–6), the time will come to sing of a new pleasant vineyard (27:2), as Jacob takes root and Israel blossoms and puts forth shoots (27:6).

It has been pointed out that while Jeremiah is regarded as "prophet to the nations" (Jer. 1:5), the title would almost fit the prophet Isaiah better. At the same time, Isaiah is presented not so much as a prophet to the nations but as the prophet who establishes Israel's God as the one God of all nations and of all the earth. The final hymn at 12:1–6 called for the addressant to make God's deeds known among the nations and to see that Yahweh's name was exalted in all the earth. This, then, is the function and theological intention of the nations section now located as the central section of First Isaiah, comprising chapters 13—27.

Isaiah 13:1—14:32
A World Judgment and the Judgment of the Lord

The material that stands at the beginning of the nations oracles in chapters 13—14 is diverse in background and content, though the governing concern of these chapters is with the nation of Babylon. What we find here is not just section one of a long series of relatively identical oracles; rather, this opening material provides a lens through which the series of nations oracles to follow is to be interpreted. This is made clear right at the outset, where a cataclysmic scene of world judgment is depicted, one without real analogy to any judgment executed earlier by Assyria or by any of the nations that follow in this section. After a brief superscription we learn of God's special commissioning of a contingent of mighty men, using the same image of the raised signal (13:2) that appeared in chapter 5, when another nation from far away was commissioned (5:26). They too come from "a distant land" (13:5), indeed "from the end of the heavens," and they come to wreak God's judgment. But their chief target is not God's vineyard, the royal house of Judah, or the city of Jerusalem. They come to destroy the whole earth (13:5). What we see here is the culmination of all previous shows of force, the final gathering of all earthly power and strength for an assault that goes far beyond any prior effort.

The Plan of God

One of the key ways by which discrete sections of the developing Book of Isaiah have been editorially linked is that of larger governing conceptions. Significant among these is a theme rooted in the prophet Isaiah's preaching of an overarching plan of God in history, specially vouchsafed to the prophet himself. This theme should be examined before we move directly to the exposition of Isaiah 13—14, since it plays a major role in providing cohesion and literary integration across sections of First and Second Isaiah.

It is not hard to see the logic that has urged many interpreters to view the core of the material in chapters 13—14 as consisting of the final two oracles concerning Assyria (14:24-27) and Philistia (14:28-31, 32). These would fit quite nicely with the material in chapters 1—12. Indeed, in the first case the links with the preceding section are obvious. Here we find the theme of the outstretched arm (14:26), reference to the "plan" of Yahweh (14:24, 26, 27), and even the same language that appeared in the royal oracle at 9:1-7: "his yoke shall be removed from them, and his burden from their shoulders" (14:25). One could well imagine that at one time this oracle formed the very conclusion of the presentation of chapters 1—12. The hand outstretched against Israel is finally turned against Assyria, and "the yoke of their burden, and the bar across their shoulders" is forever broken "as on the day of Midian" (9:4). That the reign of Immanuel is about to begin would also be strengthened by the following oracle against Philistia, which is dated to "the year that King Ahaz died" (14:28).

One should note carefully how these two nations, Assyria and Philistia, are depicted as coming to the end of their respec-

128

tive periods of domination. Assyria is defeated by the God of Israel "in my land, and on my mountains" (14:25), a fate that is confirmed by the record of the events of 701 B.C. now found in chapters 36—37, which tells of the defeat of Assyrian troops somewhere outside the gates of Jerusalem (37:36). Reference to the subjugation of the Philistines was made at 11:14. There Israel was to be the agent of Philistia's undoing, thus reversing the situation described at 9:12. But here Philistia meets its end at the hands of a foreign nation: "For smoke comes out of the north, and there is no straggler in its ranks" (14:31).

On historical grounds most have regarded the "smoke" out of the north as none other than the nation of Assyria, which subdued the region sometime after the Syro-Ephraimite debacle. Here, however, we might also be able to recognize obliquely the roots of the tradition that Isaiah prophesied a later Babylonian judgment, long after Assyria passed from the scene. On the one hand, Isaiah traditions speak of the defeat of Assyria at Yahweh's own hand, frequently in Yahweh's own land (so 14:25; see also 10:16; 31:8–9). At the same time, one also sees some suggestion that the traditions recognize the emergence of a new foe from the north who will replace Assyria at some point in the future (39:1–8). Clearly the Babylon of Isaiah's day needs to be distinguished from the later Neo-Babylonian empire that destroyed Jerusalem in 587 B.C.; Isaiah traditions themselves make such a distinction (23:13). At the same time, one can spot the vestiges of a tradition that hints at the future beyond Assyria's defeat "in my land": this tradition may well have focused on Babylon as the new "smoke" from the north with "no straggler in its ranks." Thus, what we have is not a rejuvenated Assyrian empire that defeated Philistia, but a new Babylonian foe who would begin to gain in strength and who would finally defeat Assyria and threaten in new and more powerful ways the security of the region. It is on the basis of such a tradition that much of the Babylon material in chapters 13—14 and 21—28 has been built up.

Certainly it is striking that material concerning the defeat of Assyria by Yahweh's outstretched hand (14:24–27) has been all but subsumed under the larger treatment of the Babylonian empire (13:1—14:23). Moreover, as commentators have recognized, the theme of the outstretched hand has taken on new and broader proportions in 14:24–27. Here we learn of the outstretched hand in conjunction with a plan and purpose of

129

God (vv. 24, 26, 27). Now the purpose goes well beyond the destiny of Assyria as rod of God's fury, and its ultimate defeat "in my land": "this is the plan that is planned *concerning the whole earth;* and this is the hand that is stretched out over *all the nations"* (14:26). When we then learn in the next unit that Philistia will meet its end at the hands of one from the north with "no straggler in its ranks" (14:31), while Assyria may have been originally meant, now we are pointed in the direction of a new "plan that is planned concerning the whole earth" involving a plan of God yet more mysterious. Read in the larger context of chapters 13—14, that plan involves the signaling of a new foe from the north, God's consecrated ones who are summoned to execute his anger (13:3)—not just over Philistia but over all nations on earth.

Certainly Second Isaiah is familiar with the conception of a plan of old revealed by Yahweh to his special servants in Israel, shared with them so that at a later time Israel might be able to declare the "former things"—something the idols and wise counselors of the nations cannot do (41:21–29). This plan of old involves, in our judgment, God's charting the destinies of nations in the divine council. The conception of a "plan of God" and an "eternal purpose" appears at several important junctures in this particular section of the Book of Isaiah. In the context of the oracle against Assyria, it appears three times in succession and serves to underscore that God has a purpose, not just for his own people, but for the whole earth and each one of its nations. God looks "from my dwelling" (18:4) and sees to the fate of the Ethiopians, left to the "birds of prey" (18:6)—the same term used for the destructive forces of Persia in Second Isaiah (46:11). So too God is "stirring up" the Medes against Babylon (13:17)—just as in Second Isaiah God "stirred up one from the north" (41:25), namely, Cyrus the Persian, whose task it is "to subdue nations before him" (45:1). By contrast, the plans of the nations will be confounded (19:4). For God has his own, deeper purpose in mind (22:11; 23:8–9).

From the perspective of Second Isaiah, God's eternal purpose for the nations is acknowledged as a "former thing" with special relevance for the period at hand. The domination of the Babylonian empire is at an end; God has raised up a deliverer in the person of Cyrus; all of this had been foretold in days of old; no other people proclaimed it—their gods and their wise counselors are nothing (41:24). The only people who heard this from the beginning were God's own people (41:27).

130

Because of the distinctive way in which the various oracles are configured in chapters 13—14, we see the outlines of a plan of God that operates in several discrete phases. Assyria is defeated by God's outstretched hand (14:24–27)—a theme deeply rooted in Isaiah tradition (chaps. 5—10). Then the defeat of Philistia is spoken of: the oracle is distinctive insofar as Philistia is warned not to rejoice over the destruction of "the rod that struck you" (14:29)—clearly a reference to the preceding oracle and the destruction of Assyria. Instead, Philistia is to fear because "smoke comes out of the north, and there is no straggler in its ranks" (14:31). This image in turn is picked up at the beginning of chapter 13, where a host for battle is mustered from a distant land (13:3–4), whose forces will wreak a judgment felt by all the earth. Finally then, a yet more fearful nation will be dispatched to bring the mighty Babylon, destroyer of all the earth, to its knees (13:17–22). From Assyria, to Babylon, to Persia, chapters 13—14 link the original proclamation of Isaiah, regarding the rod of God's anger, with the coming Babylonian threat and the final destruction of Babylon by Persia—all of this accomplished under the conception of God's "plan that is planned concerning the whole earth" (14:26).

We have on occasion referred to the puzzle of the growth of the Book of Isaiah. One reason for the extensive development of the book may have been the conviction by later interpreters that Isaiah had prophesied the rise of the Babylonian empire as agent of judgment against Judah and Jerusalem. Or, the rudiments of such a position may more generally have existed in Isaiah's conception of Yahweh's plan concerning the nations. It is clear that Isaiah prophesied the end of Assyrian domination. Though this is usually described as an act of direct divine intervention on Israel's behalf, it cannot be ruled out that Isaiah also prophesied the emergence of a yet greater foe from the north who would eventually wreak an awesome judgment against Assyria and the whole region—indeed, against the entire earth. Chapter 39 is an important text in this regard, and we will need to examine it in detail below. As the material concerning Babylon in chapters 13—14 now stands, it has clearly come under the influence of later enrichment in the light of the events of 587 B.C. and the later fall of Babylon, not to mention the rise of the Persian empire. But there may well have existed in the original Isaiah traditions a conception of Yahweh as controlling the destiny, not just of Assyria, but of wider nations and peoples. Consistent with this notion, a specific interest then developed in the

131

role of Babylon and Persia within God's larger plan which he "planned concerning the whole earth."

It is interesting to note that a similar conception of stages of destructive violence can be found in the opening chapters of the Book of Habakkuk, together with a meditation on the theological purpose behind such a commissioning of nations in all their awesome might. As in the superscription to Isaiah 13—14, here too we hear of an "oracle" *(massā')* that "the prophet Habakkuk saw" *(hāzāh)*. The prophet complains of violence and injustice in the earth (Hab. 1:2–4). God responds by rousing up the Chaldeans, "that fierce and impetuous nation" (Hab. 1:6). Yet the prophet is left to puzzle how this represents any kind of solution, since the Babylonians are "dread and fearsome" and "their justice" proceeds "from themselves" (Hab. 1:7); they too "come for violence" (Hab. 1:9). The prophet rightly sees that God has ordained them as a judgment (Hab. 1:12), but he cannot understand how justice is done when "the wicked swallow those more righteous than they" (Hab. 1:13). Will the Chaldeans go on forever slaying nations mercilessly? With this final question the prophet is left to take his stand and wait for an answer. He learns that final justice will come, but in the meantime the prophet and all those who are upright must live by faith (Hab. 2:2–4). The time will come when a taunt shall be taken up against the Babylonian plunderer, when "all that survive of the peoples shall plunder you—because of human bloodshed, and violence to the earth" (Hab. 2:8).

In sum, it may appear that God's sending forth of the Chaldeans in judgment over Assyria, Judah, or even the whole earth does nothing less than unleash a terrible cycle of senseless violence. But as in Habakkuk, God stands firm on the conviction that all takes place according to a mysterious plan of old and that in the end justice will be done, as violence and destruction finally eliminate all forms of pride and arrogance on earth—including the arrogance of those who themselves wreak the judgment. Such is the vision that the prophet Habakkuk, and the prophet Isaiah, saw.

A World Judgment (13:1–22)

132

If the above interpretation is correct, then we have confirmation of the view held by Clements and others that the nation dispatched to execute Yahweh's indignation in chapter

13 is not the judge of the Babylonians but the Babylonians themselves. On the other hand, we disagree with Clements's emphasis on the judgment as specifically shaped in the light of the destruction of Jerusalem in 587 B.C. As in chapters 24—27, the destruction decreed by God at the hands of his "consecrated ones" is much more comprehensive than the fall of Jerusalem or the defeat of any single capital by the powerful Babylonians. All hands become feeble; every heart—not just the heart of Judah's king or Judah's people—will melt in fear (13:7; cf. 7:2, 4; 8:6). This "day of the LORD" comes to put an end to all sin (13:9), and the evil of the whole world is to be punished (13:11). All human pride and arrogance is under assault, and even the heavens and the earth will feel the effects of God's awesome judgment (13:10, 13). This scene of massive judgment is reminiscent of God's assault on human pride and the haughtiness of all people such as was found in chapters 2—4.

Then, without warning, the terrifying Babylonian judge is himself brought before a new judge of all the earth. At 13:17, using a new verb (the same term appears in 41:25 of Cyrus the Persian), God stirs up the Medes (Persians) against Babylon. The awesome judgment executed by Babylon is now executed against it. The image of thorns and briers, familiar from chapters 1—12, is exchanged for that of wild beasts, as the land without inhabitant (13:20) is taken over by howling creatures, ostriches, satyrs, hyenas, and jackals. The key terms in this unit are found at 13:19, which speaks of the glory, splendor, and pride *(gā'ôn)* of the Chaldean kingdom. God had promised to put an end to "the pride *(gā'ôn)* of the arrogant" (13:11) through the agency of his "consecrated ones"—little did they realize that that same charge would apply with special force to themselves.

In chapter 1 we were introduced to the image of God's vineyard, with only a single booth left standing (1:8). A survivor confesses that if it were not for that single booth, "we would have been like Sodom, and become like Gomorrah" (1:9). This oracle against Babylon, "the glory of kingdoms," prophesies the total destruction of a people, "like Sodom and Gomorrah when God overthrew them" (13:19). Such is the extent of God's judgment over extreme forms of pride and arrogance. Using the same imagery that was found in Habakkuk ("there is still a vision for the appointed time; it speaks of the end, and does not lie," Hab. 2:3), the oracle concludes with an assurance that the

133

fulfillment of the prophecy "is close at hand, and its days will not be prolonged" (13:22). Violence will come to an end when the mighty Babylon is fallen, and God's justice will again rule the earth when all forms of pride and idolatry are vanquished.

The Taunt Against Babylon (14:1–23)

Habakkuk the prophet was promised that the vision of final justice was not ephemeral: it was plainly written so one could see it even if running (Hab. 2:2). But it would require patience, and in the time of waiting "the righteous live by their faith" (Hab. 2:4). The prophet is warned that "if it seems to tarry, wait for it; it will surely come, it will not delay" (Hab. 2:3). As a guarantor of the vision, the prophet hears the taunt that will be taken up against the arrogant Babylon (Hab. 2:6–20) consisting of a series of five long woes proclaiming an end to injustice and plunder. Instead, as if directly alluding to the promise of the righteous reign of the shoot of Jesse in Isa. 11:1–9, "the earth will be filled with the knowledge of the glory of the LORD, as the waters cover the sea" (Hab. 2:14). The glory of God will mean "shame will come upon your glory" (2:16).

A similar movement can be detected in our Isaiah text. Isaiah 14 opens with a promise of return and restoration of God's people Israel. Their harsh service is brought to an end (cf. 40:2), they are again comforted and chosen by God (cf. 40:1), and those who were their captors are now ruled by them (cf. chap. 47). Aliens will cleave to the house of Jacob (cf. 45:14–17). When final rest is granted to Israel, a taunt will be taken up against Babylon, as was the case in Habakkuk. Here we learn of the extent of Babylon's unjust dominion over the earth.

The taunt opens with the general claim that, by bringing an end to the dominion of the oppressor Babylon, God has broken "the staff of the wicked, the scepter of rulers" (14:5). The first royal oracle (9:1–7) had spoken of the staff and scepter of Assyria, broken as on the day of Midian. But Babylon's staff and scepter are the epitome of unjust oppression, the culmination of all evil, wielded by a nation "that struck down the peoples in wrath . . . , that ruled the nations in anger with unrelenting persecution" (14:6). This is no mere instance of earthly persecution, or even an outstanding example of absolute power corrupting absolutely: the whole earth was made to feel the oppressive weight of Babylon's rule, and now the whole earth breaks into singing. Even the cypresses and the cedars of Lebanon—once brought low when God hewed down the Great Forest Assyria (10:33–34)—are free to rejoice at Babylon's demise (14:8). It appeared as though no force on earth could contend with the might and terrifying force of Babylon the Great: all great cedars experienced this unprecedented display of force.

But now in the underworld all the former leaders of the earth are roused from their shadowy existence to greet Babylon the Great and to proclaim, "You too have become as weak as we!" (14:10). Babylon had climbed high into the heavenly reaches, high above the highest cedars of Lebanon, claiming an ascendancy equal to the Most High. There in the assembly of the deities of the nations, in the abode of the Most High God in the far north, Babylon sought identity with God. Instead, its king found himself in Sheol among the graves of kings long dead. The portrayal of Psalm 82 stands close at hand. God stands in the midst of the divine council and holds court among the gods of the earth. The charges are brought forward: injustice, lack of attention to the plight of the poor and afflicted, the weak and the needy (Ps. 82:2–4). Perhaps in ironic condemnation, Yahweh addresses these unjust gods as divine sons of the Most High: "Nevertheless, you shall die like mortals, and fall like any prince" (Ps. 82:7). For, as the psalm concludes, all nations stand under the sovereignty of Israel's God.

Here we see mighty Babylon as dead as any dead prince on earth, pondered over by those who once stood in dread of his might. This powerful Babylon who made the earth tremble, who returned the earth to a state of wilderness, who refused to release prisoners—this Babylon is denied a place of resting even among the dead. Special in his display of power and oppressive might, special too is his final destiny: unburied, his sons slain, his name and the name of his descendants erased from memory, lest they "rise to possess the earth" (14:21). The final scene depicts a wasteland, Babylon without name or remnant, offspring, or posterity (14:22), swept clean by a broom of eternal destruction.

One must ask in conclusion how such a portrayal of Babylon's final destiny could have been generated. What has given rise to such a relentless picture of destruction? The answer must be sought in the actual historical experience of Israel and the nations of the world who were forced to endure Babylon's unprecedented assault on humanity and common codes of justice.

135

Habakkuk and Isaiah agree that in the nation of Babylon even the awesome violence of Assyria is thoroughly overshadowed. From Israel's perspective, this was a nation that sought to rule the world at any cost. And it did so without regard for the most minimal standards of justice, arrogating to itself the status of the divine with a justice that proceeds from themselves (Hab. 1:7). The taunt of Isaiah 14 affirms that no nation on earth, however powerful and however terrifying, can finally void the justice that created the earth and all its peoples. If the vision seems slow, wait for it (Hab. 2:3); God's justice will surely come, it will not delay (Hab. 2:3); its time is at hand, and its days will not be prolonged (Isa. 13:22); behold, the one whose soul is upright will not fail (Hab. 2:4).

An Ominous Ending (14:24–32)

After such a sustained indictment of Babylon, it seems curious to return to the plight of Assyria. But the intention of such a move has already been discussed: we learn that with God's purpose concerning Assyria he has a wider purpose for the whole earth. Yahweh will break the yoke and burden of Assyria, as promised in the first royal oracle, and by this action God's final defeat of Babylon is also foreshadowed (14:5). For the hand that was stretched out against God's vineyard (5:25) remains stretched out to counter all national pride and arrogance, wherever it is found: "This is the hand that is stretched out over all the nations" (14:26).

We then move to an oracle against Philistia (14:28–32). Most assume that King Ahaz died at some point in the mid-720s B.C. (14:28). The oracle's original circumstance of delivery may well have been the death of Tiglath-pileser, also in the mid-720s: Philistia is not to rejoice over the death of "the rod that struck you" (14:29). An adder is about to appear to replace the serpent (14:29). The following verse (14:30) has caused much confusion, since it speaks of security for the firstborn and the needy but also of famine and slaying for Philistia's remnant. It is striking that the image of the adder and the young child was also employed in 11:8, at the conclusion of the second royal oracle. We wondered at that time whether the animals mentioned in 11:6–9 were symbols of national powers threatening Israel. We may have a link to that passage here: in fulfillment of the prophecy of 11:6–9, when the adder appears, the innocent need not fear. Rather, the threat exists for Philistia specifically.

136

Whatever the original circumstances that gave rise to this oracle, the placement of it after the oracle against Assyria achieves a new effect. It is difficult to avoid the impression that the "rod which struck" Philistia is not just any single individual Assyrian king, about to be replaced by some new obscure Assyrian ruler. Rather, Assyria as a whole is implied, and a new adder will come forth from the roots of the Assyrian kingdom, whose fruit will be a flying serpent! With the ominous next to last verse, "for smoke comes out of the north, and there is no straggler in its ranks," we are prepared for the scene of awesome destruction spoken of in 13:1—14:23, executed by the Babylonian empire. Only in Zion will the afflicted find rest (14:32). This is the response to be given the messengers who inquire about the state of affairs under the terrifying reign of that army from the north with "no straggler in its ranks."

Conclusion

The diverse material in Isaiah 13—14 has been assembled in a distinctive manner so as to emphasize that in the prophet's original vision of the outstretched hand (14:24–27) and the destruction of Philistia (14:28–32) there lay the seeds for a much more comprehensive plan of God, involving the rise of the Babylonian empire and its final destruction. As in 1:1 and 2:1, a certain temporal flexibility is achieved at 13:1 with the use of the term *ḥāzāh:* "The oracle concerning Babylon that Isaiah son of Amoz saw *(ḥāzāh)."* Those who shaped the diverse material in chapters 13—14 did so with the conviction that the rudiments for a vision of Babylonian judgment lay in the proclamation of Isaiah concerning the purpose of God. The prophet "saw" beyond his own day to a coming day of the Lord yet greater than anything that had transpired during the period of Assyrian domination. One could detect a certain analogy between Assyria, arrogant rod of judgment judged, and Babylon the Great. But in the case of the latter, the violence and pride of Assyria was far outstripped. A world judgment is executed to eliminate all vestiges of human pride and arrogance, and in the end the agent of judgment is itself brought low—to lower estate than anything ever imagined for Assyria (cf. 10:33–34). We will have occasion to see the effects of Babylon's rule in more specific terms at the conclusion of the nations section (chaps. 21—27), especially as this involves God's vineyard Israel. For the time being we are left to ponder on the response given the

137

messengers of the nation: The Lord has founded Zion and in Zion the afflicted of his people find refuge (14:32). More will be said about the nature of that refuge in the final section (esp. chaps. 24—27).

Isaiah 15:1—16:14
Oracles Concerning Moab

While it is possible in at least general terms to have some sense of the historical background of the oracles in Isaiah 13—14, the same is not true of the material related to Moab in chapters 15—16. Dates have been put forward for as wide-ranging a period as the early eighth century, prior to the activity of Isaiah, to the late second century B.C. The fact that portions of the Isaiah text (esp. 16:6–11) are paralleled fairly closely in the nations section of the Book of Jeremiah (48:29–38) may well suggest that we are dealing with traditional material related to the kingdom of Moab, thus frustrating the search for precise historical background.

Most divide the two chapters into three units: an opening lament on the occasion of a Moabite defeat (15:1–9); a sort of reply to the lament, with a focus on the throne of David (16:1–5); and a further lament with consideration of Moab's pride (16:6–11). The material is concluded with two further notes in 16:12–13.

The final note (16:13–14) may help determine the proper context for the diverse material that proceeds. The collection of oracles regarding Moab is interpreted as relating to a period now past. This would lend strength to the view that the oracles have emerged from some older traditional setting, not necessarily closely related to historical events in Isaiah's day, though this cannot be ruled out. The laments delivered for Moab in the past are contrasted with a coming period of yet worse contempt.

In our judgment, the reason for the lengthy Babylon section at the head of the nations section in Isaiah is to make clear that, whatever military losses any nation might have experienced in the past, especially at the hands of Assyria, these will pale in comparison to the destruction about to be experienced at the

138

hands of Babylon. As such, traditional material has been taken up concerning the defeat of Moab and placed in a new context, that of a world judgment about to be wrought by the Babylonian empire.

In the first oracle (15:1–9) the sudden defeat of Moab is reported in the opening verses. Already, there is weeping and sackcloth, as the various cities of Moab are crushed; even the mountain villages of Nebo and Medeba wail in anguish. The rapid accounting of Moabite cities and regions, from principal towns to lesser-known villages, serves to stress the degree of penetrating assault: Ar, Kir, Dibon, Nebo, Medeba, Heshbon, Elealeh, Jahaz, Zoar, Eglath-shelishiyah, Luhith, Horonaim, Nimrim, Eglaim, Beer-elim. What region has not been affected? Little wonder every head is baldness and every beard shorn (15:2). Everywhere there is wailing and crying, tears and blood. Nothing is left for the fugitives that escape. Even the remnant of the land is to be hunted down by the lion—perhaps an Assyrian foe (5:29). From beginning to end, the tone of lament is obvious.

The interpretation of the following unit (16:1–5) is less clear. It appears to pick up with the reference to escaped citizens fleeing from the previous destruction (15:9). Gifts have been sent across the river Arnon, dividing Moab from Judah, and with them a plea for asylum. As the text stands in the NRSV (there is difficulty with the translation), the final verses (vv. 4b–5) represent a continuation of the direct speech of those seeking asylum. They look forward to a day when oppression ceases and the Davidic throne is secure, issuing sure justice and righteousness on behalf of all.

If this is direct speech from Moabite refugees, then it is interpreted as disingenuous in the ensuing reply (16:6–11) and is swiftly rebuffed. Refuge is apparently refused on the grounds of Moab's great pride: the term is repeated four times in the space of one verse (16:6) and is joined by charges of insolence, arrogance, and boasting. No—the wailing is to continue. The catalog of destroyed villages is picked up again: Heshbon, Sibmah, Jazer, Elealeh, Kir-heres (16:8–11).

While many view these three oracles (15:1–9; 16:1–5; 16:6–11) as unrelated, such a conclusion is probably unwarranted. In their present configuration the logic of the material is clear: wailing begins as a consequence of a terrible defeat; a request for asylum is then made of Judah; the request is refused

139

as the great pride of Moab is recounted; and so the lamenting continues where it had first begun. The unknown mourner of 15:5 resumes his cry, which continues up to 16:11. A final response is then made from the perspective of Judah, as was the case in 16:6–7.

The interpretive key to the Moab oracles is provided in the final verses (16:12–14). In 16:12 we find confirmation of the view set forth at 16:6–7, namely, that Moab's lament will not soon come to an end. No appeal at high place or sanctuary will alter the verdict. Then at 16:13 we learn that the Moabite laments that precede actually stem from a time now past, from the standpoint of the final editor: "This was the word that the LORD spoke concerning Moab in the past." The next phrase, "but now" *(wĕ'attāh),* underscores that a contrast is being set up between this past time of lamentation and a new period of humiliation, one that will come within three years. Then the great multitude of Moab and all its glory will be brought low, leaving only a few survivors (16:14).

In sum, it is not clear that this older material concerning a Moabite defeat and ensuing lamentation is utilized at this point in the Book of Isaiah out of specific historical interest in the destiny of the Moabites as such. It is extraordinarily difficult to place the oracles in a clear historical setting that would aid in their interpretation. What is of interest to the shapers of the material is God's judgment over all forms of human pride, of which Moab has its share (16:6). To this end, traditional material has been selected and placed in a larger nations context.

At the same time, it appears that the material has been selected not so much to memorialize an isolated instance of Moabite defeat, however thoroughgoing; rather, that defeat is set in contrast to a coming period of yet worse desolation when "the glory of Moab will be brought into contempt" (16:14). This serves to confirm the vision of world judgment provided in the opening chapters (chaps. 13—14). However terrible and haunting a lament went up from Moab in days past, the future is darker still. The Babylonian smoke from the north will soon descend upon Moab and "those who survive will be very few and feeble" (16:14).

Isaiah 17:1-14
Oracles Concerning Syria-Ephraim

There is general agreement that, in contrast to the foregoing material concerning Moab, one can fairly easily reconstruct
the historical circumstances that have given rise to the oracles
in chapter 17. The pairing of Syria (Damascus) and Ephraim is
of course familiar to us from the Isaiah memoir (chaps. 7—8),
and indeed most have urged that the interpretation of these
oracles be guided by the circumstances of the Syro-Ephraimite
assault on Judah in 734–732 B.C. In this respect, the oracles
against Syria and Ephraim found here are treated in similar
fashion as the oracles against Assyria and Philistia found at the
end of chapter 14 (14:24–32). That is, they stem from the period
of Isaiah's early ministry and concern themes and historical
events familiar to us from chapters 5—12.

At the same time, as with the material in 14:24–32, we must
also reckon with secondary shaping and editorial intervention
in chapter 17, carried out in order to work this traditional material into a new context concerning the destiny of the nations at
large. The marks of such editorial intervention are clear; less
clear is how such secondary shaping is to be interpreted.

The opening superscription mentions only Damascus
(17:1). Yet clearly the Northern Kingdom must also be understood as the object of the oracle; indeed, Ephraim is the prime
interest of the oracle from verse 4 onward, while Syria-Damascus virtually drops from view. We have an opening oracle of
judgment against Syria-Ephraim (vv. 1–3), followed by a series
of three "on that day" oracles concerning Israel (vv. 4–6, 7–8,
9), and a concluding unit in which the grounds for Israel's judgment are made clear (vv. 10–11). Then there is a decided shift
in tone. The final verses (vv. 12–14) depict the defeat of the
nations who rush against Israel. The imagery is familiar from
chapter 8, where the assault from Assyria was likened to a river
with overflowing banks; here the nations "thunder like the
thundering of the sea" (17:12), "like the roaring of many waters" (17:13). Just as there, so here, mysteriously and suddenly
the nations are halted in their assault: "At evening time, lo,
terror! Before morning, they are no more" (17:14).

141

Especially within chapters 28—31 it is possible to trace a similar motif, whereby the nations rise up against Zion, at God's behest, and then suddenly are turned back without warning (29:5–8; 31:4–5). We will examine this motif in detail below. Unfortunately scholars are divided in their assessment of this theme in Isaiah, especially as it is related to so-called Zion theology. Does the motif of Zion's protection from the nations' assault predate Isaiah, forming a central part of the Jerusalem cult traditions? Or, does it develop as a result of God's sparing of Jerusalem in 701 B.C.? Or, does it reach mature expression only in the postexilic period? Above we indicated our general acceptance of the first position, though with the proviso that Isaiah has used Zion traditions quite carefully and never with an emphasis on God's unconditional defense of Zion.

The curious thing is that here the motif is used, not in connection with Zion, but in the context of an oracle concerning Syria and the Northern Kingdom of Israel. Moreover, in a context where the emphasis is on a coming world judgment, why does this material conclude on a note of hope?

The answer probably lies with the fact that here within a section dealing with foreign nations Israel itself is the object of discussion. It may well be the case that the intention of the superscription in naming only Damascus is to suggest that, for all intents and purposes, Israel has been subsumed under the rubric of a foreign nation, the one with which it entered into treaties against its own people to the south. The oracle makes clear that God stands firm against all shows of military grandeur—so the fortress of Ephraim must fall (17:3), just as the kingdom of Damascus is brought low. The "glory of Jacob" must be brought down just as the "glory of Moab" was brought into contempt in the previous section (16:14). Only a few small gleanings will remain (17:6). But this will be sufficient for Israel to return and again "regard their Maker" (17:7).

The final verses (7:12–14) make clear that although Israel has forgotten the God of their salvation (v. 10)—in contrast to the hymnic confession at 12:2—they will not be completely consumed in the coming debacle. This hope may well have originated in the context of Isaiah's own proclamation, since it is clear that he cherished distinct visions of reunification involving the final restoration of the vineyard once destroyed: "Ephraim shall not be jealous of Judah, and Judah shall not be hostile towards Ephraim" (11:13). As such, it may well have been the case that he adapted the promises of Zion's final deliverance to the situation of Israel's final survival from the assault of the nations (see 13:4 for the theme of the mustering of the nations).

In sum, the fate that lies in store for Damascus Israel will share as well. Both examples of pride and military arrogance must fall. Israel was tempted to join with Syria in an effort to avoid the Assyrian judge, and in so doing they turned on their own people to the south. Here in the nations section Israel too is condemned as one of the nations, just like Moab, Syria, or Egypt. Yet elsewhere we hear of God's final plans for Israel (14:1–2), that is, the wider vineyard, including the Northern Kingdom. In the assault of the nations that lies ahead, even beyond the days of Assyrian hegemony, Israel will be preserved from final destruction, just as Zion was delivered in the days of Hezekiah (37:33–38).

Isaiah 18:1—20:6
Oracles Concerning Ethiopia and Egypt

Introduction (20:1–6)

The next three chapters of Isaiah (chaps. 18—20) treat the nations of Ethiopia and Egypt. The material is somewhat unique in the nations section insofar as Ethiopia and Egypt are first handled individually (chaps. 18—19), and then in a short prose narrative (chap. 20) both are treated together. Most assume that the latter narrative is the most original. There we see the familiar motif of Isaiah acting as "a sign and portent," as this theme was first introduced in 8:18. The narrative is explicitly set at the time of an Assyrian assault against Ashdod, led by the commander-in-chief of Sargon. This would locate the narrative sometime in the late eighth century B.C.

But there are several important chronological problems. Sargon defeated Ashdod, a Philistine coastal city, in 711 B.C., after a failed attempt at rebellion. Because of the way verse 2 is now phrased, it looks as though Isaiah's three-year sign act of walking naked and barefoot—an act now already completed— was executed in order to foretell the fate of Ashdod at the hands

143

of the Assyrians. Yet as the narrative presently stands, the prophet's sign act is directed at Egypt-Ethiopia. The shift occurs at 20:3. Moreover, the "inhabitants of this coastland" who are referred to in 20:6 have been interpreted by many as being the same Ashdod Philistines referred to in 20:1. Here, however, they bemoan not their own fall but the fall of Egypt and Ethiopia, in whom they had trusted. Their question "And we, how shall we escape?" points to a future, not a past, defeat.

For these and other reasons it is to be concluded that the original tradition of a sign act directed at Philistia has been edited in order to relate the preceding oracles concerning Egypt and Ethiopia to the prophet's past action of walking barefoot and naked for three years. In the present form of the narrative, those who are dismayed at the fall of "Ethiopia their hope" and "Egypt their boast" are either the people of Judah (20:5), as some have argued, or the "inhabitants of this coastland" (20:6), which seems more likely because of the final shaping of the text. This latter group is no longer the Philistines of Ashdod, from Isaiah's day, but the familiar people of the coastland spoken of in Second Isaiah (41:5; 42:4), representing the nations at the limits of the known world. They contrast the treatment of the Egyptians-Ethiopians at the hands of Assyria with the situation in their own day ("on that day") and wonder how they will escape. A narrative that originally concerned Ashdod in 711 B.C. has been secondarily linked to the anticipated defeat of Egypt and Ethiopia. This narrative has in turn been related to the future concerns of the people of the coastland who wonder how they will survive "in that day." The people of the coastland represent those at the outer edges of God's sovereign rule: their concern is with the coming world judgment spoken of in chapters 13—14.

It is remarkable just how resilient the original Isaiah tradition is and the degree to which material related to past events has called forth fresh interpretations. Isaiah walks naked and barefoot as "a sign and portent" against Ashdod, insisting that they too will fall to the Assyrian lion, as did the Northern Kingdom and as would all of Judah. This sign act has then been connected with the anticipated defeat of Egypt and Ethiopia, also at the hands of Assyria. At this level of the text, the primary concern is with denouncing all interest in foreign coalitions as a way of throwing off the divinely ordained Assyrian judgment. This theme receives rich treatment in chapters 30—31, where

144

Judah's rulers are condemned for preferring the horses and chariots of Egypt to the Holy One of Israel (31:1). Then, finally, the entire narrative has been coordinated with the motif of coming world judgment introduced in chapters 13—14. The assault of the Assyrians against Ashdod, Egypt, Ethiopia, and Judah itself is contrasted through the speech of unknown "inhabitants of this coastland" with a coming period of destruction when all must wonder: "how shall we escape?"

In sum, it is possible to regard the narrative in chapter 20 as the "original" tradition concerning Egypt and Ethiopia only in a limited sense. In its final form, it has received considerable enrichment intended to coordinate its portrayal of Isaiah's sign act both with the preceding oracles concerning Ethiopia (chap. 18) and Egypt (chap. 19) and also with the larger presentation of the nations section, concerning a coming world judgment from which no one will be absent (20:6). We are beginning to see a distinct pattern in the nations oracles. Older traditions concerning the defeat of foreign nations, at the hands of Assyria (chap. 17) or perhaps even earlier (as in the Moab oracles in chaps. 15—16), have been recast so as to accommodate a larger world judgment perspective now introducing the entire nations section (chaps. 13—14). Past military defeat is spoken of in order to set the stage for a yet fiercer display of force and final judgment (16:13–14; 20:6), one that lies in the future but is soon to come. This pattern is also to be detected in chapters 18 and 19.

Swift Messengers Dispatched (18:1–7)

Problems of Interpretation

As with the foregoing material concerning Syria-Ephraim, the tendency of scholars has been to interpret the oracle concerning Ethiopia in the context of a reconstruction of historical events that involve the prophet Isaiah and his "foreign policy." That is, the oracle is said to address certain policy matters regarding foreign alliances as these form options for the royal house and the nation of Judah in the days of Isaiah.

Admittedly, there are several minor problems of a literary nature that seem to frustrate a straightforward reading; detailed historical reconstructions attempt to sort these out. Are the ambassadors who are sent by Ethiopia (Cush) the same swift

145

messengers who are charged with a mission in 18:2? Who is the nation "tall and smooth, . . . mighty and conquering"—Cush, Assyria, some other nation? If Cush, is the point of the oracle that the ambassadors presumably dispatched by it are then sent back to it with a message? Further, does the depiction of God looking quietly from his dwelling (18:4) imply neutrality and/or smug assurance? To what end? Who is the agent of judgment who "will cut off the shoots with pruning hooks" (18:5*b*)—Yahweh, the king of Assyria, some other king? Does the final verse offer an interpretation that is consistent with the oracle itself, or has it misunderstood the force of the material found in 18:1–6? These and other questions have been raised by a close reading of the oracle in 18:1–7.

It has been argued that the main oracle (18:1–6) should be situated in the historical period of Isaiah and interpreted in the light of policy options confronting Judah. Ambassadors are sent to Judah to encourage Judah to join a coalition against Assyria (18:2). Isaiah addresses these ambassadors with the following message: even though a battle cry is raised against Assyria (18:3), God will merely look on; he will not take part in the fighting (18:4). However, in due time he will hew away the "spreading branches" of Assyria (18:5), but only on his own time frame.

In such a reading the "nation tall and smooth" (18:2) is none other than Judah. Yet this is a strange characterization of Judah. Moreover, the final verse (18:7) is clear in its insistence that the "people tall and smooth" are those who bring gifts to Judah, "to Mount Zion, the place of the name of the LORD of hosts." It is difficult to avoid the conclusion that the "nation mighty and conquering" is Ethiopia (so explicitly 45:14).

A modified version of this reading would have the ambassadors dispatched from Ethiopia, though not necessarily by the Nile (this is an interpretation of the NRSV; the Hebrew reads simply "by the sea"). The "swift messengers" (18:2) are either the same ones referred to in verse 1, and the prophet is adjuring them to return home; or, these are divine messengers sent not to Ethiopia but to Assyria. Assyria is then the "nation tall and smooth." The point of the oracle is: Yahweh will take no part in coalitions involving Ethiopia, Egypt, and Assyria, and neither should Hezekiah. The final image of a calm and serene summer evening is meant to point to the total indifference of Yahweh to the notion of a coalition with Ethiopia. Yet the next two verses (18:5–6) certainly offer a different picture of Yahweh's indifference. And the final verse (18:7) must be viewed as problematic, since the nation tall and smooth is not Assyria but Ethiopia. As such, it is judged to be a misinterpretation based on Isa. 45:14.

In our judgment, neither reading is entirely satisfactory, especially with respect to the handling of the final verse (18:7). Clearly the entire nations section is now under the influence of a later Babylonian-period redaction. Yet how could such a gross misinterpretation have been generated, whereby "a people tall and smooth" are wrongly identified as the Ethiopians, not the Assyrians or even perhaps Judah, as these readings maintain? As for Isa. 45:14–17, the direction of influence seems far more likely to run from Isaiah 18 to Second Isaiah, not the reverse. Isaiah 45:14 is a summarizing verse that speaks of "the wealth of Egypt and the merchandise of Ethiopia, and the Sabeans, tall of stature," the latter clearly a reference to the nation "tall and smooth."

Moreover, in both of these readings the final emphasis is really shifted away from Ethiopia, despite the opening superscription and the final interpretive verse. The oracle turns out to be more about Assyria and possible coalitions for Hezekiah to consider, even though these are never explicitly mentioned. Finally, the interpretation of Yahweh as serenely detached seems overstated: what is divulged to the prophet is that God is in fact looking on and, as the next verse makes absolutely clear, is about to render swift judgment before any growth can take place. In sum, the "coalition interpretations" are dependent upon historical reconstructions that finally play too indirect a role in the text of Isaiah 18 as such.

A Unitary Reading

Is it possible to interpret the passage in such a way as to take the various literary problems seriously and at the same time produce a more unitary reading, involving the entire chapter, including verse 7? Is the primary context for interpretation a historical reconstruction involving alleged coalitions and political options; or, can our passage best be understood by appeal to the larger nations section and the interpretive context it provides?

It is striking, for example, that the image of the signal "raised on the mountains" (18:3) is already familiar from the

147

very opening verses of the nations sections: "On a bare hill raise a signal" (13:2). The wider "world perspective" that dominates the introductory Babylon section (13:5, 9, 11; 14:7, 9, 16, 21) is also found here: "All you inhabitants of the world, you who live on the earth, . . . look! . . . listen!" (18:3). The image of Yahweh looking down from his dwelling (18:4) is clearly attached to the following scene of swift judgment (18:5), already well established as a motif in this wider section (see 17:14). That is, before any growth can take place the young shoots will be cut off and the spreading branches will be hewn down (18:5).

In contrast to the material concerning Moab, Syria, and Ephraim, the degree to which older material concerning Ethiopia has been put to use here is not altogether clear. Certainly the opening description of Cush as a land of whirring wings, noted for sending forth ambassadors by boat, may well represent a traditional description, even perhaps with relevance for the period of Isaiah's ministry. So too the depiction of Cush as "a nation mighty and conquering, whose land the rivers divide" (18:2) is quite possibly a familiar epithet, as is the description of the Ethiopians as "a nation tall and smooth"—hence the use of this description in 45:14. But, as in the case of the Moabite material, the oracle does not emphasize an event or a set of circumstances with primarily historical (past) relevance. Swift messengers are sent to a nation famed for its own messengers, in order to transmit a more fearful piece of news than anything heard in Isaiah's own day; the swift messengers are probably sent from the divine council itself. All the inhabitants of the world are to know that a terrible world judgment is upon them: the signal has already been raised (18:3; so 13:2) or is about to be raised. God's judgment is to fall "like a cloud of dew in the heat of harvest" on the spreading branches of Ethiopia (18:4). That is, the woe pronounced on the land of whirring wings (18:1) is about to be visited upon the nation tall and smooth.

The images of 18:6 are not quite so clear. Do these essentially offer an amplification of the scene of judgment in 18:5, as wild beasts and birds of prey fall upon the nation? Or, do we see some kind of further staging here, after the judgment of 18:5? The image of beasts of the earth (18:6) was utilized at the scene of Babylon's destruction at the hands of the Medes (13:21), as wild beasts, howling creatures, ostriches, hyenas, and jackals took over the pleasant palaces of Babylon. We know from Isa. 46:11, a passage probably based on descriptions found in the nations section, that Cyrus the Persian is called a "bird of prey from the east" who will come to put an end to Babylonian tyranny. As such, one likely interpretation of 18:5–6 is that, first, the Babylonian agent of judgment will thoroughly hew away the spreading branches of the Ethiopian nation; then, the beasts of the earth and the birds of prey will summer and winter upon Ethiopia, after the Babylonian world judgment has passed. The reference is to the coming reign of Media-Persia, agent of judgment over Babylon.

Such an interpretation is further strengthened by the final verse (v. 7), which has not misunderstood the preceding oracle but offers a final comment consistent with it. During the coming period of Persian dominion "on that day," the Ethiopians will bring gifts to Mount Zion, to the Lord of hosts. In precisely this spirit Second Isaiah has interpreted the oracle of chapter 18. It is not surprising that in Second Isaiah the paying of tribute to Israel's God by Egypt, Ethiopia, and "the Sabeans, tall of stature" (45:14–17) takes place in the larger context of the calling of Cyrus the Persian "my anointed" (45:1). This matches the same description provided in 18:1–7.

An Oracle Concerning Egypt (19:1–25)

Introduction

We noted above how in chapter 20 the motif of a sign act directed at Ashdod was modified to give prominence to a theme that finds clearer expression in Isaiah 30—31: the condemnation of trust in foreign alliances on the part of Judah. In those chapters the prophet's denunciation is specifically targeted at those who "take refuge in the protection of Pharaoh" and "seek shelter in the shadow of Egypt" (30:2). So too in chapter 20 one can still see the clear marks of a tradition whose main concern was to condemn trust in Egypt and Ethiopia. Anyone who puts trust in these nations "shall be dismayed and confounded because of Ethiopia their hope and of Egypt their boast" (20:5). Just as the prophet walked barefoot and naked, so will the king of Assyria lead away captive the Ethiopians and the Egyptians.

Despite the interpretation of many commentators, it cannot be firmly determined in chapter 20 whether those who are condemned for false trust are Judah's citizens (much less Hezekiah specifically) or a more general referent. In the final form

149

of the material "the inhabitants of this coastland" are the only ones specifically mentioned as having placed their hope in Egypt-Ethiopia. The same cannot be said of chapters 30—31, where it is Judah that is specifically condemned by the prophet for false trust. In the nations section, however, the perspective is much broader as the emphasis remains on God's control of the destinies of all peoples.

It should come as no surprise that many interpreters have sought to read chapter 19 within the narrower framework of prophetic condemnation of Judah and the royal house for false alliances with Egypt. The coordination of chapter 19 with the wider literary and historical context of chapters 30—31 is frequently undertaken, as the thrust of the oracle against Egypt is interpreted from the standpoint of Judah and Hezekiah's temptation to trust in foreign alliances. Judah should not trust in Egypt, since Egypt too will fall to Assyria. Precise dating of the material is complicated by the fact that the oracle is extremely vague in terms of historical reference. So too must the circumstances of possible Judahite coalition be inferred, since the oracle is silent on this matter.

In our judgment this silence is far from accidental. As with the other nations oracles discussed thus far, while it is possible to conjecture about this or that original historical setting, the oracle concerning Egypt in its present form now participates in a much broader vision of judgment. This is achieved in part by the framework in which the oracle has been set, most especially by the interpretive additions in 19:16–17 and the wider expansion in verses 18–25. Before we discuss the oracle itself in detail (19:1–15), it might be helpful to have a look at this intriguing interpretive material.

On That Day (19:16–25)

The most obvious literary division of the oracle concerning Egypt—reinforced by the decision of the NRSV to distinguish between prose and poetry—comes at 19:16. Here begins a series of five "on that day" oracles, each one relatively independent of the other. Moreover, while the first oracle maintains the general theme of judgment against Egypt (19:16–17) as this finds expression in 19:1–16, the final four are far from condemnatory and indeed speak in unprecedented terms of Egypt's inclusion with Israel as the people of one God, Yahweh, Lord of the nations.

It is not entirely clear how these five separate oracles developed, nor in what historical circumstances. The first seems to be an expansion on the preceding material; here we find the themes of the outstretched hand together with the purpose of Yahweh, as first introduced in 14:26–27. The second two appear to reflect known historical circumstances from a later period, when exiles from Israel found their way to Egypt (cf. Jeremiah 43—44). However, whether we have a reference to the fifth-century Elephantine community, where "the language of Canaan" (19:18) was indeed spoken and a temple to Yahweh was also in existence (19:21), or to some yet later community of Israelites is not clear. The final two oracles concern both Egypt and Assyria. We heard of a highway from Assyria for the remnant of Israel at 11:16, so perhaps these two oracles are a sort of midrashic expansion of that verse. The highway from Assyria for the exiles was to serve on analogy to the exodus of Israelite slaves from Egypt (11:16). Our oracle has combined these two references and created "a highway from Egypt to Assyria"—not for Israel but for the Assyrians and Egyptians who will worship together. The final oracle speaks of Israel as a blessing "in the midst of the earth" together with Assyria and Egypt, who in a remarkable phrase are called "my people" and "the work of my hands."

In the case of the final two oracles it is by no means clear that we have reference to known historical circumstances, say, in the Seleucid or Hellenistic period, as some have argued, when trade routes linked Egypt and Assyria with lowly Judah. Rather, these final two oracles may simply have been generated on the basis of known Isaianic oracles and as such speak of a day that still lies in the future. They are midrashic expansions on texts that can be identified elsewhere in the Isaianic corpus, even as they go far beyond these in terms of their depiction of an age of commonweal. Here we see the longed-for fulfillment, still "on that day," of the first explicit nations text in the Book of Isaiah (2:1–5), where the nations stream to Mount Zion so that the God of Jacob "may teach us his ways and that we may walk in his paths" (2:3). We mentioned in discussing this text that Israel would have to join the other nations—it would have no place of special privilege, on account of its rejection by God (2:5–6). So here Israel is a "third with Egypt and Assyria" even as it is "a blessing in the midst of the earth" and remains "Israel my heritage" (19:24).

151

Prior to Israel's sanctification as depicted in 4:2–6 we learned of a cleansing of Jerusalem "by a spirit of judgment and by a spirit of burning" (4:4). So too Egypt must be properly prepared before it is found acceptable by the Lord of the nations. The conclusion of the third oracle therefore sets up the transition to Egypt's inclusion with a scene of cleansing: "The LORD will strike Egypt, striking and healing; they will return to the LORD, and he will listen to their supplications and heal them" (19:22). Here we have virtually a reversal of the exodus theme whereby Egypt refused to turn and was therefore hardened of heart and resolve against Israel and their God. Instead, God smites Egypt *so that* they might be healed and might turn and offer supplication to Israel's God.

As it now stands, this remarkable picture of Egyptian and Assyrian worship of Israel's God is only to come following a scene of judgment, to be visited on both nations. The following oracle in chapter 20 reminds the reader that this scene of judgment must first come to pass before "that day" of glorious international peace and common worship occurs. It is difficult to account for this extraordinary depiction of Egypt and Assyria except to say that it must have been considered consistent with Isaiah's own original prophetic vision, from which it developed. At the same time, this is no simple picture of universalism, depicting a time when various religions and various gods are exchanged and found mutually enriching. Egypt and Assyria turn and worship Israel's God and are incorporated as God's people only by virtue of an extreme case of divine initiative and grace. Such is God's will "on that day": to bring all nations under his sovereign rule and benefaction. This is the other side of the world judgment to be visited on all nations, the beginning of the streaming of the nations to Zion such as found expression in 2:1–5. That beginning is sketched here with the nations of Egypt and Assyria, the two nations in Isaiah's own day that presented such a stiff challenge to Israel's faith and trust in God.

There is another key place in the Book of Isaiah where we find a series of "on that day" oracles, namely, in the memoir material from the period of the Syro-Ephraimite debacle (7:1—9:7). Following the Immanuel promise and the word of judgment to Ahaz (7:14–17) we hear of days to come in a series of four "on that day" oracles (7:18–25). Like the oracles in chapter 19, they are a combination of weal and woe, though the emphasis is decidedly on the latter. This contrasts with the series in chapter 19. It is striking that here too the nations of Egypt and Assyria play the significant roles. In chapter 19 a highway is established so that Egypt and Assyria might become with Israel a blessing in the midst of the earth. In 7:18, however, Yahweh whistles for the fly of Egypt and the bee of Assyria, who come and settle in Israel in a scene of hostility and judgment. The images are ones of scarcity, a sweeping away, wilderness, briers and thorns (7:20–25). In sum, not only is the series of "on that day" oracles in chapter 19 an extension of certain aspects of Isaiah's preaching; it also offers a clear reversal of the "on that day" series from the days of Ahaz.

We spoke above of 19:16–25 as offering an interpretive framework for the poetic material in 19:1–15. Two purposes are achieved by the "on that day" series. On the one hand, the first oracle (19:16–17) clearly connects the original poetic material (19:1–15) to the larger conception of world judgment so pivotal in the nations section. Just as we saw in the Moab (16:13) and Ethiopia oracles (18:3–6), this "on that day" oracle links the scene of judgment described in 19:1–15 to a coming catastrophe. This catastrophic judgment involves the larger "plan that the LORD of hosts is planning against them" (19:17). By the use of the same language and imagery of 14:26–27, we know that God's judgment against the Egyptians is only one part of a much broader "plan that is planned concerning the whole earth" (14:26) and that this hand "that the LORD of hosts raises against them" (19:16) is the same hand "that is stretched out over all the nations" (14:26).

At the same time, this larger nations perspective is also maintained in Egypt's case by the remarkable depiction of coming weal now provided in 19:18–25. God's final word for the nations is not desolation but worship and healing and incorporation. Such healing will come only as God chooses to make himself known by his own act of free grace, enabling those who once persecuted his people and blasphemed his name to offer supplication and be heard.

I Will Confound Their Plans (19:1–15)

The main portion of the oracle concerning Egypt, if it should be called that, is found in 19:1–15. Most detect three separate sections in the oracle: verses 1–4, concerning political turmoil and eventual defeat for Egypt; verses 5–10, concerning the drying up of the Nile; and verses 11–15, concerning the

153

foolish counsel of Egypt's wise men. Attempts to separate authentic sections from secondary developments in 19:1–15 have not been particularly successful. Even scholars who posit a specific historical setting for the oracle, or its subsections, readily acknowledge the speculative nature of such proposals. The one reference in verse 4 to the handing over of Egypt "into the hand of a hard master" unfortunately does not narrow things down greatly; as G. R. Hamborg puts it, "Most of the great Assyrian kings could be described as hard masters" (p. 147). Others have conjectured that a Cushite dynasty is to be sought behind this reference; they connect the Egyptian oracle closely with the preceding Ethiopia passage (18:1–6).

Rejecting an interpretation of the passage as simply reflective of Israel's nationalism—a reading that would be sorely troubled by the inclusion of verses 18–25!—others have sought to understand the oracle against Egypt in the context of Isaiah's rejection of foreign alliances. Yet surely this is a very oblique reading. Nothing in the oracle itself suggests that Egypt is condemned because of Judah's inclination to trust in her. On the other hand, is it clear that Egypt has not in fact committed a grave sin, especially when the larger context of the nations section is taken into account? Both 19:3 and 19:11–15 show specific interest in the theme of mistaken counsel and misguided wisdom. Is such wisdom misguided because of the political schemes that are dreamed up in its wake, say, involving Judah or other possible coalitions against Assyria? The text is as silent here as it is in identifying the hard master of 19:4.

Rather, Egypt's wisdom is condemned purely because it in no way jibes with "what the LORD of hosts has planned against Egypt" (19:12). Egypt has its famous plans (19:3) endorsed by their many idols, sorcerers, mediums, and wizards. But from the standpoint of Yahweh's plan and purpose "concerning the whole earth" (14:26), "the princes of Zoan are utterly foolish; the wise counselors of Pharaoh give stupid counsel" (19:11). We are not told what this counsel and wisdom is about. The emphasis is simply on the esteem in which Egypt holds its trusty counselors, wise men, wizards, sorcerers, mediums, and princes, some of whom claim to have access to the secrets of the ages: "I am one of the sages, a descendant of ancient kings" (19:11b).

154

Here we touch upon a theme that is developed in great detail elsewhere in the Book of Isaiah, that is, the notion that the plan of Yahweh is a plan that has been set from eternity: "Have you not heard that I determined it long ago? I planned from days of old what now I bring to pass" (37:26). In the context of chapters 36—37 the motif is employed to argue that Yahweh controls the destiny of Assyria and has commissioned Assyria from eternity for a task vis-à-vis the nations, "that you should make fortified cities crash into heaps of ruins" (37:26). As we have seen, in the nations section Assyria is replaced by Babylon, who is to wreak a world judgment greater than anything experienced in Isaiah's day: "This is the plan that is planned concerning the whole earth" (14:26). An integral part of the motif of the plan of God is that the plan has been set from eternity—so sure is its foundation. Moreover, because Yahweh has revealed the plan only to Israel, to his servants the prophets, other nations are powerless to know their final end. Nor can they know the former things that were revealed long ago to Israel and are now on the point of fulfillment.

The place where this theme appears in its most developed form is in Second Isaiah. The wise men of the nations are challenged to set forth their proofs: "Tell us the former things, what they are, so that we may consider them" (41:22). The nations are to gather themselves and bring forth their witnesses (43:8–9), but they cannot, for "you are my witnesses . . . and my servant whom I have chosen" (43:10). No one is like Yahweh, the first and the last, "who told this long ago" and "declared it of old" (45:21). In the oracle that tells of Egyptian and Ethiopian tribute (45:14–17), these nations make supplication (cf. 19:22) and confess "God is with you alone, and there is no other" (45:14). Isaiah 19:3 indicated that God would confound the plans of the Egyptians, their idols and sorcerers; 45:16 speaks of the fulfillment of this oracle: "All of them are put to shame and confounded, the makers of idols go in confusion together." Yet consistent with the final images of chapter 19, Second Isaiah also speaks of the nations' final acknowledgment of Yahweh: "Turn to me and be saved, all the ends of the earth!" (45:22).

In its present form, the oracle concerning Egypt (19:1–15) cannot be located at one specific period in past history. As in the case of Moab, it may well be that we are dealing with older traditional material concerning Egypt and its famed wisdom, which are about to collapse. As 19:4 puts it: "I will deliver the Egyptians into the hand of a hard master; a fierce king will rule over them." Who this fierce king and hard master is remains—

155

perhaps intentionally—unclear. Various Assyrian or Cushite rulers have been proposed.

At the same time, by placing the oracle in the broader framework now provided at 19:16–25, the judgment over Egypt is shifted to the future "on that day." The hand of Yahweh stretched out against all the nations (14:26) will cause the Egyptians to tremble with fear (19:16). The purpose of the Lord which is planned against the whole earth (14:26) has now reached to Egypt (19:17). As in 20:6, so too here Egypt is to become a byword for any survivors in that day: "Everyone to whom it is mentioned will fear because of the plan that the LORD of hosts is planning against them" (19:17). The Egypt-Ethiopia complex closes in 20:6 with the haunting question, posed by the surviving "inhabitants of this coastland" upon seeing the fall of Egypt, "And we, how shall we escape?"

In the final presentation of these three chapters (chaps. 18—20) we can see how an original sign act, once directed toward Philistia, has been redirected to address the fate of Egypt and Ethiopia within God's larger purpose "that is planned concerning the whole earth." The prophet wears sackcloth as a sign of warning and distress against Ashdod. Then he is stripped even of these meager garments of mourning; walking naked and barefoot, he directs a word of judgment to Egypt. Finally, we learn of a yet greater day of judgment in store for Egypt and Ethiopia and all the nations "on that day" (19:16–17; 20:6). On this plaintive note the presentation of chapters 18—20 is drawn to a close. Yet the motif of prophetic mourning, linked to the person of Isaiah and termed a sign and portent (20:3), is instrumental in the chapters to follow as well (chaps. 21—22). Here we see the fulfillment of God's word to Isaiah in 8:18, that, like his children Shear-jashub and Maher-shalal-hash-baz, he would be a sign and portent in Israel from the Lord of hosts. In the same way their names carried double meanings, so too the prophet's name would mean salvation for some (12:2) but judgment for others (20:3).

Isaiah 21:1—22:25
The Valley of Vision and the Wilderness of the Sea

Introduction

At the opening of our discussion of chapters 18—20, we noted the unusual feature that the nations of Egypt and Ethiopia have been treated in a three-chapter presentation, with both nations the subject of chapter 20. On the face of it, there seems to be little reason to treat the next two chapters as a unit (chaps. 21—22), on loose analogy with chapters 18—20. Chapter 21 appears to culminate in the cry that Babylon has fallen (21:9), thus suggesting that the oracle is to be historically located near this event (ca. 540 B.C.). Chapter 22, on the other hand, tells of an assault on Judah (22:8) and Jerusalem (22:11). Though some have tried to relate the material to the fall of Jerusalem in 587 B.C., there is general recognition that the diverse traditions of chapter 22 are at least partly linked to events in Isaiah's day, namely, the 701 Assyrian assault on Judah-Jerusalem. In either case, why link the fate of Judah-Jerusalem with the fall of Babylon? Are not the two chapters clearly unrelated?

Unfortunately the historical background of this material is extremely confusing and offers little help with the question just posed. To take one example, the mention of Elam and Media in 21:2 has been taken by many as referring to the Persian defeat of Babylon. The reference to Media would be consistent with the picture of Babylon's defeat as set forth in 13:17 ("See, I am stirring up the Medes against them") and also with the cry at 21:9, "Fallen, fallen is Babylon." Chapter 21:1–10 is then an oracle telling of the fall of Babylon.

Yet the emphasis in 21:2–4 on the depiction of the prophet makes the much later historical circumstance (ca. 540 B.C.) somewhat difficult. Moreover, why is the prophet in such anguish about the defeat of Babylon, the notorious oppressor of 14:4–21? Still more problematic is the further reference to Elam, now with the obscure Kir, in 22:6. For here Elam is

157

described as fighting, not against Babylon, but Jerusalem. If there were Elamites fighting with Assyria against Judah in the days of Isaiah, does this call into question an assured later date for the material in 21:1–10? Perhaps this material describes the fall of Babylon in the days of Isaiah, at the hands of Assyria, assisted by Elamite and Median mercenaries, as many have suggested (most recently Hayes/Irvine). On the other hand, for those who propose a 587 B.C. setting for chapter 22, how could Elamites be fighting on the side of the Babylonians against Jerusalem in 22:6 and then fighting on the side of Media in 21:2 against Babylon? These two chapters represent a serious historical puzzle, and there has been no shortage of proposals. Keeping the interpretation of the two chapters completely unrelated helps in part, but there remain difficult historical problems nonetheless.

Moreover, it is striking how many intriguing features the two chapters hold in common. These features exist quite apart from the many historical problems just mentioned. First, both chapters are introduced with enigmatic superscriptions, a distinctive feature that appears only here within the nations section. Both of these superscriptions appear to have been developed on the basis of references within the oracles themselves: the "wilderness of the sea" based on the reference to whirlwinds "from the wilderness" ("desert," NRSV) in 21:1; the "valley of vision" based on the reference to "tumult and trampling and confusion in the valley of vision" in 22:5. Moreover, as A. K. Jenkins has pointed out, there may be a connection between the stern vision the prophet sees in 21:2 and the "valley of vision" at 22:1, 5—though the nature of that connection is not clear. Second, whatever we make of it in historical terms, both chapters refer to the Elamites as agents of destruction (21:2; 22:6), a fact that can hardly be coincidental.

More important, however, is the depiction of the prophet in both chapters. Where one might have expected rejoicing and thanksgiving at the fall of Babylon, the prophet is all but undone by anguish and dismay (21:3–4). Alternatively, the prophet appears chastising in chapter 22 over the exultation and shouting that he hears (22:1–2), presumably due to the deliverance of Jerusalem (22:8*b*–11). Instead, he weeps bitter tears (22:4) and calls for "weeping and mourning," "baldness and putting on sackcloth" (22:12). Eating and drinking, joy and gladness on this occasion (22:13) represent for him an "iniquity" that "will not be forgiven you until you die" (22:14). The final oracle against Shebna also seems concerned with what the prophet regards as incorrect deportment on the part of the steward (22:15–25).

The motif of sackcloth and mourning is familiar from chapter 20. The prophet was remembered in the tradition as one who did not gloat over the fall of foreign nations to whom he was sent. Rather, he saw in the judgment of the nations the righteous hand of his Lord, not simply the avenging defeat of peoples antagonistic toward Israel. This tradition was then extended to include God's judgment over all the nations, even those whose contact with Israel was in fact minimal. Chapters 21 and 22 represent two complex examples of the way this motif has been further extended. Because in our view chapter 22 and its depiction of the prophet has given rise to "the oracle concerning the wilderness of the sea" in chapter 21, we will treat this second chapter first. This will give us an opportunity to explain how the two chapters are closely related in the final presentation of the material.

Isaiah 22:1–25

Despite the position of some scholars, chapter 22 remains closely attached to the events of 701 B.C., when Jerusalem was miraculously delivered. There is very little evidence of a substantial 587 B.C. redaction in chapter 22 intended to link these earlier events with the fall of Jerusalem. This can be demonstrated by attention to the details of the chapter.

The first unit (22:1–4) describes a situation of rejoicing that the prophet judges to be inappropriate. The "tumultuous city, exultant town" is likely Jerusalem. It rejoices because its rulers were not slain in battle. The prophet, however, states that they were captured all the same, having fled the scene of battle. Therefore he weeps for the "destruction" of his "beloved people." The next unit (22:5–8a) describes this destruction in more detail. We hear of "a battering down of walls" and the removal of "the covering of Judah." The breaking down of walls and the removal of Judah are clear references to Sennacherib's destruction of "all the fortified cities of Judah" such as we hear in 36:1. Jerusalem rejoices because it has been delivered. But the prophet is not impressed.

159

As we learn in the next unit (22:8b–11), the citizens of Jerusalem did not in fact trust that Yahweh would deliver the city as he had planned from long ago (so 8:9–10). They did not look to their Lord but to their own defenses: weapons from the royal arsenal; water reservoirs; and wall fortifications. Moreover, where God called for mourning and sackcloth as proper to a state of siege, the people chose instead to cry, "Let us eat and drink, for tomorrow we die" (22:13). Then when the city was in fact delivered, they rejoiced inappropriately, for Judah had been overrun, and the prophet could only weep bitter tears for the destruction of his beloved people (22:4).

The final unit (22:15–25) is consistent with this reading. There too the emphasis is on the inappropriate deportment of one Shebna, who holds the office of steward (cf. 36:3). The steward had built for himself a stately tomb and had collected for himself splendid chariots (22:16–18). The prophet considered this shameful behavior at such dire times as Jerusalem and Judah were experiencing at the hands of the Assyrian judge. As such, he is summarily removed from office and replaced by one Eliakim son of Hilkiah (22:20). All authority is transferred to him, and he will rule properly, like "a father to the inhabitants of Jerusalem and to the house of Judah."

As at other points in Isaiah, so too here there are problems of chronology and identification. In chapters 36—37, Eliakim is already considered steward, the one "who was in charge of the palace" (36:3, 22; 37:2), that is, prior to the 701 B.C. Assyrian assault. In these same chapters we also hear of a Shebna "the secretary" and Joah the son of Asaph "the recorder" (36:3, 22; 37:2). Yet there is absolutely no suggestion that this Shebna stands under prophetic rebuke. Much to the contrary, this Shebna, along with Eliakim and Joah, presents an exemplary picture during the siege of Jerusalem. In fact, all three appear in sackcloth when the assault is under way (37:2), as does King Hezekiah (37:1). That is, they conduct themselves precisely as Isaiah requests in the context of chapter 22: "In that day the Lord GOD of hosts called to weeping and mourning, to baldness and putting on sackcloth" (22:12). In fact, there is every reason to assume that Hezekiah and the threesome of Eliakim, Shebna, and Joah are purposely depicted as conducting themselves in the manner called for by Isaiah, in imitation of the prophet's own contrite demeanor. For this and other reasons, I have argued elsewhere that the Shebna of chapter 22 cannot be the same Shebna the secretary who appears with Eliakim and Joah in chapters 36—37 (Seitz, *Destiny,* pp. 100–116).

It is not clear whether the end of chapter 22 has received secondary comment. The final two verses (vv. 24–25) appear to reverse the positive oracle addressed to Eliakim ben Hilkiah. But apart from this one single instance, there is very little evidence of major secondary transformation in chapter 22. Rather, the material can be interpreted fairly straightforwardly out of the context of the 701 B.C. assault on Judah-Jerusalem. The point of the material is to argue that the deliverance of Jerusalem was not a cause for unconstrained exultation, especially given the destruction of Judah (22:8a) and the poor conduct of Jerusalem's citizens before and after the crisis. Such an interpretation dovetails perfectly with our reading of chapter 1. There too the people are condemned for not responding appropriately to the deliverance of 701 B.C. Instead of giving rise to repentance and justice (1:27), the survivors in the lone "booth in a vineyard" (1:8) continue to rebel and be smitten (1:5). Israel's rulers are especially to blame (1:10, 23, 26). Shebna the steward is a good example of unjust leadership, more concerned with his splendid chariots and his exalted tomb (22:16–18) than with defending the widow and the orphan (1:23).

The oracle concerns a valley of vision (22:1). In this "valley of vision" the day of the Lord comes upon Judah, just as had been prophesied earlier in Isaiah's career (7:17–25). Jerusalem was spared as promised (8:9–10). But the Lord of hosts, rather than proving to be a sanctuary, became for those who trusted in weaponry, reservoirs, and fortified walls a snare, a trap, a stone of offense and a rock of stumbling (8:14). The prophet's word is directed to them in chapter 22. Shebna stands as a representative of those who stumble, fall, and are broken, who are "snared and taken" (8:15). Only for those who heeded the prophet's call to sackcloth and mourning would God prove to be a sanctuary. In chapters 36—37 we learn that first and foremost among those faithful ones was to be found King Hezekiah.

We mentioned above that a significant problem exists with the identification of Elam and Kir in 22:6. Kir has never been satisfactorily identified. Elam, on the other hand, appears together with Media in 21:2 as the conqueror of Babylon. Cyrus the Persian is known to have defeated the Medes in the middle of the sixth century. Before that, he was king of Anshan, whose capital was at Susa in the eastern or northern district of Elam. Yet Sargon the Assyrian is also known to have defeated Elam in the eighth century (721 B.C.). It is therefore likely that Elamite soldiers served with the Assyrians during Sennacherib's assault on Judah in 701 B.C.

It must be admitted that the nonmention of Assyria in chapter 22 remains one of the strongest reasons that confusion exists over the correct historical circumstances behind the chapter. Instead, we have only the obscure reference: "Elam bore the quiver . . . , and Kir uncovered the shield" (22:6). The purposeful decision to title the oracle "concerning the valley of vision," apparently based on the reference in 22:5, also lends an air of mystery to the entire chapter. The emphasis shifts away from specific historical circumstances to concern with the proper response to military assault and the mixed news of partial defeat (22:8b) and partial victory (22:2). In our judgment it is this concern which has triggered the secondary development of the material, just as in chapter 20 the portrayal of the prophet as clothed in sackcloth has given rise to new interpretations of him as "a sign and portent" against Egypt and Ethiopia, and against all the nations.

Isaiah 21:1–17

In chapter 21 the obscure "valley of vision" gives way to the even more obscure "wilderness of the sea" (21:1). The vision of the tumultuous day of the Lord in the "valley of vision" (22:5) is trumped by a yet more "stern vision" revealed to the prophet (21:2). Where once the prophet weeped bitter tears for the destruction of Judah (22:4), now he is thrown into total disconsolation (21:3–4). Picking up the reference to the Egyptian reaction to the awesome hand of the Lord (19:16), the prophet likewise is seized with pangs "like the pangs of a woman in labor. . . . The twilight I longed for has been turned for me into trembling" (21:3–4; cf. 19:16). The wrongful eating and drinking of 22:13 appears now as preparation for military assault (21:5), though the reference is obscure. The Elamite warriors who bore the quiver in the assault on Judah-Jerusalem now join the Median soldiers in a more gruesome assault on the oppressor Babylon.

These multiple linkages can hardly be accidental. What triggered the initial interest in constructing some sort of analogy between the valley of vision and the wilderness of the sea is not clear. Perhaps it was the ironic appearance of the Elamites, first as hostile to Judah-Jerusalem and then conceivably

162

as fighting on its behalf against the oppressor Babylon. Yet precisely here the analogy takes its most ironic twist. Where one might have expected rejoicing (as in 22:2) over the final destruction of the nation who claimed "I will make myself like the Most High" (14:14), instead we see even greater anguish than accompanied the Assyrian assault on Judah-Jerusalem.

At the same time, the portrayal of the prophet in chapter 21 (vv. 3–4) conforms almost exactly to the descriptions of reactions to the day of the Lord as these were set forth in chapters 13—14.

> Wail, for the day of the LORD is near;
>   it will come like destruction from the Almighty!
> Therefore all hands will be feeble,
>   and every human heart will melt,
>   and they will be dismayed.
> Pangs and agony will seize them;
>   they will be in anguish like a woman in labor.
> They will look aghast at one another;
>   their faces will be aflame.
>
> (Isa. 13:6–8)

In the context of our discussions of chapters 13—14 we noted that some regarded the oracle concerning Babylon in chapter 13 as a description of Babylon's defeat, while others interpreted the awesome day of the Lord as accomplished by Babylon itself. Only in 13:17–22 do we hear of Babylon's final defeat at the hands of the Medes, a theme that is then pursued in detail in chapter 14.

Yet herein lies the mystery of the prophetic reaction in chapter 21 and its linkage to chapter 22 and the Assyrian assault on Judah-Jerusalem. Both the world judgment by Babylon and its own judgment by Persia are parts of the same day of the Lord. This is not an instance of keeping score on who receives what just punishment at the hands of what just judge, with Israel on the sideline ready to cheer the results when they tip in their favor. God has allowed the nations to do their worst, and the result is a return to chaos where there are no obvious winners or gloating victors. The prideful display of power and might has brought about its own horrific end. In this sense it is wrong to understand the long poem against Babylon in 14:4–21 as a "taunt" (NRSV), if by that is meant a derisive gloating over Babylon's downfall on Israel's part. Instead, the long poem is a *māšāl*, a lesson, a parable for all ages, meant to give rise to sober

163

accounting and even anguish and dismay (21:3–4). There is no place here for the "tumultuous city, exultant town" (22:2), at least not initially. The prophet sees a stern vision, more appalling than what he saw in the valley of vision when the covering of Judah was taken away. This vision involves a world judgment and the world judge Babylon.

At the outset we mentioned the problem of historical distance in chapter 21, whereby the depiction of the prophet Isaiah is emphasized, yet the vision concerns the fall of Babylon centuries away (ca. 540 B.C.). It is as though the prophet sees in the actions of Elamite and Median troops some dreadful foreshadowing of later events, when the world oppressor Babylon is finally defeated: "Go up, O Elam, lay siege, O Media; all the sighing she has caused I bring to an end" (21:2). One thinks here of the great visions of Daniel which, because they concern events beyond his days and his comprehension, produce such anxiety and confusion: "As for me, Daniel, my spirit was troubled within me, and the visions of my head terrified me" (Dan. 7:15); "As for me, Daniel, my thoughts greatly terrified me, and my face turned pale; but I kept the matter in my mind" (Dan. 7:28); "So I, Daniel, was overcome and lay sick for some days" (Dan. 8:27). Daniel too knows the importance of "prayer and supplication with fasting and sackcloth and ashes" (Dan. 9:3) if he is to understand the stern visions vouchsafed to him—also visions concerning the world powers, their rising and their falling. It cannot be ruled out that part of the reason for the prophet's anguish involves the motif of future revelation, that is, that Isaiah sees a vision concerning days to come whose precise content and significance remain obscure to him. The theme is of course quite explicit in the case of Daniel, but we may see something of it in rudimentary form here.

There is one further feature of chapter 21 concerning future revelation that bears comment. We noted in our discussion of chapters 13—14 how the theme of world judgment through the agency of violent empires finds similar expression in the vision of the prophet Habakkuk. Habakkuk meditates on the moral dilemma of how God can send forth such a ruthless nation as the Babylonians for a task of world judgment (Hab. 1:12–17). In response, a vision whose content is not divulged, but whose burden seems clearly related to the sureness of Babylon's eventual fall, is vouchsafed to the prophet: "For there is still a vision for the appointed time; it speaks of the end, and does not lie" (Hab. 2:3). In Hab. 2:6, as in Isa. 14:4, a "taunt" is then taken up against the Babylonian oppressor in the form of an extended woe oracle (Hab. 2:6–20).

Several ancient commentators (Rashi; Ibn Ezra) had also noted the important relationship between Habakkuk and Isaiah 21, especially in verses 6–8. Some kind of link clearly exists between Isa. 21:8 and Hab. 2:1:

> Upon a watchtower I stand, O LORD,
> continually by day,
> and at my post I am stationed
> throughout the night.
> (Isa. 21:8)

> I will stand at my watchpost,
> and station myself on the rampart;
> I will keep watch to see what he will say to me.
> (Hab. 2:1)

To explain the obscure reference to a lion at Isa. 21:8 ("and the lion cried"; see NRSV note), Rashi goes so far as to appeal to the principle of gematria (i.e., involving the numerical value of the Hebrew letters) as pointing to the name "Habakkuk" (with the same numerical value)—a view regarded as idiosyncratic by most modern commentators, despite the fact that "lion" is clearly intended in the Masoretic text.

What is striking is that Isaiah does not himself play the role of the "watcher" (21:6, 8). Rather, he is charged by God to "Go, post a lookout, let him announce what he sees" (21:6). The watchman is to be especially alert for riders, "horsemen in pairs, riders on donkeys, riders on camels" (21:7). Precisely in Hab. 1:5–11 the onslaught of the Babylonians is described with special attention to the swift riders of "that fierce and impetuous nation":

> Their horses are swifter than leopards,
> more menacing than wolves at dusk;
> their horses charge.
> Their horsemen come from far away;
> they fly like an eagle swift to devour.
> (Hab. 1:8)

The question is therefore raised for the reader who knows the vision of Habakkuk: Whom is the watchman about to announce, the coming of the Babylonians, "that fierce and impetuous nation"? Then the answer comes to the "lion" stationed on the

165

watchtower, brought by horsemen and riders in pairs: "Fallen, fallen is Babylon; and all the images of her gods lie shattered on the ground" (Isa. 21:9). Not the onslaught but the defeat of Babylon is announced by the watchman. It is not surprising that the woe oracles directed at Babylon in the vision of Habakkuk close with a peroration concerning Babylon's idols and images (Hab. 2:3–19). These God has "shattered on the ground" (21:9).

The use of the vision of Habakkuk in Isaiah 21 accomplishes several things. First, it allows the prophet Isaiah to hear of the future from the Lord of hosts and then in turn announce what he hears to Israel, "my threshed and winnowed one" (21:10). The vision of Habakkuk promised an end to Babylonian violence, following a period when Babylon would itself serve as an agent of judgment ordained by God (Hab. 1:5–6). Second, by the charge to the prophet to "Go, post a lookout, let him announce what he sees" (21:6), the historical distance from the prophet Isaiah to the actual fall of Babylon is covered, without doing violence to the integrity of Isaiah's known historical location. Isaiah is not stylized as a soothsayer with proud talents at discerning the distant future. The stern vision that he receives disturbs him so greatly that he can neither hear nor see (21:3). Instead, the anonymous watchman hears and sees (21:6–9). In this manner the prophet Isaiah is made able to hear and then announce what he has heard from the Lord of hosts (21:10), even though it concerns events well beyond his own days. Finally, by announcing the fall of Babylon in specific terms, the earlier visions of Isaiah concerning Babylon are confirmed, using the message of the watchman Habakkuk. In chapter 13, Isaiah "saw" an oracle concerning Babylon that told of the destruction of the whole earth and then of the judgment of this world judge (13:17–22). There the vision of the future is vouchsafed to the prophet without concern for historical distance. Yet the descriptions of world judgment remain generalized, even as they are horrific in their import, and they are still dependent upon the prophet's original conception of the hand of Yahweh and his "plan . . . concerning the whole earth" (14:26) derived from his understanding of the role of Assyria. In chapter 21 we learn in no uncertain terms that Yahweh's plan concerning the whole earth extends to the kingdom of Babylon and involves its sure and certain downfall.

166

The opening superscription (21:1) has from ancient times occasioned much discussion (Macintosh). What exactly does "the wilderness of the sea" mean? With Theodoret, Ibn Ezra, and Qimqi, we take "sea" to be a cipher for Babylon, which is soon to become a wilderness. The Akkadian phrase "land of the sea" in reference to South Babylonia might also confirm this reading. More relevant is the extensive material in Jeremiah 50—51 concerning Babylon's fall, where we hear of the inhabitants of Babylon "who live by mighty waters" (Jer. 51:13). And in Jer. 51:36–37, God promises to "dry up her sea and make her fountain dry; and Babylon shall become a heap of ruins." The great "sea" is to become a wilderness. Such is the burden of the oracle concerning the wilderness of the sea vouchsafed to Isaiah through the agency of the watchman (21:1–10).

The watchman motif is then extended into 21:11–12 to link the preceding material to three oracles concerning Arabia (Dumah: vv. 11–12; Arabia-Dedan-Tema: vv. 13–15; and Kedar: vv. 16–17). Again we learn from a comparison with the nations material in Jeremiah that Nebuchadrezzar, king of Babylon, is credited with the destruction of the land of Kedar (Jer. 49:28–33) in fulfillment of his plan and purpose (Jer. 49:30). As such, we move back to the period before Babylon's fall, when it remains actively engaged in its role as world judge consistent with the larger presentation of the nations section in Isaiah. It is intriguing to note that the Arabians are depicted as fleeing from battle in 21:15, much in the same way as the rulers of Judah-Jerusalem in 22:3. But as in 20:6, where an unknown inhabitant cries out "And we, how shall we escape?" so too here there can be no avoiding the judgment of Yahweh, whether at the hands of the Assyrians (22:3) or their replacement, the Babylonians (21:16–17).

Within the space of two chapters we move through historical periods that range from the Assyrian assault on Judah (chap. 22), to the Babylonian assault on Arabia (21:11–16), to the fall of Babylon itself (21:1–10). Clearly, strict chronological organization has taken a backseat to other concerns in the final presentation of chapters 21—22. Chief among these is an interest in the proper response to the day of the Lord, as modeled by the prophet Isaiah during the Assyrian assault of 701 B.C. and then again upon receiving the stern vision of Babylon's coming fall. With 21:11–17 we return to the theme that predominates in the nations section, that is, the coming world judgment executed by Babylon. The oracle concerning the wilderness of the sea (21:1–10) provides us with only a brief glimpse of days to come, when the mighty Babylon falls and its many idols lie shattered on the ground. We must wait until the presentation of chapters 24—27 to hear more of this theme. There too we can detect a concern with the proper response to the day of the Lord (24:14–16), as this involves both a judgment over the whole earth and also the promised end of Babylon's reign of terror.

Isaiah 23:1–18
The Oracle Concerning Tyre

Related to the question of final organization in the nations section is the placement of this last oracle concerning Tyre, the final in a long series of pronouncements against foreign nations (Babylon, Assyria, Philistia, Moab, Syria-Ephraim, Ethiopia, Egypt, the Wilderness of the Sea, the Valley of Vision). As with other nations oracles, one can attempt to place the oracle against Tyre in the period of Assyrian hegemony and even argue for Isaianic authorship if Sennacherib's assault on Phoenicia in 705–701 B.C. forms the precise background. But in its present form such a reading is excluded, since 23:13 makes clear that the significant judgment against Tyre was executed by Babylon: "Look at the land of the Chaldeans! This is the people; it was not Assyria." As such, the final editor probably had in mind Babylon's siege of Tyre in the early sixth century as the occasion when Tyre was "destined for wild animals" (23:13).

The Babylonian assault on Tyre also forms the background of prophecies concerning Tyre in Jer. 27:3 and 47:4. But the most extensive treatment of Tyre to be found is in the Book of Ezekiel, where an extensive three-chapter section (outdone only by attention to Egypt in chaps. 29—32) clearly understands Tyre's defeat to come at the hands of the Babylonians: "I will bring against Tyre from the north King Nebuchadrezzar of Babylon, king of kings, together with horses, chariots, cavalry, and a great and powerful army" (Ezek. 26:7). In Ezekiel it is the fame and renown of Tyre that comes to the fore and especially its great riches, accumulated through a lively sea trade. So we hear of "your riches" (Ezek. 26:12), "merchant of the peoples on many coastlands" (Ezek. 27:3), "perfect your beauty" (Ezek. 27:4), "your riches, your wares, your merchandise, your mariners and your pilots, your caulkers, your dealers in merchandise" (Ezek. 27:27), "signet of perfection, full of wisdom and perfect in beauty" (Ezek. 28:12). Among those who trafficked with Tyre could be counted many, many nations: Tarshish, Javan, Tubal, Meshech, Beth-togarmah, Rhodes, Edom, Judah, Damascus, Dedan, Arabia, Kedar, Sheba, Raamah, Haran, Canneh, Eden, Asshur, and Chilmad (Ezek. 27:12–25). Truly it could be said that Tyre was a nation without peer in the realm of trade and international exchange.

Many of the same images can be seen in Isaiah 23, where Tyre is termed "the merchant of the nations" (v. 3), "the bestower of crowns" (v. 8) "whose traders were the honored of the earth" (v. 8), "exultant city whose origin is from days of old" (v. 7). Here we may well have the explanation for the final position occupied by the oracle concerning Tyre: Tyre is the nation without peer in terms of "pride of all glory" (v. 9); it is truly the "honored of the earth" (v. 9). Surely, then, such an internationally renowned nation, shrewd trader with doubtless many in its debt—surely it could avoid the judgment of Babylon, through bribe or sweet deal!

Yet the final word on the nations of the earth is one of total judgment, without exception, and precisely on the nation that believes it is exempt by dint of strength or international prestige:

> The LORD of hosts has planned it—
> to defile the pride of all glory,
> to shame all the honored of the earth.
> (Isa. 23:9)

The original theme of "the plan that is planned concerning the whole earth" (14:26) appears here in conjunction with "the hand that is stretched out over all the nations" (14:26):

> He has stretched out his hand over the sea,
> he has shaken the kingdoms.
> (Isa. 23:11)

Indeed, the oracle concerning Tyre is shaped in such a way that it serves as the culmination of God's word to the nations, a fitting conclusion for all that precedes.

169

We noted above that the appellation "wilderness of the sea"

served the ironic function of emphasizing that the nation Babylon would soon become the opposite of a great sea, that is, a desert. Jeremiah 51:36 makes something of the same point (see above). Yet later in this extensive Jeremiah treatment (Jer. 50:1—51:64) we find another image employed to stress the total destruction of Babylon, one in which the sea functions as a symbol of chaos and of all the destructive powers latent in creation (consistent with Gen. 1:6–8 and the Noah story; also with Yam, the Sea, in Canaanite mythology). Ironically, the unleashing of the sea as an agent of destruction makes the earth a "land of drought and a desert":

> How Sheshach [i.e., Babylon] is taken,
> the pride of the whole earth seized!
> How Babylon has become
> an object of horror among the nations!
> The sea has risen over Babylon;
> she has been covered by its tumultuous waves.
> Her cities have become an object of horror,
> a land of drought and a desert.
>
> (Jer. 51:41–43)

Given the very subtle and complex way in which language functions in the Book of Isaiah, we would not want to rule out the possibility that "sea" has a double meaning in the context of chapter 21. The "sea" will create a "wilderness"; and Babylon, the "sea," will become a wilderness. Both meanings appear in the context of the oracle against Babylon in the Book of Jeremiah.

The image of the sea also appears frequently in the oracle concerning Tyre—it is not surprising, given Tyre's reputation for international sea trade and its enviable location as a coastal port. Unfortunately, at several junctures the text is almost untranslatable (23:4). But God appears to bring about Tyre's destruction by the very sea that is also Tyre's boast:

> Cross over to your own land,
> O ships of Tarshish;
> this is a harbor no more.
> He has stretched out his hand over the sea,
> he has shaken the kingdoms.
>
> (Isa. 23:10–11)

170

It appears that several meanings flow together (so to speak) when the image of sea is employed. First, there is the image of sea as a force of destruction. This image is employed in Isaiah's proclamation concerning Assyria as agent of judgment: "The Lord is bringing up against it the mighty flood waters of the River, the king of Assyria and all his glory" (8:7). Babylon is also the sea soon to become a desert (cf. Jer. 51:36). Finally, Tyre "in the heart of the seas" (Ezek. 27:25; 28:2, 8) is also "wrecked by the seas, in the depths of the waters" (Ezek. 27:34). The same imagery so clearly employed in Ezekiel may also be detected in Isa. 23:4, 10–11, even though the text is at times difficult to interpret.

It is important to grasp the various shades of meaning for the term "sea" and its equivalents in the context of chapter 23, for here we find another possible reason for the final position of this oracle within the nations section of Isaiah. Within the following section (chaps. 24—27) the world judgment is clearly depicted in terms of a return to chaos. As in the days of Noah, "the heavens languish together with the earth" (24:4) and "the windows of heaven are opened, and the foundations of the earth tremble" (24:18). These images strongly reminiscent of Genesis are prepared for in part by chapters 21 and 23 and their employment of the language of sea as a destructive image.

The final image of chapter 23 is not one of destruction, however, but one of reversal leading to commonweal. In the days following Tyre's judgment we learn that all the merchandise of which Tyre was so proud will "be dedicated to the LORD; her profits will not be stored or hoarded" (23:18). Instead, all these goods will be set aside for those "who live in the presence of the LORD." At the conclusion of Second Isaiah, God remembers the days of Noah, not as days of judgment and a return to chaos, but as days when he "swore that the waters of Noah would never again go over the earth" (54:9). In the final chapter, "everyone who thirsts" is invited to "come to the waters" (55:1). Those who have no money are to "come, buy and eat! Come, buy wine and milk without money and without price" (55:1). Here, quite possibly, Second Isaiah draws on the twin images of the oracle concerning Tyre: the waters are now no longer waters of destruction but waters where the thirsty are to congregate; they can drink, and also eat from the storehouses that are found at Zion. The threats of the nations oracles have been reversed, and the age of commonweal promised there is about to dawn.

Isaiah 24:1—27:13
A Tale of Two Cities

Introduction

We have adopted an approach in this commentary that pays particular attention to the role that literary context plays in the interpretation of individual passages. We have not done this to the exclusion of interest in historical context, as this has traditionally influenced the exegesis of passages in Isaiah. But we have pressed on to inquire about the final form of the material and the sorts of historical concerns that are reflected in the text as a whole. When one tries to appreciate the total perspective of the nations section, certain specific historical factors begin to come to the fore. Chief among these is the interest in a coming world judgment, massive in scope, affecting all nations, accomplished by the Babylonian empire. At two specific points (chaps. 14 and 21) we also learn that God's judgment against national pride extends to include Babylon as well. This is not a cause for rejoicing but rather a sign of how comprehensive and far-reaching are God's sovereignty and justice.

If the term "Babylonian redaction" is relevant anywhere, it is not so much in chapters 1—12 but rather in the nations section. By this we mean, not just an interest in Babylon as judge over Judah and Jerusalem in the events of 587 B.C., when the capital fell and kingship came to an end. Rather, we mean an interest in Babylon as world judge, as executing God's punishment over all nations, and as finally brought before the throne of justice itself. More than at any other point in the presentation of First Isaiah, the nations section reflects a thoroughgoing interest in the destiny of the nations vis-à-vis Babylon and in Babylon's own final destiny.

That interest extends to chapters 24—27. Indeed, in many respects these four chapters represent the culmination of a Babylonian redaction, if we might call it that. Here too, in chapters 24—27, literary context plays a decisive role. Scholars have already noted the clear and extensive relationship between these four chapters and other texts in Isaiah, particularly

172

the preceding chapters 13—23. As we will demonstrate below, that relationship is most evident in the case of chapters 13—14, which is not surprising, since these chapters deal with the rise and fall of Babylon. The close connection between chapters 24—27 and the preceding nations section prompted one recent interpreter to consider the former "the key to the redactional understanding of the foreign nation oracles in Isaiah 13—23" (J. Becker, quoted from Sweeney, "Isaiah 24—27," p. 40).

Appreciation of the role that context plays in the proper interpretation of chapters 24—27, especially vis-à-vis the nations section, is fairly recent. Older commentators were persuaded that chapters 24—27 represented an absolutely distinct section in the Book of Isaiah, one of the latest—if not the latest—to be added to a nearly completed book. Older commentators were also in agreement that chapters 24—27 were written in the form of an apocalypse, close in circumstance and time of composition to the Book of Daniel. Obviously such a judgment would render the relationship between chapters 24—27 and the rest of the book, consisting of prophetic speech, secondary and arbitrary. Finally, it should also be noted that more recent commentators who see a close literary relationship between chapters 24—27 and other sections of the Book of Isaiah do not necessarily reject a postexilic date and setting for the composition of these chapters, even as they regard the classification "apocalypse" to be misleading or too confining.

One of the persistent problems of interpretation in chapters 24—27 involves the identity of the obscure city mentioned at several points in the presentation (24:10; 25:2; 26:5; 27:10). It is also not clear whether the same city is consistently referred to. In addition, 26:1 speaks of a "strong city" that is found in the land of Judah and that, in contrast to the other references, clearly merits God's approbation—it is a city where "the righteous nation that keeps faith may enter in" (26:2). Recently, many have sought to identify the destroyed city, at least in chapter 24, with Jerusalem. Another clear alternative is to see Babylon as the city about to be desolated. In both of these cases, one could argue for a sixth-century date, with the fall of Jerusalem (587 B.C.) or the fall of Babylon (ca. 540 B.C.) as the relevant historical points of reference. Also at issue is whether the oracles are true prophecies, that is, addressing a future set of circumstances not yet come about; or, by contrast, actual descriptions of known historical events, now in the past. A fur-

173

ther alternative, which has been defended vigorously over the years and continues to find strong support, is to regard God's hostility toward the city in more general terms. Plöger, for example, considers the reference to God's judgment against the city (24:10, 12) as amounting to punishment of "city life . . . in general" (quoted from Johnson, p. 12). Those who hold for a more general referent are of no common mind about the correct date for the composition; nor do they agree over whether the oracles address future circumstances or past events already experienced by the community.

These debates about the identity of the city are important ones. Here we have a significant recurring literary motif that helps provide unity and structure in the four-chapter complex. In each chapter, there is a clear reference to a city (24:10, 12; 25:2; 26:1, 5; 27:10). It would be nice to know just what city—or cities—is being held up for special consideration.

Without engaging the debates on their own terms, what might we conclude about the city in chapters 24—27? First, with the exception of 26:1-2, the city stands in opposition to God's will and justice and therefore must be destroyed. In 26:1-6 the lofty city brought low (26:5-6) stands in clear contrast to the strong city where salvation is set up (26:1-2). In all other instances, the unnamed city is to be destroyed. Second, the fact of the city's not being named must be taken into consideration. What would prevent the author from being clearer about his intention to name Jerusalem or Babylon as the city about to be destroyed? The nonspecific way in which the city is mentioned would seem to support the view that city life in general is being condemned. Moreover, we can see elsewhere the obvious decision to speak in general and broad-scale terms about God's judgment. This is most apparent in the references to God's punishment of the earth and the world, which far outnumber references to the city in these four chapters ("the earth": 24:1, 3, 4, 5, 6, 13, 16, 17, 18, 19 [x3], 20, 21; 25:8; 26:9, 21; "the world": 24:4; 26:9, 18; 27:6; "the nations, peoples, inhabitants": 24:1, 5, 6, 13, 17; 25:3, 6, 7, 8; 26:2, 5, 9, 18, 21). It is difficult to avoid the impression that a more general referent for the city is intended, to match the far-ranging scenes of destruction and desolation that await "the earth," "the world," and all its inhabitants. At the same time, these references to the destruction of the city—and indeed the desolation of all the earth and its peoples—may well have originated in response to

174

some specific historical event or its anticipation. As the material is now presented, that historical event appears to lie in the future.

As we noted in our discussion of chapters 13—14 above, there is a considerable degree of agreement between the perspective of these two opening chapters and that which is found in chapters 24—27, such that we spoke of a conscious framing around the larger nations section. The larger world judgment scenario is clearly to be noted in chapters 13—14. God will destroy "the whole earth" (13:5); he will "make the earth a desolation" (13:9); the world will be punished for its evil (13:11) as the heavens and earth tremble (13:13). When Babylon is finally broken, "the whole earth" is at rest (14:7). When Babylon's king descends to Sheol, "all who were leaders of the earth," "all who were kings of the nations" (14:9), rise to meet him. Babylon was a nation "who made the earth tremble, who shook kingdoms" (14:16). Babylon made "the world like a desert" (14:17). And Babylon "overthrew its cities" (14:17).

Because of the similarities between the perspectives of these two sections (chaps. 13—14 and 24—27), we would argue that the same world judgment is being referred to. So the city that is destroyed is in some sense Jerusalem, but it is also any city overthrown by Babylon (14:17), and from what we know of the nations section, these were many. We also learn in the nations section that God sends forth Babylon as an agent of judgment against the entire world—this is his purpose concerning the whole earth and all nations (14:26). The same purpose is referred to in 25:1 as a plan of old "faithful and sure," namely, that God has "made the city a heap, the fortified city a ruin" (25:2). Throughout the nations section we heard of a coming judgment directed against all forms of human pride and military strength, a judgment from which no one would be exempt (14:26; 16:14; 18:6; 19:16–17; 21:17). We also learned that, ironically, this judgment would finally include the agent of judgment as well: "See, I am stirring up the Medes against them" (13:17); "Fallen, fallen is Babylon; and all the images of her gods lie shattered on the ground" (21:9). In chapter 14 "the man who made the earth tremble" (v. 16) is brought to lowest estate. So it is also against the mighty city Babylon that God's final act of judgment is rendered.

175

One other matter was clarified in the nations section and that concerned the future of God's vineyard. God would not permit the nations to destroy his own people utterly but would rebuke the mighty waters of the nations "that thunder like the thundering of the sca" (17:12–14). For this reason a certain distinction must be made regarding the fate of Jerusalem in the context of God's laying waste the earth (24:1) and bringing low the lofty city (26:5). While it is possible to see in chapter 24 the world judgment spoken of in chapter 13, extending to Judah-Jerusalem as well, it would be incorrect to limit the interpretation of "desolation . . . in the city" (24:12) to Jerusalem or in any way suggest that the city broken down in chapter 24 is primarily to be understood as the capital of God's vineyard. Especially when one focuses on the interpretation of chapters 24—27 as a whole, it is clear that while God has in mind a judgment of the whole earth, he himself intends to "reign on Mount Zion and in Jerusalem" (24:23). A contrast is then set up in chapter 25 between the fortified city that God destroys and "this mountain" (25:6–12) where the reproach of God will be taken away. Chapter 26 maintains this contrast by speaking of a strong city where salvation is set up (26:1) and the lofty city whose inhabitants will be brought low (26:5).

Here again the larger context of the Book of Isaiah plays an important role. Within the presentation of chapters 1—12, the final chapter serves the function of permitting an unknown "inhabitant of Zion" to testify to God's ultimate salvation and comfort for his people (12:1–6). In our discussion of this passage we noted the threefold repetition of the Hebrew root from which the prophet Isaiah's name ("Yahweh is salvation") is taken: "God is my salvation" (12:2); "he has become my salvation" (12:2); and "you will draw water from the wells of salvation" (12:3). This final hymnic piece brings the first major section (chaps. 1—12) to a close by allowing us to see something of God's ultimate protection for Zion, playing on the name "Isaiah," which was to serve as a sign and portent in Israel (8:18).

Within chapters 24—27 we see not one but several hymnic pieces (25:1–5; 25:9; 26:1–21; 27:1–6). As in chapter 12, where an unknown inhabitant of Zion testifies to God's final salvation, so too at 25:9 an unknown voice cries out:

176

Lo, this is our God; we have waited for him, so that he *might save us.*
This is the LORD for whom we have waited;
let us be glad and rejoice in *his salvation.*

(Isa. 25:9)

In step with the presentation of the nations section, now the whole world is to testify to God's salvation and sovereign rule as well as Israel and the anonymous "inhabitant of Zion":

> Therefore strong peoples will glorify you;
> cities of ruthless nations will fear you.
> (Isa. 25:3)

> Open the gates,
> so that the righteous nation that keeps faith
> may enter in.
> (Isa. 26:2)

> For when your judgments are in the earth,
> the inhabitants of the world learn righteousness.
> (Isa. 26:9)

These passages testify to the coming fulfillment of the charge in chapter 12 to "make known his deeds among the nations" (12:4) so that his praise might "be known in all the earth" (12:5).

If this appeal to the wider context of the nations section for aid in interpreting chapters 24—27 is essentially correct, then several other matters fall into place. The proper interpretation of 24:14–16 has frequently puzzled readers. In the midst of a dirge over the destruction of the earth, a chorus of voices suddenly begins to sing God's praises. Is this an appropriate or an inappropriate response on the part of those "in the coastlands of the sea" (24:15)? In the very next verse a first-person voice gives exactly the opposite response, reminiscent of the prophet's reaction in the commissioning scene (6:5): "Woe is me! For the treacherous deal treacherously, the treacherous deal very treacherously" (24:16). Another set of texts also comes to mind, from the more proximate chapters 21—22. There too the proper reaction to the assault on Jerusalem and to the larger world judgment was of particular concern (21:3–4; 22:1–4, 12–14). There too the prophet saw a stern vision, "the betrayer betrays, and the destroyer destroys" (21:2), which, far from being a cause for rejoicing, appalled the prophet and rendered him unable to see or hear. The same motif has clearly been utilized in chapter 24. We will have more to say about the exact interpretation of 24:14–16 in the context of our discussion of chapter 24 below. Here is a further instance where the wider context of the nations section has influenced the composition of chapters 24—27 and its presentation as the culmination of God's word and purpose concerning the whole earth.

177

Finally, the appeal to the foregoing perspective of chapters

13—23 also helps determine the historical setting of the material in chapters 24—27. We know that God's full judgment over human pride and national arrogance will not be completed until Babylon is itself brought before Yahweh's throne of justice. Yet the world judgment, described in such similar terms in chapters 13 and 24, is also executed by this same Babylon, the "warriors" who execute God's anger (13:3). As such, the author of chapters 24—27 stands at a historical point when Babylon is at its greatest military strength and as God's agent threatens to "waste the earth and make it desolate" (24:1), in the poetic language of the text. Yet the author also stands sufficiently close to the collapse of Babylon's might as to envision God's final act of justice as involving it, quite specifically. In this respect, interpretations of the doomed city (24:12), the fortified city (25:2), and the lofty city (26:5) as Babylon are essentially correct, insofar as the judgment of Babylon represents God's final assault on human pride. In sum, the author of chapters 24—27 probably stands somewhere after the fall of Jerusalem in 587 B.C. and before the Persian capture of Babylon around 540 B.C. It also seems likely that this same "author" stood in close proximity to those who were responsible for the final editing of the diverse material in chapters 13—23. This would help explain their similar working perspectives and their common interest in the theme of God's final judgment over his own agent of judgment, Babylon.

As has been pointed out, the defeat of Babylon at the hands of Cyrus the Persian was a relatively peaceful affair, compared with the destruction of Babylon by Xerxes (ca. 485 B.C.) and by Alexander the Great in 331 B.C. For those who regard the oracles as composed on the basis of past events, the Persian defeat of Babylon would be the least likely historical candidate for giving rise to the oracles of chapters 24—27, with their emphasis on the total annihilation of the whole earth and especially the lofty city. But in our judgment the oracles refer to both past and future destruction, that is, the past destruction accomplished by the Babylonian empire, a punishment regarded by the author of chapters 24—27 (and chaps. 13—23) as directed at the whole earth and terrifying in its force; and also the coming judgment of Babylon, the lofty, fortified city. In a manner of speaking, the author is caught up in a vortex of world violence. That the oracles may have found more appropriate historical fulfillment in the assaults on "the lofty city" that followed the Persian takeover of Babylon is only a testimony to their long-range accuracy and ongoing vitality. In an oblique sort of way, the lack of specific fulfillment in the Persian capture of Babylon also testifies to the future orientation of the material concerning the desolation of the city. As Dan Johnson has pointed out in defending a future orientation in chapter 25, anticipating the overthrow of Babylon by Cyrus, "because the 'description' of the destruction does not square with the actuality it is 'unthinkable' that it had been composed after the event" (Johnson, p. 60).

In the central panel of this four-chapter presentation (chaps. 25:1—26:6), a clear contrast is set up between the destruction of "the fortified city" (25:2) and the worthy establishment of "a strong city" whose gates open to "the righteous nation that keeps faith" (26:1–2). A further contrast exists between the mountain where God prepares a feast for all peoples (25:6–9) and the high fortifications that are Moab's pride (25:12). These "will be brought down, laid low, cast to the ground, even to the dust" (25:12). The strong city where salvation has been set up is to be contrasted with the lofty city, which likewise God "lays low. . . . He lays it low to the ground, casts it to the dust" (26:5). This contrast between the strong city and faithful mountain, on the one hand, and the lofty city with its inhabitants of the heights, on the other, is the central theme of chapters 24—27. For this reason, "A Tale of Two Cities" is an appropriate title for chapters 24—27, the conclusion of the nations section in the Book of Isaiah.

Isaiah 24:1–23
A Return to the Days of Noah

While efforts have been made to describe the development of tradition in chapter 24, with core material identified only at verses 1–6 and 14–20 (Wildberger), there is also evidence of a certain structural unity and compositional integrity in the present form of the chapter. It is true that one main theme of the chapter can be located in verses 1–6 and 14–20. This theme centers on a cosmic judgment that is the consequence of the breaking of God's "everlasting covenant" (24:5). What follows

179

upon this breach of contract is an awesome world judgment, one that affects every level of society (24:1–3) and the cosmic order itself (24:4–6, 17–20).

Commentators have debated which covenant the author had in mind at 24:5. The reference to specific laws and statutes having been violated has urged some to see here a reference to the Mosaic covenant (Clements; Johnson). On the other hand, several key features of chapter 24 argue in favor of the Noah covenant as the "everlasting covenant" that has been broken. The Noah covenant is specifically termed an "everlasting covenant" (Gen. 9:16). The references to the earth lying polluted (24:5) and a curse devouring the earth (24:6) also seem to pick up from the descriptions of the Noah story: "Now the earth was corrupt in God's sight, and the earth was filled with violence" (Gen. 6:11). Further, as Clements has pointed out, the guilt spoken of at 24:6 "is regarded as a universal condition, so that there is no necessity to specify what particular sins have occasioned such guilt" (Clements, *Isaiah 1—39*, p. 202). The cosmic proportions of the judgment occasioned by the breach of covenant also resemble the Noah story; in 24:18 we even hear that "the windows of heaven are opened, and the foundations of the earth tremble." This sounds like a direct allusion to Gen. 7:11: "On that day all the fountains of the great deep burst forth, and the windows of the heavens were opened." In addition, we mentioned above the key role the sea played as agent of destruction in chapters 21—23, threatening to return the world to the conditions of chaos that obtained before God separated "the waters from the waters" (Gen. 1:6).

But quite apart from these specific references, the most compelling reason for regarding the "everlasting covenant" as the covenant with Noah is the national and cosmic scope presupposed by the chapter. This is not a covenant with Israel only (Mosaic) that has been broken, but one with the entire cosmos and every nation on earth. The chapter makes quite clear that it is the "inhabitants of the earth" generally, not the inhabitants of Israel specifically, who have acted in such a way as to merit God's fierce judgment. It is not so much that the reasons for their guilt are universal and unstipulated (Clements) as it is that these reasons have already been articulated and discussed in the context of chapters 13—23, which were concerned, above all, to expose the sins of the nations beyond Israel's borders.

Here the Noah story offers a perfect analogy. We stand long

180

before God's specific election of Israel. God's concern is with the nations at large and the entire created order. He saw "that the wickedness of humankind was great" (Gen. 6:5); "the earth was corrupt . . . , and the earth was filled with violence, . . . for all flesh had corrupted its ways upon the earth" (Gen. 6:11–12). The final judgment of God is revealing in its similarity to the situation recounted in Isaiah 13—27:

> And God said to Noah, "I have determined to make an end of all flesh, for the earth is filled with violence because of them; now I am going to destroy them along with the earth" (Gen. 6:13).

> Now the LORD is about to lay waste the earth and make it desolate.
>
> (Isa. 24:1)

> The earth lies polluted
> under its inhabitants.
> (Isa. 24:5)

> A curse devours the earth,
> and its inhabitants suffer for their guilt.
> (Isa. 24:6)

> [The earth's] transgression lies heavy upon it,
> and it falls, and will not rise again.
> (Isa. 24:20)

As in the Noah story, all creation is affected, not just earth's human inhabitants:

> The earth dries up and withers,
> the world languishes and withers;
> the heavens languish together with the earth.
> (Isa. 24:4)

> The wine dries up,
> the vine languishes.
> (Isa. 24:7)

> The windows of heaven are opened,
> and the foundations of the earth tremble.
> The earth is utterly broken,
> the earth is torn asunder,
> the earth is violently shaken.
> (Isa. 24:18b–19)

The only thing missing is the explicit use of the forty-day flood image. But even it is somewhat latent in the description of judgment in Isaiah 13—27, which comes about because of the

181

nations' violence and destructive force, likened at Isa. 17:12 to "the thundering of the sea" and "the roaring of mighty waters." Only God will be able finally to rebuke these waters (17:13), just as in the days of Noah "God made a wind blow over the earth, and the waters subsided" (Gen. 8:1).

In defending a Mosaic covenant interpretation of Isaiah 24:5, Johnson argues that it "was impossible for humanity to break the Noachic covenant" (p. 27)—which is precisely what the poet argues humanity has done. Johnson goes on to state that the Noachic covenant "was simply a promise by God never again to destroy the world by a flood" (pp. 27–28). Yet perhaps this is exactly the point the author of chapters 24—27 wishes to make. God has not broken the everlasting covenant; the nations have, through their displays of pride and national might. What was seemingly unthinkable—the breaking of an everlasting covenant—has tragically occurred. Humanity has encroached upon a covenant that God had established as inviolate. In the poetic language of chapter 24, the author argues that the nations have returned to the violent ways of their forebears in the days of Noah. The world is not destroyed again by a forty-day flood, as God had promised, but rather by the centuries-long assaults of the nations.

One question remains, given the Noah background of chapters 24—27. Where is Noah? Is there any remnant symbol in the presentation of chapters 24—27? Is the strong city with walls and bulwarks of salvation (26:1) to be regarded as an ark of sorts? Who is addressed in Isa. 26:20 as "my people"—a people who are to "enter your chambers, and shut your doors behind you; hide yourselves for a little while until the wrath is past"? Are we to think here of those whom God set apart in the ark, together with Noah, before "the LORD shut him in" (Gen. 7:16)? In Isa. 26:20 the people are to enter their chambers and shut their doors for—in language most reminiscent of the Genesis story—"the LORD comes out from his place to punish the inhabitants of the earth for their iniquity; the earth will disclose the blood shed on it, and will no longer cover its slain" (26:21; cf. Gen. 6:11–13).

The remnant that functions on analogy with Noah and his family in Isaiah 24—27 is a portion of the people of Israel. It includes those who sing out God's praises following the world judgment, as the "strong city" of Jerusalem again reclaims a place of honor (26:1–6). In fulfillment of the powerful language of Isa. 2:1–5 and 4:2–4, Zion is to become a final refuge for the righteous nation (26:2) and those "whose mind is stayed on thee" (26:3, RSV). Chapter 26 functions to depict God's intention for the emergence of a "strong city" that will stand in absolute contrast to the proud city that must be destroyed and brought low, that is, Babylon and every city whose mind is set not on God but on human achievement and military might divorced from God's justice. Insofar as the Israel of Isaiah's day is to be properly indicted on these charges, so too it will share the fate that lies in store for Babylon. As a whole, then, chapters 24—27 also function as a warning that will hover over the presentation that follows in chapters 28—39, where the question of Israel's allegiance to Yahweh or attraction to the nations is continually before the reader.

Chapters 24—27 also remind the reader that another choice is possible for Israel and that is the choice to be like Noah. Israel need not be swept up in the world judgment that culminates in Babylon's destruction and the fall of Jerusalem. There is another option. Already in chapters 6—8 we heard of the possibility that a remnant would emerge (6:13; 8:16-22). This was not a remnant that would be spared direct experience with a coming judgment; on the contrary, this remnant would also feel the sting of destruction and desolation and would be called on to testify to God's presence and teaching during difficult times of trial and challenge. They would "be burned again," to use the language of Isaiah's commissioning (6:13). They would have to face difficulty and abuse at the hands of the nations but also at the hands of an Israel who preferred consultations with the dead, the mediums and wizards (8:19-20).

Moreover, in the context of Babylon's destruction foreshadowed in chapter 21 we learned that an inappropriate response to the extension of God's judgment to include the perpetrator of violence was one of simple rejoicing (21:3-4). Instead, the prophet was consumed with anguish and dismay at the vision of judgment vouchsafed to him. So it is that when the same vision of judgment begins to be fulfilled in chapter 24, as the world is rocked by the twin waves of judgment by Babylon and judgment of Babylon, we again find a commentary on what should be the proper response. At 24:14-15, unknown remnant voices at the ends of the earth "sing for joy" and shout out praises, presumably at the character of God's world judgment that extends beyond Jerusalem's fall to include Babylon the Great.

Caught up in this vortex of violence, however, the prophet's

183

remnant voice gives utterance to a quite different response—a response that puts us in mind of the heavenly council scene of chapter 6: "I pine away, I pine away. Woe is me!" (24:16). It is as though the vision of judgment seen there is now being witnessed, in fulfillment of the description at 6:11: "Until cities lie waste without inhabitant, and houses without people, and the land is utterly desolate." In chapter 24 the prophet sees the fulfillment of God's word of judgment as first vouchsafed to him during the commissioning scene of chapter 6. This is no cause for celebration. It is a time for painful, sober recognition and acknowledgment of God's necessary judgment—it had to come to this. The word vouchsafed to the prophet did not lie.

The scene of destruction reported by the divine voice in chapter 6 was especially comprehensive. It appeared to speak of a destruction not limited to the vineyard alone but touching all humanity and every nation on earth, until "vast is the emptiness in the midst of the land" (6:12). Chapter 24 testifies that such a scene of judgment has come to pass: cities now lie waste without inhabitant (6:11; 24:10, 12); the land is utterly desolate (6:11; 24:1, 3, 19); men and women have been removed far away (6:12; 24:2, 6, 18). But within this same vision of destruction we learned there would be a tenth that remained, to be burned again, that a holy seed might emerge in the end. So it is within the scene of world desolation reported in chapter 24 that brief glimpses of a remnant can be identified. Few men are left (24:6); unknown voices are lifted up (24:14); the prophet himself speaks (24:16). But this is not a time for gloating over the destruction of Babylon or the fall of any other "city of chaos." The prophet's voice is the voice to be heard now. What he sees he knows to be the fulfillment of the vision of judgment vouchsafed to him on the eve of the Syro-Ephraimite crisis. If a remnant is to emerge, it must be burned again. Only then will God again reign on Mount Zion, "and before his elders he will manifest his glory" (24:23). Only then, like Noah, will the burned remnant emerge from the ark to offer sacrifice and praise.

Isaiah 25:1–12
An Appropriate Response

In chapter 24 a contrast is clearly visible between voices that sing out songs of praise and a lone first-person voice that tells of ongoing treachery (24:14–16). What is not so clear is how we are to evaluate this contrast. The voices of joy appear to celebrate not just the fall of the city of chaos, related in the preceding unit, but also "they shout from the west over the majesty of the LORD" (24:14). Moreover, an imperative form is used in verse 15, as the coastlands of the sea are expressly charged to "glorify the name of the LORD, the God of Israel" (24:15). What may well be accepted as an appropriate response, then, on the part of the nations at the ends of the earth is, on the other hand, set in contrast to the voice of the prophet who must continue to endure desolation and destruction. From his perspective, treachery continues, and he must continue to endure it.

It is one thing for the nations to give praise, but what of Israel, for whom this lone voice stands as representative? They must apparently bear the brunt of violence and treachery. It is quite possible that the experience of 587 B.C., involving the destruction of Judah and Jerusalem, stands behind this cry of treachery. What the nations at large had to endure at the hands of Babylon, Judah and Jerusalem endured in particularly acute ways. Babylon's own demise is not an occasion for hymns of joy, unless that joy finds its origin in comprehension of the plan of God. Without penetrating the divine purpose, hymns of joy are peremptory, misguided shouts of hope but not cries of conviction. The hymn that Israel will sing must be a hymn that springs from understanding God's ultimate purpose. Such a hymn is now found in 25:1–5. It is as though the skies clear for a moment and the first-person voice of 24:16 finally grasps the meaning of God's activity in the midst of this world judgment.

It may be that the final unit of chapter 24 (vv. 21–23) is the pivot on which the following hymn turns. Two key pieces of information are provided here. First, God plans a punishment of "the host of heaven in heaven, and on earth the kings of the

185

earth" (24:21). Here a link is established with the perspective of chapters 13—14, at the head of the nations section. Babylon, it is to be recalled, had boasted of its great strength and described how it had climbed to the heights of heaven to set its throne within the divine assembly, proudly stating, "I will make myself like the Most High" (14:14). But the prophet promised another destiny for Babylon: "How you are fallen from heaven, O Day Star, son of Dawn!" (14:12). The one who laid the nations low is cut down to the ground (14:13). Isaiah 24:21–23 picks up this same motif. The image of gathering together the kings of the earth like prisoners in a pit (24:22) is also reminiscent of the "kings of the nations" who lie in their tombs and greet the great Babylon who now joins them in the pit (14:18–21). What had been promised concerning Babylon's final destiny in the context of chapters 13—14, the prophet learns is finally coming to pass.

Second, the final verse of chapter 24 made clear that Yahweh of hosts would again reign on Mount Zion and manifest his glory before his elders. The promise of the restoration of righteous leaders was delivered in chapter 1 (1:24–26). This would happen once God had vent his wrath on his enemies and avenged himself on his foes (1:24). Israel too would be cleansed of its dross so that Zion could once again be called the faithful city (1:26).

In chapter 24 the prophet sees the vision of utter worldwide judgment come to pass, such as had been vouchsafed to him at the commissioning of chapter 6. While this might have given rise to shouts of joy for those at the ends of the earth (24:14–15), it meant treachery and woe for the prophet. Yet by the conclusion of the chapter another set of promises came to mind that likewise appeared on the verge of fulfillment. These included the final victory over Babylon, Day Star, son of Dawn, and the promised reign of God on Mount Zion in a city cleansed and restored with proper leadership. The coalescing of these three earlier visions, now in the context of chapter 24, may explain the location of the hymn of thanks found at 25:1–5.

It is not surprising, then, that right away we hear reference made to "plans formed of old, faithful and sure" (25:1). The voice of thanksgiving sees that with the destruction of Babylon and the promise of the restoration of Zion, God is not acting mysteriously or arbitrarily. He is acting as he had promised to act. What was required of the prophet and the righteous community was patience and steady vision. That steady vision now proclaimed that plans of old were being fulfilled in the "wonderful things" witnessed in the present day. The destruction of the "fortified city"—whether Babylon or a Jerusalem primarily conceived of in this mode of military might—was a cause for rejoicing because it was the fulfillment of earlier promises. Now these destructions belonged to the past—such cities of might would never be rebuilt (25:2). As a consequence, those who trusted in cities of strength might now see the true source of strength, might now fear and revere the God of Israel, the God of the nations. Here again one can pick up the strains of Psalm 2 just below the surface: "Now therefore, O kings, be wise; be warned, O rulers of the earth. Serve the LORD with fear, with trembling" (Ps. 2:10–11).

The final refrain of Psalm 2 can also be heard as the hymn continues: Blessed are all who take refuge, not in military strength nor strong cities nor palaces, but in him (Ps. 2:11). We learn in the final verses of the hymn that God has remained a refuge for some during these times of desolation and distress, perhaps even during those days when Jerusalem itself was overrun. The poor and the needy have known God as their stronghold. He has been their shelter and their shade from the blast of the ruthless.

Many scholars rightly claim that the proper historical backdrop for these oracles in chapters 24—27, with their description of destruction and the utter desolation of the earth, is the fall of Jerusalem in 587 B.C. We have argued above that it is impossible to separate neatly another act of destruction, another bringing low of a strong city, from the destruction of Jerusalem, namely, the overthrow of Babylon not long thereafter. The irony is that both acts of destruction are capable of linkage in the first place, since Babylon was itself responsible for the fall of Jerusalem in 587 B.C. But the prophet speaks out against all forms of human pride and any recourse to military strength when it comes without proper attention to the will of God and his claim on his people and the nations. Israel and the nations are together to see in the destruction culminating in the overthrow of Babylon, and including Babylon's own assaults on the nations, the act of the one God who stands against human pride and idolatry in any form.

187

What is striking, then, is that the fall of Jerusalem is never singled out as a particularly isolated example of God's destruction and punishment. The Book of Isaiah contains not one historical report or one extended narrative in which the fall of Jerusalem is explicitly referred to. The closest thing to this can be found at 39:5-7 where the prophet is made to prophesy the future ransacking by Babylon of royal storehouses in Jerusalem. Yet even here the focus remains on the royal house as such, whose end is predicted by the prophet. All the traditional accounts of the destruction of the temple, the exiling of the people, the military assaults against Jerusalem in specific form—for these we must turn to other sources, especially II Kings, Jeremiah, Lamentations, and Ezekiel. The fall of Jerusalem is an *implicit motif* in the Book of Isaiah. But it never forms the center of explicit attention as it does elsewhere in the canon. And it tends to be seen within the broader framework of God's activity with the nations at large.

There appear to be two chief reasons for this. One we have already alluded to, namely, that the destruction of Jerusalem is seen to be just one act of divine punishment of human pride. To be sure, Jerusalem retains its identity both in punishment and in restoration. Its destiny is not swallowed up into the common destiny of the nations, if such a term is even apposite. The nations at large do not lose their own individual identity and historical profile, as we saw in chapters 13—23. The point to be emphasized is that the Book of Isaiah strains at a much larger conception of God's relationship to the nations than can be found in other prophetic collections. Especially in that section of Isaiah presently under discussion (chaps. 13—27), Yahweh the God of Israel shows himself to be Lord over all the nations. The destruction of Jerusalem is but one poignant chapter in God's dealing with the nations and the cosmos itself.

Moreover, it is not a destruction for which there is long lamentation. The Book of Isaiah insists that Jerusalem's destruction has a larger purpose, is part of a plan "formed of old, faithful and sure" (25:1). Jerusalem's desolation is but a preparation for a new and better Zion, where the "LORD of hosts will reign . . . , and before his elders he will manifest his glory" (24:23). The city that claimed to be strong will receive a new sort of strength (26:1), and as a consequence Zion will become the capital, not of a restored vineyard, but of all the nations on earth. In short, Jerusalem's destruction was a necessary prelude to its restoration as a new and transformed city of salvation, where "the righteous nation that keeps faith may enter in" (26:2).

188

Second, the radical end to life in Zion-Jerusalem, as it is depicted in Jeremiah, Ezekiel, and the Deuteronomistic History, is treated in a more mysterious manner in the Book of Isaiah. To be sure, we hear of exiling and deportation, as Israel is scattered to the four winds. But this theme is handled more broadly in the Book of Isaiah. Beginning with the Syro-Ephraimite crisis itself, the vineyard begins to break up and deteriorate. Slowly and surely the hand of the Lord works its judgment against Israel and the nations. But the punishment comes in stages, first involving the Northern Kingdom, then Judah, and then finally Zion-Jerusalem.

Yet when it comes to the final destruction of Zion-Jerusalem, we are lacking the kind of explicit record that is so familiar from the sources just mentioned. Moreover, the First Isaiah section closes with a narrative complex that chooses to highlight Zion's mysterious durability within God's plan and purpose for his vineyard and the nations at large (chaps. 36—37). Zion is not destroyed by the Assyrian forces, but wondrously withstands the blasphemous assaults of the nations (37:33–38). This too is part of God's plan of old, something he determined long ago (37:26). When in the chapters under discussion (chaps. 24—27) Jerusalem's destruction is suggested, and indeed appears to be presupposed, there remains an air of mystery about what in another place is described as sitting down and weeping at the memory of Zion (Psalm 137). In my judgment, the only explanation for this is to be found in Isaiah's unique remnant theology. A tenth was to be left and burned again. It would then become a holy seed. The voices of this holy seed begin to speak up in chapters 24—27.

This is not to suggest that Zion-Jerusalem did not endure a horrible desolation at the hands of the Babylonians in 587 B.C., only that this desolation is understood differently in Isaiah than it is in other sources. It is accepted as a terrible but necessary prelude to God's final establishment of Zion as a city after his own heart, the capital of the nations. All human pride needed to be swept away by the very epitome of human pride itself, Babylon, before God could begin to do a new thing—not just with Israel but with every nation on earth. In the midst of this vortex of destruction, voices remain in Zion to declare, first painfully and then more profoundly, that God's plan of old is coming to fruition. The beginning of that purpose consists in a judgment that must be endured, but its end consists in the final establishment of Zion, whose destiny had been adumbrated "from of old" but still awaited concrete earthly fulfillment.

189

In the final unit of chapter 25 (vv. 6–12) we hear of the fulfillment of "the word that Isaiah son of Amoz saw concerning Judah and Jerusalem" back at 2:1–5. There we learned that the mountain of the house of the Lord would be established as the highest of the mountains. Isaiah 25:6 simply speaks of "this mountain" without need of further clarification (cf. vv. 7, 10). The laying low of Moab in the final unit (vv. 10–12), as well as the larger context's depiction of God's breaking down every lofty city, serves to underscore the singular status of "this mountain," an obvious theme in 2:1–5.

The opening unit (vv. 6–8) depicts the streaming of the nations, but in language that goes beyond the imagery of pilgrimage and judgment such as we had in 2:1–5. The poet speaks of a grand feast for all people, a feast beyond comparison for its richness of food and extravagance of drink. The veil and the covering referred to in verse 7 are symbols of the vast destruction that God has wreaked on all nations and peoples but is about to remove. It is not a symbol of spiritual blindness or hardheartedness, as has been maintained from time to time, but rather of the concrete desolation visited upon all people. It is from this perspective that the imagery of verse 8 is to be interpreted. The poet is speaking of a complete reversal of God's activity and intention for the nations in the past, an intention that led to their utter annihilation. In the age that is to come, death will be replaced with life, sorrow with joy, as at a feast of unimaginable proportions.

The reference to "the disgrace of his people" (25:8) has occasioned discussion. Is the reference to Israel's exile, about to be terminated? or, to Judah's sense of being a minority among the nations? or, to the ongoing oppression from foreign nations that plagued Israel long after the exile? Given a context in which all peoples and all nations are the focus of attention—just as in 2:1–5—the question is: Is the reproach to be narrowly interpreted as involving only Israel or Judah, over against the nations, or as involving the nations at large—again, consistent with our interpretation of 2:1–5? In the first half of verse 8, where "death is swallowed up forever," interpreters agree this is a death that afflicts all nations, not just Israel. The reason for a shift in emphasis back to Israel is presumably to be found in the reference to "his people." All the earth will cease in its reproach of Israel, as the second two options for interpretation mentioned above see it.

190

We would argue that a more likely interpretation of "his people" is one not in contrast to all nations but inclusive of them. Earlier in the nations section, a similar transformation took place. Israel retained its identity and its specific role in the age to come, but at the same time, and precisely because of Israel's place in the age to come, God could address Egypt as "my people" and Assyria as "the work of my hands" (19:25). The reproach of the nations involved their necessary punishment, described in detail in the wider nations section. Now that reproach is to be taken away. With that action, God now addresses as "his people" not just Egypt and Assyria but the nations at large. Verse 8 closes on the same note: their reproach will be taken away, not just from Judah or Israel but "from all the earth."

If this interpretation is correct, then the confession that follows immediately in 25:9 is uttered not by an inhabitant of Judah alone but by the nations who now address Israel's Lord as "our God." Again, this is consistent with themes developed earlier in the book. The knowledge of God and his salvation was to extend to the nations, who were to stream to Zion that they might learn the ways of the God of Jacob (2:3). The inhabitant of Zion, to be sure, was to sing God's praises "in that day" (12:4). And we must assume that he or she leads the singing on this day. But the inhabitant of Zion was likewise charged to "make known [God's] deeds among the nations" (12:4). The confession at 25:9 provides evidence that that charge has been taken up, and we might well imagine that in a context where the emphasis falls on the coming feast for all the nations and peoples, new voices began to sing along with the inhabitant of Zion.

To be sure, it is not always possible to distinguish neatly between the more universal strains of the prophet's message, here and elsewhere, and those which continue to insist upon the specific role Israel is itself to play "in that day." We have wrestled with this tension elsewhere in the prophet's proclamation. It forms one of the main themes, if not the main theme, of the Book of Isaiah, where the God of Israel, in judging his own people through the agency of foreign nations, proclaims his sovereignty over all the earth and in turn his will for recognition and acknowledgment by these same nations, now through the agency of his people Israel. Here we can see a foreshadowing of what one interpreter has called a "fruitful paradox" of the Book of Isaiah "essential for Paul's presentation of a universal

191

gospel which at the same time insists on the particularity and priority of Israel" (Johnson, p. 62). The "fruitful paradox" of the Book of Isaiah is one of the chief reasons this prophet, more than any other in the canon, is used so widely and effectively in proclaiming the gospel in the New Testament. Here we touch upon the mystery commended to Augustine by Ambrose, who regarded Isaiah not as a prophet of the past but as first apostle and evangelist.

Seen in this light, the final unit of chapter 25 (vv. 10–12) serves the express purpose of offering a check on any simple view of universalism that would misunderstand the mystery of the prophet's proclamation of coming salvation for all nations. Any whiff of human pride or residue of national arrogance will be judged severely by the Lord of the nations. So it is that Moab's pride and skill must be leveled. If this mountain is to be established above all mountains, then the high fortifications of Moab's walls must be brought down, laid low, cast to the ground, even to the dust (25:12).

If by Isaiah's universalism is meant an exchange of religious values and beliefs common to all humanity, then the term is misplaced. God's promised feast for all peoples is no orgy of inclusion, where what is good and proper in one nation is commended to another. This feast follows hard upon a terrible scene of judgment where all that humanity might judge as high and lofty is brought low, even to the dust. Death is swallowed up forever precisely because it has had its day, as the reproach of the earth threatened to consume it altogether, as in the days of Noah. The final unit of chapter 25 reflects the seriousness with which God judges any trace of human pride that threatens to undo his plan for a feast of grand proportions where all nations will confess him as Lord and give thanks for his salvation. A statue must be built to an unknown God before the one God can show his true existence and proclaim his final will that all worship him and eat at his table, where death is swallowed up forever and the tears of all peoples wiped away.

Isaiah 26:1–21
The Way of the Righteous

There is general agreement that chapter 26 is comprised of two psalmic units (vv. 1–6, 7–19) and a final appeal (vv. 20–21). The first unit is generally recognized as a psalm of thanksgiving or hymn of trust. More difficulty surrounds the form-critical designation of the long central unit in verses 7–19. Portions of the unit appear to be psalm-like reflections on the fate of the righteous (see Psalm 1, e.g.), and the unit opens with this theme (vv. 7–10). But scholars have been quick to note the shift to lament and supplication in verses 11–19, causing more than one interpreter to regard chapter 26 in its entirety as a national lament.

In view of our concern here with the role that context plays in understanding the final form of the material, one main problem confronting the interpreter is how to integrate the foregoing chapter, with its themes of national feasting and acknowledgment of the Lord, with chapter 26, where the tone shifts to concern over the fate of the righteous, surrounded by adversaries (vv. 11–14), their final deliverance in question (vv. 17–18). There seems to be a temporal shift as well, made clear in the concluding unit (vv. 20–21). Whereas in chapter 25 God's total desolation of the "fortified city" lay in the past, giving rise to songs of praise (25:1–5, 9), chapter 26 appears to view the desolation and judgment as still on the horizon. This is most explicit in the final unit, where the day of Yahweh has not yet come, compelling the righteous to take cover "until the wrath is past."

In our judgment, this question of proper temporal perspective is more pressing than the matter of diverse genre within the chapter. It is by no means unusual for individual psalms of lament to reflect, strictly speaking, a mixture of different genre, including meditations on the fate of the righteous and the wicked, set next to complaint and lament, on the one hand, or clear statements of trust, on the other (see among others Psalm 3—5; 7; 9—10). It is striking, when one reviews the many psalms that reflect a similar mixture of genre as chapter 26, how fre-

193

quently the temporal movement of the psalm is likewise never fixed. Sometimes the psalmist ends on a note of conviction, sure that the righteous will finally emerge victorious as God's plan is vindicated (Psalm 10); but just as often the psalmist is left to wait—in mid-appeal or in mid-lament—as the psalm closes, with God's final victory still in the future (Psalm 25).

The problem of the relationship between chapters 25 and 26 may be less acute than it first appears. Chapter 25 closed with an oracle of judgment against Moab (25:10–12), underscoring that God's intention for a feast for all nations would not necessarily go unchallenged. The hymn of thanksgiving that opens chapter 26 (vv. 1–6) employs language quite close to that found in 25:10–12 when it speaks of bringing low the inhabitants of the height and the lofty city: God "lays it low to the ground, casts it to the dust" (26:5; cf. 25:12). Those who sing the song of salvation in Judah open the gates, not for any nation, but for "the righteous nation that keeps faith" (26:2). The key word here is "righteous," and it is this character of God's people that concerns the poet in 26:7–15. Note the frequency with which the term is used (ṣaddîq), together with "judgment" (mišpāṭ), in the opening verses of this unit (vv. 7, 8, 9, 10).

For this reason, too severe a break ought not to be posited at verse 7. Nor is there strong evidence of an intended break at verse 11, forcing the unit at verses 11–15 to be interpreted as a lament, in contrast with both 26:1–6 and 26:7–10. Statements of trust can be detected at verses 12, 13, 14, and 15. The main shift comes at 26:16, signaled by a change from the first-person perspective of 26:1–15 to a sudden third-person perspective: "O LORD, in distress they sought you, they poured out a prayer when your chastening was on them." At this juncture clear signs of lament begin to predominate. As the first-person voice resumes its place (vv. 16–17), the unknown speaker tells of birth pangs, but no birth, of no deliverance or judgment over the nations, when this had been longed for. Only after this complaint is lodged does the voice break forth with a statement of trust, assured that those who have died will finally "awake and sing for joy" (26:19). The final unit then places the righteous at a point in time before God's judgment of the nations, as the language of chapter 24 is resumed. The "earth will disclose the blood shed on it" (26:21). We have returned to the days of Noah.

In sum, the key break in chapter 26 is to be found at verse 16; otherwise the chapter is to be divided into two sections

194

(26:1–15 and 26:16–21). The first section emphasizes that only the righteous nation that keeps faith will have a place at God's banquet on Mount Zion. A similar note was sounded in 2:1–5, where the nations stream to Zion to be taught God's law. The psalm language is employed at this juncture to emphasize the nature of life lived under God's rule: the lofty city is replaced by a mind set on God, a mind like that of the psalmist, who "trusts in you" (26:3). The righteous know that God's judgments are intended to give life and to teach righteousness to those who otherwise do not know God. Only in this way can the "inhabitants of the world" understand righteousness as Israel understands it and be brought thereby to "see the majesty of the LORD" (26:10). For those who do not recognize the hand of God in the destruction visited upon them, there can be no enfranchisement, but only death and lack of final memorial (26:14). This statement predicates or otherwise clarifies the vision given in the preceding chapter, where we learned that death would be swallowed up forever (25:8). Only for the righteous nation that keeps faith or the righteous individual who acknowledges God's name is such a statement apposite.

With verse 16 the reader is returned to the situation of chapter 24. That is, we see again the anguish of those righteous inhabitants who stand before the world judgment of God but do not fully comprehend what its final issue will be. Their complaint is reminiscent of the lone first-person voice at 24:16, which lamented over the treachery of the treacherous. The prayer of these supplicants has had no final effect, so far as they can see (26:16). They writhe in pain like a woman in childbirth but never give birth (26:17). The world judgment seems to have touched only them: the inhabitants of the earth have not fallen, and there is no sign of final deliverance (26:18).

The response to the lament, as in the Psalter, is not formally marked, but comes without warning at 26:19. Taking up the promises of 25:8, the supplicants are promised that death is not the final word, not for those who wait on the Lord in the midst of the cosmic judgment. Those in anguish at the time of the great desolation, who lament their lot and see no final purpose but remain steadfast—light will finally shine on them, even in "the land of shades."

The final unit (26:20–22) clarifies the temporal perspective 195 of the larger pericope from verse 16 on (26:16–22). The day of wrath, at fullest measure, lies still in the future. It will finally encompass, not just Judah and Jerusalem in the events of 587 B.C., but all the "inhabitants of the earth" (26:21). The complaint of 26:18 is here addressed: there will be a yet greater judgment, extending beyond the righteous inhabitants of Judah and Jerusalem, whatever their number, to disclose the blood shed on all the earth (26:21). Using language reminiscent of the Noah story, the righteous supplicants are urged to shut their doors behind them (cf. Gen. 7:16). A time of patient waiting is called for. Just as the prophet and his disciples had to "wait for the LORD" (8:17) patiently during times of trial that lie ahead, so the righteous inhabitant of Jerusalem must continue to pour out prayer and petition until the wrath of God has passed (26:20).

Though the final chapter of this tradition complex (chap. 27) will give us another glimpse of God's ultimate intention beyond the coming judgment, 26:16–21 situates us temporally before that day of wrath. Isaiah 26:16–21 calls for an attitude of psalm-like trust and waiting, one that may frequently give rise to lament and supplication, for the righteous ones in Israel's midst. This attitude, we learn in 26:1–15, is also required *following* the day of wrath, as the new Zion strains to be born amidst nations that still refuse to acknowledge God's sovereignty over all the world (26:11). Yet God's promises are identical for both groups, as are his final demands that "the inhabitants of the world learn righteousness" (26:9). Then a strong city may truly be set up, one that has walls and bulwarks of salvation, a fitting memorial to the prophet Isaiah and those who with him waited patiently for the Lord in their own day. When the majestic strains of chapter 27 are fully sounded, we return to the world of that prophet and those with him (chaps. 28—39) with a fuller perspective of God's final purpose for Israel and the nations of the earth.

Isaiah 27:1–13
A New Vineyard, Sing of It!

Following a brief "on that day" oracle (27:1), chapter 27 opens with a magnificent poem celebrating God's establishment of a new vineyard, reversing the images of fruitlessness and inattention that dominated the former vineyard (5:1–7). This new "Song of the Vineyard" extends at a minimum through verse 5, and probably includes (as gloss or integral conclusion) verse 6 as well. So too the final unit of the chapter (27:12–13) recapitulates much of the heady enthusiasm of previous such oracles, as the people of Israel are gathered from afar, from Egypt and Assyria, so that they might again worship God on his holy mountain. We are put in mind of the promises uttered at several points in chapters 1—12, but most especially at 2:1–5 and 11:12–16. Israel will not be lost in the coming dispersion but will finally be gathered to make its way back at the head of the nations, as if in response to the appeal, "O house of Jacob, come, let us walk in the light of the LORD" (2:5).

Given the relative clarity of both the opening and closing units of this final chapter (27:1–6 and 27:12–13), it is unfortunate that the intervening pericope (27:7–11) has given rise to such difficulties of interpretation. Curiously, many scholars read the reference to "Jacob" in verse 9 as pointing specifically to the Northern Kingdom. They in turn find two possible historical situations in which to place the oracle: as concerning the old northern kingdom of Isaiah's earlier preaching or as emerging from the Jewish-Samaritan conflict of the late postexilic period. Needless to say, these historical periods are widely separated one from another and are both equally curious in the context of chapters 24—27. Suddenly the "fortified city" (27:10) is Samaria, capital of the erstwhile Northern Kingdom or later rival to Jerusalem in the Hellenistic period.

These are historical observations. More troubling is the drastic shift in tone and content implied in these readings of 27:7–11, over against the opening and closing units. Following hard upon a glorious new "Song of the Vineyard" we are plunged suddenly into a mood of judgment, recalling the sad fate of the Northern Kingdom or anticipating the future demise of Samaria. Just as suddenly the chapter ends with a fresh vision of return and restoration, focused neither on the Northern Kingdom nor on the Southern Kingdom but simply on the people of Israel "lost in the land of Assyria" or "driven out to the land of Egypt" (27:13). Is it possible to see a more consistent perspective maintained throughout the chapter?

The first thing to note is that all three pericopes that frame this difficult central unit (27:1; 27:2–6; 27:12–13) are concerned to underscore God's victory over forces hostile to the restored

197

vineyard or to his people in dispersion. Leviathan "the dragon that is in the sea" is most likely a cipher for Babylon. The mythological monster of the deep, dragon of the waters of chaos and challenger of God's sovereignty over creation, has here been transferred to the realm of history to serve as a symbol of those national forces at war with the rule of God. God puts an end to this challenge decisively and forever with "his cruel and great and strong sword" (27:1).

In the new "Song of the Vineyard" the striking feature to be noted, over against the first song, is the degree to which God has become keeper, and protector, and guardian of the vineyard. Gone is God's hostility toward the vineyard: the briers and thorns, which the old vineyard became, are now weapons of divine defense on behalf of the vineyard (27:4). Gone too is the vineyard's old freedom. The vineyard is not fully outfitted by God (so 5:1–2) and then left to itself, God watching to see what kind of grapes it would yield (5:3–4). God now stands guard over the vineyard night and day, watering it every single moment (27:3), now not leaving it unattended in order to determine its yield. The hostile forces, we now know from the larger presentation of the Book of Isaiah, are the nations bent on destruction, intoxicated by their grand military designs and accumulated successes. They have a choice: make peace with God and share in his protection, together with Israel, or be burned up altogether (27:5). Unlike the old vineyard, Jacob/Israel (again reunified) will blossom and put forth shoots (cf. 5:4). These shoots will fill *the whole world* with fruit (27:6).

In the final brief unit we see a similar concern to guard Israel against possible extinction. Israel will be gathered in the same way grain is threshed and preserved, the chaff left to blow away.

In the central unit (27:7–11) we might well expect something of the same general picture. Certainly the image of the "fortified city" (27:10) has elsewhere not referred to Samaria but to any city of pride, quintessentially Babylon. At 25:1–5 a hymn of praise was sung for the ruination of the fortified city (25:2), carried out that the nations might learn the fear of God. The fortified city that here sits solitary, forsaken and deserted, like a wilderness (27:10), is neither Jerusalem nor much less Samaria, in the strict sense, but rather the symbol of strength broken down before the majesty of Israel's God.

It is on this same note that the pericope opens, when the

rhetorical question is raised: Have those who were smitten received the same penalty reserved for the agent of judgment? Here as elsewhere in the long nations section, the answer is no. Assyria's punishment will overshadow Israel's (10:15–34); Babylon's will overshadow that of Assyria and all the nations (14:4–21). The fate of the slayer will be worse than the fate of the slain (27:7).

The NRSV's rendering of the following verse (27:8) is an interpretation; the words "by exile" do not appear in the Masoretic text. Moreover, the vague third-person "them" is somewhat confusing. Johnson translates more literally, "When he drove her away, cast her forth, he contended with her; he removed her with his fierce blast on the day of the east wind" (Johnson, p. 108). This action by God, whomever it involves, accomplishes the removal of the sin of Jacob, as the next verse makes clear (27:9). In searching for a referent for the third-person feminine singular form, repeated three times in verse 8, the nearest possible candidate is the fortified city of 27:10, now solitary, forsaken and deserted—as one might expect if this city were the object of the actions described in verse 8. In sum, 27:8 does not speak of an "exile" of "them"—that is, the Northern Kingdom, either in Isaiah's day or at the time of the Jerusalem-Samaria schism centuries later. Instead, it speaks of the desolation of the "fortified city," in the same general sense as was intended in the preceding chapters. Again, it is "its" boughs that are broken and burned in 27:11.

The final indictment of "a people without understanding" has been interpreted as pointing to Israel, and indeed the divine predication employed here ("he that made them"; "he that formed them") would appear to suggest that God's own people are being referred to. But we have seen how the expression "my people" has taken on new meaning in the context of chapters 24—27, extending on occasion (see esp. 25:8) beyond Israel to include the nations as well. In the context of our discussion of chapter 25, we noted the expressions used earlier in the nations section, particularly for Egypt and Assyria: "Blessed be Egypt my people, and Assyria the work of my hands" (19:25). References to God's forming and making a people need not refer only to Israel. Indeed, the final verse, which speaks of both Egypt and Assyria as places where the dispersed dwell, may well have interpreted the previous verse (27:11) along the lines we are suggesting.

199

The point of the central pericope (27:7–11) is not to be set in contrast with the framing pieces (27:1; 27:2–6; 27:12–13). The first speaks of God's halting the fierce dragon; the second, of God's appeal to the nations to make peace, or be destroyed by the guardian of the vineyard; the third, of God's destruction of the slayer, a destruction which exceeds that reserved for the slain, "for this is a people without understanding" (27:11); the fourth, of Israel's final preservation and return. The desolation of altars and Asherim described in verse 9 is not to be restricted to the territory of the Northern—or Southern—Kingdom, however much such practices played a role in Israel's own just condemnation. The broad scope of chapters 24—27 is not suddenly restricted here. Wherever the worship of rival "gods" is carried out, there can judgment be expected. In this way, the "guilt of Jacob" will finally be expiated—namely, when all false worship practiced by God's people is extinguished, wherever it is found.

As our discussion of chapters 24—27 is brought to a close, several striking things should be noted about the function and placement of these four chapters.

First of all, in temporal terms we are brought within the final sweep of the Book of Isaiah, even though we remain before the midpoint of its literary presentation. Babylon is about to be judged, the slayer will be slain, and a new vineyard promises to emerge. Zion will be restored as promised and take on its new role as capital of the nations. All peoples are invited to the banquet of fat things God has prepared for just this occasion. Death will be turned to life, sorrow to joy. Still, amid the feasting, Israel faces challenge: from the wicked who refuse to learn righteousness, and from the nation that does not make peace or lay hold of God's protection.

The challenge to the prophet Isaiah and his disciples is brought to mind here. Yahweh's protection of the vineyard is increased precisely at the moment when an invitation to all nations on earth has been extended. It is a time for feasting and restoration but also for vigilance and steadfastness. The complex ends on a note of warning, even as Israel is gathered from among the nations and brought back to Zion. The challenge from false worship is recalled, as well as days of destruction. It is on this note that we reenter that temporal sweep of the Book of Isaiah which places us back in the days of the prophet, his teaching and his disciples. It is to that material that we are about to turn (chaps. 28—39).

The reader has learned in the course of the nations section (chaps. 13—27) just how fruitless it is for Israel to conceive of the nations as potential allies or independent military forces, beyond the scope of God's control, governed by their own gods and under these, determining their own individual destinies. As we know and as Israel must experience firsthand, Assyria cannot be played off against Egypt or Egypt against Assyria (chaps. 30—31). Even Babylon will put in an appearance in the final chapter (39:1-8), an ominous reminder of the desolation yet to come. Yet the reader knows the final destiny of each of these foreign powers, for it is to Israel alone that God's plan concerning the nations has been revealed, in accord with his purposes established long ago (14:26; 25:1).

We know that trust in foreign alliances is a false route. But in what does trust in Yahweh truly consist? What does it mean for Israel to believe and therefore be established? Again, the examples given thus far have been largely negative ones, as in the case of the house of Ahaz (chaps. 7—8). We have been promised righteous rule (9:1-6). Will we finally see it? Will we get some glimpse of what it means for false alliances to be rejected and trust in God preferred? We know of God's final vision of the new vineyard (27:2-6). Is it possible to see some example of righteous trust in the prophet's own day, or must the fulfillment of God's designs for the vineyard always be deferred to a time in the distant future, after the desolation described in chapters 24—27 has come about? To answer these and other questions better, we turn now to the final section of First Isaiah, chapters 28—39.

PART THREE

A King Will Reign in Righteousness

Isaiah 28—39

Overview

We have tried to show thus far in the commentary that chapters 1—12 and 13—27, while containing material from a variety of historical periods, have nevertheless been meaningfully organized in such a way as to present Isaiah and his message to posterity. That is, chapters 1—12 and 13—27 are truly subdivisions of the larger Book of Isaiah, consciously intended and editorially shaped—not just randomly organized literary blocks or catch basins for older tradition and newer commentary erratically juxtaposed.

Can the same be said in any way for chapters 28—39? A quick survey of structural outlines for the Book of Isaiah would show that the tendency has not been to detect some larger organization in these final chapters but rather to see smaller collections of tradition. Even here opinion can be divided.

The final narrative material in chapters 36—39 is frequently seen to be one such smaller collection. The chapters concern the 701 B.C. deliverance of Jerusalem and the figure of King Hezekiah. The fact that they have a counterpart in the Books of Kings (II Kings 18:13—20:19) reinforces our sense of a well-marked tradition complex. Chapters 34—35 are likewise frequently interpreted together and, on the basis of common language and historical perspective, argued to reflect the concerns of Second Isaiah chapters, if not also authored by the same circle that has composed chapters 40—55. About the remaining material in chapters 28—33 there is less consensus.

But the ability to detect clear subsections in chapters 36—

39, 34—35, and even 28—33 has frustrated, not enhanced, any sense of larger organization across chapters 28—39 as a whole. Most feel that in the first subdivision (chaps. 28—32; 33) we return to the historical period of the prophet Isaiah, during the reign of Hezekiah. Many speak of two cycles of preaching activity, one represented by material in chapters 1—12 and another by material in chapters 28—32 (33). Some conjecture that the prophet had a period of withdrawal from public proclamation between the production of these two tradition complexes (perhaps hinted at in 8:16–22 which tells of Isaiah binding up the teaching and waiting patiently with his disciples). This is pure speculation, however, since the text itself is silent about any period of withdrawal as an explanation for two separated preaching cycles (chaps. 1—12 and 28—33).

By the same token, the judgment that material in chapters 28—33 should be placed in the prophet's lifetime has met with general assent, even as it drives a historical wedge between these chapters and the material in chapters 34—35. The view that chapters 34—35 represent an apocalypse on analogy with chapters 24—27 (so-called little and big Isaiah apocalypses) has been largely replaced by the notion that chapters 34—35 play some sort of anticipatory or "bridging" role vis-à-vis Second Isaiah chapters. But in either instance we remain several centuries removed from the circumstances of chapters 28—33.

Finally, discussion of chapters 36—39 has, until recently, been largely carried out with an eye toward certain specific historical problems, chief among them determining what happened to Jerusalem in 701 B.C. As such, interest in chapters 36—37 has overshadowed concern with chapters 38—39. At the same time, the former two chapters in Isaiah have themselves been overshadowed by the material in Kings that deals with the same historical circumstances (II Kings 18:13—19:37). There are a number of reasons for this judgment, but chief among them is the existence in Kings of a tiny piece of tradition not found in the Isaiah record (II Kings 18:14–16), which tells of Hezekiah's submission and sending of tribute to the Assyrian king Sennacherib. This tradition is regarded as historically accurate, while two other accounts reconstructed from Isaiah and Kings are considered later theological reflections. We will have more to say about the details of this reconstruction below.

One of the consequences of granting priority to the Kings' record, and especially the small tradition found at II Kings

18:14–16, is that chapters 36—37 and 38—39 are frequently analyzed separately. And because Hezekiah is depicted in negative terms in II Kings 18:14–16 (so the judgment runs), his portrayal across chapters 36 39 has not until recently been regarded as a unifying feature in these four chapters, urging one to interpret them in a more synthetic manner. Moreover, because the alleged negative depiction of Hezekiah in II Kings 18:14–16 is considered the true starting point for historical reconstructions, a decidedly negative impression emerges concerning the royal house. Even those who see a clear contrast between Ahaz and Hezekiah intentionally structured into the final form of the text (cf. chaps. 7—8 and 36—39), nevertheless regard this as a late, exilic, or postexilic enhancement without foundation in history.

This reconstruction is rehearsed because it has an impact on the question under consideration, that is, the question of possible structural shape for chapters 28—39 as a whole. The negative judgment rendered over Hezekiah on the basis of II Kings 18:14–16 is filled out by appeal to a much broader reconstruction of events in ancient Near Eastern history for this period. Hezekiah's tribute payment in II Kings 18:14–16 finds confirmation, it is argued, elsewhere in the Book of Isaiah. When the prophet Isaiah condemns those "who set out to go down to Egypt" (30:2) and "those who trust in chariots . . . but do not . . . consult the LORD" (31:1), he has in mind chiefly the royal house and the figure of Hezekiah, who prefers to strike military deals rather than consulting the prophet—that is, until he is hedged in by an angry Assyria and must pay them allegiance as well. God finally rescues Jerusalem, but not on the strength of anything the royal house has done but only for his own sake or in confirmation of the prophet's word.

Related to the question of Isaiah's attitude toward the royal house is his assessment of Zion. Does the prophet have a "Zion theology" that tells of God's ultimate protection of Zion, or is that a secondary editorial embellishment, akin to Hezekiah's later enhancement? The prophet's word to Zion is especially prominent in this section of the larger book (28:16–22; 29:1–10; 31:4–9; 32:9–20; 33:5–6, 20–22; 34:8–12; 37:30–32) and indeed might rightly be considered a unifying theme or concern of these various chapters. Or does the prophet hold a decidedly negative view of "Zion theology," one in which God, rather than protecting Zion, fights against Zion on the side of the nations? In the end, then, God delivers Zion in the events of 701 B.C. only because of his own final mercy, not because of some compelling commitment to Zion or Zion theology. Or is the prophet's "Zion theology" fundamentally mysterious, meaning both chastisement and final protection? And how are these two aspects to be isolated in a way that is exegetically responsible?

A correct appraisal of the prophet's royal and Zion theology is of fundamental importance for the question of possible larger structural purpose in chapters 28—39. To put the question bluntly: Do chapters 28—33 present a view of Zion and king that is fundamentally confirmed by chapters 36—37 and the circumstances of Jerusalem's deliverance? Is the king who is to reign in righteousness (32:1) the same king who experiences the deliverance of Jerusalem and indeed brings it about through prayer and contrition (37:1-4; 38:1-6)? Is the prophet's word concerning Zion countermanded by Jerusalem's deliverance, fulfilled by the events of 701 B.C., or only secondarily modified and adjusted to produce a false sense of continuity?

There may well be a more formal structural component to these questions about the organization and purpose of chapters 28—39. Like chapters 24—27, chapters 34—35 play a specific role in the larger presentation of this section: they point to the future judgment of the nations and the eventual return to Zion of God's people. Presupposed is the Babylonian desolation of 587 B.C., as well as Babylon's own eventual downfall at the hands of the Persian empire. In this sense the historical perspective of chapters 24—27, 34—35, and 40—55 is similar.

Prior to the introduction of this later perspective, we can see the formal organization of a six-chapter unit (chaps. 28—33). Each of these chapters is introduced with the single-word interjection *hôy* ("woe") or, in the case of chapter 32, *hēn* ("see"). Yet a further "woe" introduction can be seen at 29:15. It may well be that this collection of six woe oracles—directed at the Northern Kingdom (28:1), the defenses in the city of David (29:1), those who hide counsel (29:15), those who go to Egypt instead of to Yahweh (30:1; 31:1), and finally the national powers bent upon treachery—is meant consciously to evoke the earlier pattern of woe oracles found in chapter 5 (5:8, 11, 18, 20, 21, 22) (Stansell). There the prophet was finally cleansed and set apart from the judgment called for by the woes (6:5-7).

The pattern having been established in the presentation of chapters 1—12, it is picked up and used as a formal device here.

Only now the exception is not made for the prophet—that would be redundant, given 6:5–7—but for the royal house, in an explicit way, as was only promised and foreshadowed in chapters 1—12. The *hēn* ("see") at 32:1 breaks the pattern of woe introductions in order to introduce the figure of the king who will rule in righteousness. The figure of the king is to stand apart from the faithlessness and foolishness that infect Israel: Northern Kingdom, military designers, seekers of false counsel and false alliance. The king will withstand the assaults of the nations (33:1). In the coming debacle (32:9–14), the palaces and fortresses will be forsaken, and "the hill and the watchtower will become dens forever" (32:14). But a new spirit will also come upon those who have waited for righteousness and justice (32:15–20). The eyes of the people "will see the king in his beauty" (33:17). Gone will be fortress and tower, replaced by a new Zion, "the city of our appointed festivals . . . , a quiet habitation, an immovable tent" (33:20).

The following subsection (chaps. 34—35) relates the full deliverance of Zion to the period following Babylonian judgment and desolation. Only then will the promised way be built (35:8; cf. 11:16; 19:23). Only then will sorrow and sighing finally flee away (35:10; cf. 25:8).

But the reader is given a clear foretaste of the final deliverance of Zion in the presentation of chapters 36—39, which closes off the First Isaiah material. And with respect to the royal house, it is precisely in chapters 36—39, not in later tradition in the Book of Isaiah, that our "eyes will see the king in his beauty; they will behold a land that stretches far away" (33:17). These chapters give concrete testimony to the king who stands in utter contrast to Ahaz and his house, King Hezekiah, who truly reigns in righteousness (32:1) and fulfills the promises uttered by the prophet in the context of judgment during the Syro-Ephraimite crisis. We return to the fateful "conduit of the upper pool on the highway to the Fuller's Field" (36:2) where before Ahaz had faltered and refused to stand fast (7:3). It is a time of crisis, just as before, with the Syro-Ephraimite coalition forces replaced by the mighty army of the Assyrian king Sennacherib. Now a sign is accepted by the royal house (38:7), where before it was refused (7:12). The "zeal of the LORD of hosts" (37:32) accomplishes Zion's deliverance, as had been promised by the prophet in the context of his royal proclamation (9:7). Assyria reached "up to the neck" (8:8) but was finally halted (37:36), Sennacherib escaping with his life only to lose it shortly (37:37–38). In every way, Hezekiah forms a fitting contrast to Ahaz and, in so doing, gives concrete witness to the validity of the word of God. He believes and Zion is established.

The final chapter opens the tradition onto the period of Babylonian desolation, as had been foretold in the opening chapters of the nations section. Is Hezekiah personally responsible for the later Babylonian threat, as some have suggested, through his actions with the emissaries of Merodach-baladan? Or does this chapter have a far more complex function than the simple assigning of blame? It is interesting that the Chronicler judges this to have been a time of testing for Hezekiah to see how he would respond to the prophetic word of judgment (39:5–8). In the Chronicler's estimation, Hezekiah passed the test (II Chron. 32:31) and proved himself worthy of the earlier evaluation of the Deuteronomistic Historian: "He trusted in the LORD the God of Israel; so that there was no one like him among all the kings of Judah after him, or among those who were before him" (II Kings 18:5). Hezekiah was truly a king who reigned in righteousness (Isa. 32:1).

Alongside the concern with Zion and king in chapters 28—39, there is one other important theme to be isolated in this final section. That is the theme of proper wisdom and knowledge, to be set over against foolishness and confusion. Interest in this theme is displayed at several key points (28:7–13, 23–29; 29:13–16, 22–24; 31:1–3; 32:1–8; 33:6). We hear of wisdom, proper knowledge, counsel, discernment, understanding, noble things, and the fear of the Lord. And with the coming reign of the righteous king, the harsh commission of 6:10, to make ears heavy and eyes shut, begins its reversal for the wise: "Then the eyes of those who have sight will not be closed, and the ears of those who have hearing will listen" (32:3). Also to be included under this theme are the many references to the teaching of the prophet, now in the more formal sense of a written testimony (29:11–12; 30:8–9; 34:16). As before (8:16), the written testimony will serve to validate the prophet's word for later generations, even as it is veiled to those around him who refuse to hear and see.

In sum, there is evidence of a certain loose structure governing the present arrangement of chapters 28—39, focusing on Zion's destiny, the wise, and the reign of a righteous king. We now turn to examine these themes in the context of our commentary on individual chapters.

Isaiah 28:1–29
Strange Is His Deed—Alien His Work!

There is general agreement that chapter 28 is to be divided
into four subsections (vv. 1–6, 7–13, 14–22, and 23–29). The first
consists of a woe oracle directed to the Northern Kingdom. The
second is an oracle of judgment over those who presume to
teach knowledge to Israel, the priest and prophet, and yet
speak nothing but gibberish. The third unit is an oracle of judgment over the rulers of Jerusalem. Yet the oracle also suggests
that for those in Zion who remain steadfast, God will be a sure
foundation (28:16). He is about to do a strange deed: will it mean
that Zion is to be utterly destroyed, or does its "strangeness"
consist in the fact that the judgment will fall one way for some
and another way for others? The final oracle with its parabolic
character implies that this latter meaning is intended. The wise
one knows how a field is to be plowed or how dill is to be
threshed. So too the one who is instructed aright will understand the counsel and wisdom of God (28:26, 29). Presumably
such a person will also understand the mystery of God's strange
deed and alien work directed at "the whole land" (28:22).

It is not difficult to follow the progression of the chapter,
even across what appear to be four distinct subunits. The judgment against the drunkards of Ephraim shifts at verse 7 to an
indictment against priest and prophet, crazed from drink and
unable to give proper instruction. Their own baby talk (28:10)
will soon be turned to another sort of gibberish: the foreign
speech of the invader (28:11). Having rejected their role as
leaders in Israel, the word of God likewise becomes for them a
sort of gibberish (28:13). The effect is quite clear in Hebrew,
which gives here *ṣaw lāṣāw ṣaw lāṣāw, qaw lāqāw qaw lāqāw,*
which is difficult to render in English ("precept upon precept,
precept upon precept, line upon line, line upon line") in similar
clipped phrases.

In the next unit (28:14–22), the actual judgment against
these "rulers of Jerusalem" is stipulated in more detail. But first 209
there is an additional indictment involving their "covenant
with death" (28:15, 18). Ronald Clements urges that a strictly
political interpretation be adopted, whereby the covenant with

death is in fact an alliance with Egypt. With Otto Kaiser and others, we prefer a more cultic interpretation. These leaders— the indictment continues to be aimed at priest and prophet, not at politicians—have struck some sort of deal with the forces of death and the underworld, a kind of insurance policy against the "overwhelming scourge" (28:15, 17–19). Here the opening images of hailstorm and overwhelming flood (28:2) are resumed, now directed at the whole land (28:22). The covenant of death is annulled; it will afford no protection, but only terror; no comfort, but only a bed too short to lie on (28:20).

Another important theme is also introduced at 28:16–17. Just as the overwhelming scourge will expose the lies and false refuge of prophet and priest, so too God will provide a bulwark against the storm for those who believe and stand fast. In Zion, God will establish a stone against which all other stones are tested. This stone will take the measurement of the righteous and in turn will be their sure foundation when the storm sweeps through. The lies of priest and prophet will be exposed but so too will the justice and righteousness of God's people. It must be for this reason that God's warfare is to be regarded as "strange" and "alien"—it is not directed against the Philistines, as in the days of King David (II Sam. 5:17–25), nor against the Amorites, as in the days of Joshua (Josh. 10:10–15). It is directed against his own people, "the whole land" (28:22), and it will also serve as a means of exposing righteousness and falsehood, covenants with death and testing stones.

It is important to recognize that from the beginning of this section where so-called Zion theology plays a prominent role (chaps. 28—33), the prophet's teaching on the final destiny of Zion is by no means simple. God neither protects Zion and all its inhabitants against any disaster, nor does he intend to sweep all away in the overwhelming scourge. God's work on Mount Zion and in all the land is strange and mysterious. It has its own internal logic, as it seeks to winnow out the righteous while at the same time declaring null and void the plans of those who were to have instructed God's people. They neither hear God's word any longer, except as a sort of gibberish, nor do they understand God's strange deed. They have truly become a people with heavy ears, closed eyes, and hearts without understanding (6:10).

Even as this fulfillment of the prophet's commission is taking place, a new sort of discourse is emerging alongside it. The final unit (28:23–29) asks, without a hint of irony or misdirection given the commission just mentioned (6:10), that the addressants "Listen, and hear my voice; pay attention, and hear my speech" (28:23). Proper response is possible. The one who is instructed aright (28:26) is held up by the prophet for his hearers. The image of the wise farmer who knows his crops and his fields and the seasons, and who also knows how to process what has been produced—what a contrast to the priest and prophet staggering in confusion. Instead of giving clear vision and sound instruction, they spew out either gibberish or vomit. They neither know their field nor how to process its yield: they hear canned slogans or baby talk and reproduce the same.

But the wise farmer knows his vocation, and especially what belongs where and at the proper time. When the overwhelming scourge comes—and come it will, even the drunken prophets and priests know this—the farmer falls back on his own insurance policy, which is no covenant with death but the wonderful counsel and excellent wisdom that is his by gift from the Lord of hosts (28:29).

What is striking about this opening chapter (chap. 28) is not what it says about the judgment of God for the foolish priest and crazed prophet, presumed leaders in Jerusalem. We have seen language regarding God's coming judgment at full expression already in the presentation of the Book of Isaiah. What is striking here is the sketching out by the prophet of an alternative vision, one that will be sustained by God when the coming judgment comes. God's wisdom and counsel will not be withdrawn from Israel, just because those charged with instructing Israel aright in such matters have lost all their bearings. Their covenant of death will bring about their own demise and lead to the final exposure of their many sad and empty refuges. But Israel is not wholly doomed, so long as God's wisdom is available to those who will be instructed aright. It may be a wisdom exhibited by the simple farmer who shrewdly goes about his tasks. But such wisdom will be sufficient for those tested ones to see in God's actions—strange and alien—a precious cornerstone and sure foundation. Those who believe will not falter or be swept away.

Isaiah 29:1–24
Zion Is Distressed, the Nations Are Routed

In chapter 29 we run straight into the problem of how to interpret the prophet's Zion theology. The opening unit (29: 1–8) sets forth the problem. The oracle opens on a clear note of judgment, the same "woe" employed here as in 28:1 (cf. NRSV's "ah"). The object of the prophet's woe is Ariel, the city in which David encamped. Presumably Jerusalem is intended. Second Samuel 5:6–10 tells of David's capture of "the stronghold of Zion, which is now the city of David" from the Jebusites. Just as David encamped to take the city, so too God will raise siegeworks against Jerusalem (Isa. 29:3). That the siege is intended as a hostile action is clear from the language used in verse 2: "I will distress Ariel, and there shall be moaning and lamentation." The term "Ariel" may mean "altar-hearth"; evidently it refers to the altar of burnt offering in the temple and has come to stand here for Jerusalem in more general terms. Use of the term allows the prophet to play on the image of burning: Jerusalem is to become a place of burning, "like an Ariel" (29:2).

Suddenly then, without warning except for the obscure image in verse 4, the nations replace God as agents of destruction and are utterly put to flight by the same Yahweh who was encamped against Jerusalem in 29:1–3. For this reason, many regard only the opening unit as authentic to Isaiah (29:1–4) and as representative of his negative views of Zion theology. That is to say, the prophet has transformed language about God's defense of Zion against its foes, such as is found in the Psalter, in such a way that now he is Zion's chief destroyer and the one responsible for commissioning the nations as agents of judgment. The shift that occurs here in verses 5–8 is a secondary addition, brought about in the light of Jerusalem's deliverance in 701 B.C. On that occasion, marvelously and suddenly, the Assyrian foe was turned back (37:36–37). Another alternative reading argues that the prophet modified his own negative Zion thinking once the Assyrians began their assault in 701 B.C.

In some respects, this problem is not new. We saw the clear

way in which a tension was maintained in Isaiah 5—12 between God's commissioning of Assyria as agent of judgment, on the one hand, and his limiting of Assyria, on the other, as part of his larger concern with the vineyard's final destiny. Here that tension comes to a head in the space of eight brief verses.

The problem with the secondary addition argument is that it regards the composite text we now have as corrected, yet still exhibiting a clear seam where the supplementation occurred. Both it and the modification argument also turn on evidence from historical events that is difficult to prove or disprove. What is interesting about the text that stands before us is that it has evidently tolerated the sort of tension spotted by critical readers. How is that possible? Obviously a supplementer in the position to correct a text could also have smoothed out a seam, yet precisely that has not happened.

What is striking about the text in its present form is the shift detected at verse 5. God is encamped against Ariel. Then suddenly he is encamped against hostile nations bent on Ariel's destruction. Is it possible that both are aspects of the one divine action, strange and alien, as chapter 28 would describe it? That is, God fights in judgment against his own capital, and indeed against the whole land, as we learned in the preceding chapter. Yet, at the same time, he also fights against those nations who presume to hold Zion's fate in their hand: "So shall the multitude of all the nations be that fight against Mount Zion" (29:8). The nations section had made quite clear that Israel's God was Lord over all the earth and over every nation. The "righteous" nations do not sit in judgment over the "wicked" Zion. The stakes have been set rather differently in the course of the Book of Isaiah. Assyria, and Babylon, can be summoned for a task of judgment vis-à-vis Zion. But neither judge nor judged are exempt from Yahweh's final sovereignty. In sum, the judgment leveled against Zion also stands over the nations when they countermand the will of the one God of Israel and the nations. The tension created by the movement from 29:1–4 to 29:5–8 does not concern a judgment against Zion suddenly lifted. Rather, it concerns a judgment directed at Zion that also includes "the multitude of all the nations that fight against Ariel" (29:7). Zion's fate is altered, not because of any claim to righteousness, but solely on the grounds of God's justice, evenly meted out against all human injustice.

It is by no means clear that this complex passage intends to

213

convey the message that Zion will be destroyed by God in the same way the nations are routed. In the traditional view, God's turning against the nations implied his turning toward Zion in favor, delivering Zion from "all the nations that fight against Ariel" (29:7). What fails to find clearer expression is the precise character of God's punishment of Ariel. Evidently Zion is not to endure the onslaught of the nations bent on its utter annihilation. But is Zion also not to endure God's action of distressing? The opening verses depict an act of judgment, described as siege and encampment, by God himself, one that is to produce moaning and lamentation.

Here the unfortunately obscure verse 4 in all likelihood plays a role. Is the sound that rises deep from the earth the sound of moaning and lamentation, the sound of distress at the military assault of the nations, or the sound of contrition that turns God's judgment into deliverance? Each of these views has found critical support. In our judgment, the first view fits best within the movement we are describing. That is, God does distress Ariel, and moaning and lamentation do rise as a consequence, as if deep from the earth. Admittedly, there is an air of mystery about the images used in verse 4 that has led some to interpret the verse as imitative of necromantic practices, so "your voice shall come from the ground like the voice of a ghost." Indeed, the verse does drive home that Ariel's inhabitants are as though dead. The woe leveled at them (29:1) has brought them up to the realm of death and mourning.

In sum, God's routing of the nations described in verses 5–8 is not tantamount to his delivering of Zion. Zion is distressed by God, but not destroyed; brought up to the realm of death and mourning, but not slain. And lest there be any confusion, this distressing is not equivalent with the military assaults of Assyria or any nation. The consistent use of the plural ("multitude," "all the nations") drives home that no one military assault is intended. God's distressing of Ariel has its own intention and serves its own purpose. It cannot be identified in every instance with the assaults of the nations. The force of verses 5–8 is to remind us that God acts independently of the nations and is sovereign over them. God's distressing of Zion gives way to his routing of "the multitude of tyrants." These actions are not contrasting but complementary aspects of the one divine will.

As if anticipating our confusion with the movement and logic of 29:1–8, the unit that follows speaks of the closed eyes

214

and dull perception of the prophets and of anyone who seeks to understand this vision (29:9–12). Those who claim to be able to read are as confused by the vision as those who cannot read at all. As the next unit makes clear, the wonderful and marvelous actions of God are all but lost on those who claim to be wise (29:13–14). Whatever the previous chapter meant by wisdom, it did not have the conventional wise and discerning ones (29:14) in mind. The following woe oracle (29:15–16) is similar in its indictment to the judgment of priest and prophet in the preceding chapter. Those who take secret counsel to ward off the coming distress will be exposed. Their plans are a turning upside down of the counsel and wisdom of God.

Using a different genre than the parabolic discourse that concluded chapter 28, the prophet here looks to the day when the deaf shall hear and the blind see (29:17–21). It is a day not far off. Ruthless leaders who oppress the poor through deception and injustice will be cut off, while the meek shall "obtain fresh joy in the LORD" (29:19). Chapter 29 closes on something of the same note as the preceding chapter. It looks to the future as the time when understanding and right instruction will finally come to the house of Jacob (29:22–24).

Isaiah 30:1–33
In Returning and Rest

Chapter 30 can be divided into several subunits, though there is some disagreement among scholars as to the precise delimitation. It is clear, for example, that the first half of the chapter is concerned with Judah's proper stance vis-à-vis Egypt (30:1–17). The second half (30:18–33) shifts our attention to God's future judgment of the nations, using language reminiscent of chapters 24—27, while at the same time depicting a Zion that is finally taught aright (esp. 30:18–22). Within these two sections, however, smaller divisions can also be marked out (vv. 6–7; vv. 27–28).

The governing interest of modern commentators has been in determining the proper historical setting for these several units. This is particularly true of the first half of the chapter (30:1–17). Though there is disagreement over the details of such

215

a historical reconstruction, several items are judged to be beyond dispute. First, the condemnation by the prophet of false political alliances is chiefly directed at the royal house and the figure of Hezekiah. Second, the background for this condemnation is an alleged breach of faith with Assyria, again largely the fault of Hezekiah or of pro-Egyptian forces in the capital. It is assumed that the prophet Isaiah regarded the proper political stance to be submission to Assyria, and therefore any other plan involving possible Egyptian aid is to be condemned. The admonition to return and rest (30:15) is taken to be treaty language, more specifically aimed at Hezekiah and his alleged refusal to remain loyal to Assyria. Alternatively, the language is interpreted as returning to Yahweh, though the target of such an admonition remains primarily Hezekiah and the royal house.

This reconstruction depends heavily on an assessment of ancient Near Eastern documents and their relevance for the period of Isaiah's preaching. Many assume that the more precise setting for oracles in 30:1–17 is the situation alluded to in Isaiah 36—37, that is, the siege of Jerusalem by the Assyrians in 701 B.C., or the years leading up to it. There we find a reference (in the mouth of an Assyrian official) to "relying on Egypt" (36:6).

What is intriguing, however, is a comparison of this historical reconstruction with the actual text that lies before us. It is striking that Hezekiah is never mentioned by name in chapter 30 (the relevance of the Rabshakeh's remark directed to Hezekiah in 36:6, regarding his putative reliance on Egypt, is difficult to evaluate, since it is part of a highly rhetorical piece of narrative; see more on this below). Even proponents of such a historical reconstruction have noted that "Isaiah appears surprisingly restrained in not singling out Hezekiah for individual condemnation" (Clements, *Isaiah 1—39*, p. 243). Neither is there any clear reference to the royal house as such. Indicted are "rebellious children" (30:1), "rebellious people" and "faithless children" (30:9)—language quite familiar from the introductory indictment of chapter 1 (1:2, 5, 28). There too the condemnation was a general one, occasionally emphasizing corrupt leadership ("rulers," "princes," "judges," "counselors") but never exclusively focusing on the royal house alone (much less the figure of Hezekiah).

Moreover, it is difficult to grasp Isaiah's specific political counsel to Hezekiah on the basis of the material in chapter 30.

Is it truly the case that the prophet regarded the proper political stance to be submission to Assyria, in formal terms, involving
treaties and oaths of allegiance, oaths that would then be threatened by possible alliances with Egypt? Is this really the
prophet's concrete advice to the royal house at this or at any
other period of his proclamation? Assyria may be the instrument of God's judgment (10:5), but Assyria is also infected with
pride and arrogance and is certainly not a nation with whom
Israel should conclude formal pacts, anymore than Egypt would
be a fitting political ally. In this regard, it is important to note
that the Deuteronomistic Historian does not consider Hezekiah
a noble king—without analogy except to David—because he
submitted to Assyria, but precisely because he "rebelled against
the king of Assyria and would not serve him" (II Kings 18:7) in
stark contrast to his father Ahaz, who had sent messengers to
Tiglath-pileser, saying, "I am your servant and your son" (II
Kings 16:7). The stark contrast between Hezekiah and Ahaz
forms an essential structure in the narratives of Isaiah 36—39
and Isaiah 7—8. Why would it be suddenly missing here in
chapters 28—32, which are argued to give exactly the opposite
reading, namely, that Hezekiah improperly rebelled against
Assyria and was therefore to be condemned by the prophet
Isaiah?

By the same token, we do regard chapter 30 as concerned
with proper political alignment, not just for the royal house but
for all Israel. Or, put another way, the chapter is concerned
with proper religious alignment and the correct disposition in
times of political and military crisis. The opening unit (30:1–5)
sets the stakes clearly: the prophet considers two options open
to the rebellious children, and primarily just these two. On the
one hand, there are plans and leagues that link Israel to the
nations and that conceivably gain their attractiveness from
the fact that they pit one foe against a less threatening one and
thereby level the playing field from Israel's standpoint. In this
particular case, the less threatening foe is Egypt; the more
threatening, presumably Assyria.

But the prophet speaks here and elsewhere of another
"plan" and that is the "plan" of Yahweh. This is a plan that
involves Assyria as agent of judgment but also as a nation finally
under Yahweh's control (10:12). It is a plan "formed of old,   217
faithful and sure" (25:1), involving all the nations (14:26) but
also specifically the nation of Assyria (14:25). The Assyrian

would finally be broken, the prophet had promised, and the king who would reign as a fitting contrast to Ahaz would also witness Assyria's downfall (8:9–10). This was the testimony and teaching that Isaiah was to bind up among his disciples (8:16).

Here the prophet contrasts the faithful plan of Yahweh with the plan of rebellious children who set out to garner Egyptian support against Assyria. At two key points in the presentation of Isaiah, we know this to be a failed policy. First, we have the testimony and teaching from the days of Ahaz. There we learned that the king and the nation were disestablished because of the failure of the king to trust in the counsel of God. But the nations section also makes abundantly clear that no nation can offer any final protection for another nation (30:2). Israel's God is Lord over the nations, and only his plan and protection can bring help and profit (30:5). Like the mighty beast Leviathan who is rendered powerless by Israel's Lord (27:1), so too Egypt is the great sea beast Rahab (see Job 9:13; 26:12; Ps. 89:10), monster of the deep, who is called by God "Rahab who sits still" (30:6–7).

It is not surprising that at 30:8–14 we have a reference to written testimony reminiscent of Isa. 8:16–22. As there, so here the tablet is to serve as a witness for future generations (8:20; 30:8). The "inscribed book" will testify to the final accuracy of God's word despite the rebellious disposition of his people, who chose to trust in Egyptian counsel rather than the counsel of God. If the plan of God is refused in its own day, then it will serve a purpose for a later generation, reminding them of the faithfulness of God's ways during times of crisis and testifying against their forebears who rejected God's plan in favor of the plans of humankind.

Throughout these chapters we hear of the desperate schemes of God's people, of priests and prophets who have lost their ear for the word of God, of rulers who make covenants with death rather than with God, and of rebellious, lying children who prefer to risk making alliances with foreign nations— even nations like Egypt known for their hostility toward Israel and Israel's God—rather than trusting in God's abiding care for Zion. The lesson of Ahaz is lost on them and their generation and they seem doomed to endure the same fate that he endured. Finally, when prophets and seers emerge who point them in the right direction, they prefer lies and delusions to the truth (30:10). The choice is between trust in God and trust in some other form of human security, as simplistic as that sounds. Over and over, Isaiah repeats the same theme: trust in the Holy One of Israel or be doomed to the collapse of your iniquitous schemes. The indictment is clear: Israel has commanded the prophets and seers to "let us hear no more about the Holy One of Israel" (30:11). There can be only one verdict for such a people: utter collapse (30:12–14).

It might be said that the core of Isaiah's preaching can be summed up with reference to one key verse in chapter 30: salvation and strength are the consequence of firm trust and quiet confidence in God's abiding attention and concern for Zion (30:15). The same fundamental trust is required of king, of priest and prophet, of Judah's rulers, of all of God's people. No scheme, no matter how clever or well conceived, can substitute for this basic stance of faith. Amidst the swirling claims of clever politicians, deceitful prophets, crazed priests, and unjust rulers, there remains another way, and the prophet never tires of insisting that it is the only way.

Returning and rest, quietness and confidence are the opposite dispositions of those displayed by Ahaz during the Syro-Ephraimite crisis. There we heard of hearts shaking, of fear and faintness, and of a refusal to believe. Signs of God's attention and concern offered by the prophet were rejected. The teaching of the prophet was therefore bound up for a later day. Now that later day has arrived and the same rejection and the same refusal to believe in the plan of God emerge again. Again the message of the prophet is written on a tablet as a witness for later generations. As we learn in 30:18, God continues to wait for a generation that prefers quiet trust and strength to confidence in human schemes for salvation.

The unit at 30:19–26 appears to move us ahead in time to a period when the judgment of God has already been visited upon his people, much in the same sense as in the nations section. It is likely that the judgment described is the overrunning of Jerusalem by Babylon in 587 B.C., though the scene is not located in this specific historical period in the text itself. The removal of sorrow, the defiling of graven images, the total reversal of scenes of judgment—each of these themes has already been rehearsed in chapters 24—27, under the influence of the 587 B.C. desolation and the anticipated fall of Babylon (esp. 25:8; 27:9; 25:1–12). In addition, we see a theme that develops one key aspect of the chapters presently under discussion, more specifically, the interest in proper instruction and right teaching (28:23–29; 29:11–12; 29:18; 29:24; 30:8). Isaiah 30:20 makes reference to a "teacher" who will emerge in clear sight in the coming days of affliction.

We have heard of teachings that survive generations of unbelievers to serve as a testimony for later days, both in chapter 8 and in chapters 29 and 30 (8:16–22; 29:11–12; 29:18; 30:8). To complete the picture of instruction received by God's people, we now hear of a generation that receives the teaching on the authority of this unknown instructor. Now the possibility of mishearing or manipulation of God's word, or even the simple refusal to hear at all, seems to be ruled out. The "teacher" appears under no guise; ears hear, in contrast to the image set forth in the prophet's commission (6:10); instruction is given and received (30:21). When Israel turns to the right or to the left—that is, wherever it turns—the path will be clear. The possibility of false trips to Egypt for aid is all but ruled out: the anonymous teacher presents a word to the listening ear: "This is the way; walk in it" (30:21). The image is reminiscent of Jeremiah's vision of the new covenant, which is not so much taught in the days to come as written within, requiring little formal instruction (Jer. 31:31–34). So too here, in the Book of Isaiah's vision of future days, a voice speaks to the open ear (Isa. 30:21). As a consequence, images that distract from the worship of God are swept away, just as surely as are alliances with foreign powers.

It is interesting to note that in the following scene of divine judgment (30:27–28), exactly the same image of "overflowing stream that reaches up to the neck" is employed as in the Syro-Ephraimite narrative (see 8:8). But now the image of sifting and destruction is not aimed at Jerusalem but at the nations. And the agent of destruction is not Assyria but Yahweh. In the final unit (30:29–33), the destruction of the Assyrians is more specifically mentioned. The staff and rod of God's fury is no longer Assyria (cf. 10:5); rather, God has taken back his weapons of vengeance, once embodied by Assyria, in order to wage war against Assyria itself (30:31–32). This closing unit may well have been composed on the basis of Assyria's defeat in 701 B.C. (see chaps. 36—37). Alternatively, Assyria may be a more general cipher for the nations at large, whom Yahweh will finally defeat. The routing of the Assyrians in the 701 B.C. crisis, then, serves as a concrete example of God's sovereignty over all the nations on earth and specifically over Assyria's replacement, Babylon.

So just what does Isaiah mean by "returning and rest, quietness and trust"? If this is the core of his prophetic word to royal house, priest and prophet, rulers and politicians in Judah, and all of God's people—what is one to understand by it? The answer is first of all negative: "returning and rest" are the opposite of "setting out to go down to Egypt" (30:2) or "riding upon swift steeds" (30:16). There is a place for Judah to stand that means above all else the resolute condemnation of any political treaty—be it with Egypt or with Assyria, who like the Egyptian Rahab (30:7) will be "terror-stricken at the voice of the LORD, when he strikes with his rod" (30:31). The choice is not between Assyrian domination or Egyptian treaty, as many commentators would have it, but between divine trust or trust in foreign alliance. The choice for trust in God has its own integrity and is more than a "utopian objection to all foreign alliances out of [the] rigidly conceived dogma that they betrayed a lack of faith" (Clements, *Isaiah 1—39*, p. 255). In point of fact, the prophet frequently does judge trust in foreign alliances as the surest indication of lack of faith. The prophet speaks of a true establishment (7:9) that comes precisely when king and people reject the plans of the nations and turn to the plan of God. This plan involves God's fundamental commitment to Zion, on the one hand, and his concern that Zion be cleansed through the judging actions of the nations, on the other. The latter, however, does not mean concluding formal treaties with individual nations, whether Assyria in Isaiah's day or Babylon in a later day. The prophet's assessment of Assyria's role is far more complex and cannot be reduced to the level of formal compliance to treaties or other such political arrangements.

In the positive sense, "returning and rest, quiet and trust" are dispositions of the faithful who have come to acknowledge God's mysterious but committed presence in times of crisis. They are dispositions of the wise farmer who is instructed aright (28:26) and who understands the counsel and wisdom of God (28:29). The prophet's teaching, here as elsewhere, is by no means formulaic; neither does it involve the memorization of a slogan, a creedal prophylactic against all adversity. Nevertheless the prophet keeps pointing to a wisdom, a firm trust, an open ear, a steady resolve that enables the faithful to reject political alliances while seeking to understand God's actions through the nations and to stand firm on God's commitment to Zion while acknowledging that such commitment must involve a cleansing judgment. To pull these two aspects of the prophet's

221

message apart, on historical or literary-critical grounds, is to break apart that very aspect of Isaiah's word which has given it such vitality and afterlife.

Isaiah 31:1–9
A Severe Protection

Chapter 31, in the space of nine brief verses, encapsulates most of the critical problems already under discussion. Are Hezekiah and his foreign policy under assault here? Does God fight against Zion (not just "upon" it, see 31:4) but also protect, deliver, spare, and rescue it (31:5)? Does the prophet condemn Hezekiah's refusal to submit to Assyria, evidenced by his going "down to Egypt for help" (31:1), and yet also promise Zion's deliverance and Assyria's downfall (31:8)?

As we have seen, in an attempt to preserve a consistently negative view of Zion on the prophet's part, and a consistently positive attitude toward Assyria in its role as Yahweh's instrument, several commentators view chapter 31 as composite, reflecting streams of tradition at clear odds with one another. On the one hand, we have a woe oracle aimed at Hezekiah, condemning his breach of faith with Assyria, that culminates in a judgment of Zion (31:1–4). Against the NRSV reading, the image of 31:4 is to be interpreted in the most hostile sense: "so the LORD of hosts will come down to fight *against* Zion and *against* her hill" (the Hebrew preposition *'al* can be translated "upon" or "against"). On the other hand, the remainder of the chapter reverses this image by telling of God's protection of Zion and scattering of Assyria. God's fire and furnace are in Zion, and as in the Psalter, this can only mean the final turning back of the nations who rage against God and against his anointed (Ps. 2:2).

The problem with this evaluation of the chapter's development is that it is essentially too flat. The prophet is viewed as holding a monochromatic view of Zion and Assyria, the former to be judged by the latter. The editors of the chapter, who have supplied the final verses, likewise have a monochromatic view, only it is the opposite of the prophet's. It is supplied on the basis of Jerusalem's deliverance in 701 B.C., when the Assyrians were slain "by a sword, not of mortals" (31:8; 37:36) and Jerusalem was protected; or, on the basis of the later awareness, in the days of Josiah, that Assyria's role on the national landscape was about to be severely diminished (Hermann Barth). Negative word to Zion becomes positive word; positive word to Assyria becomes negative word.

The question raised by this essentially two-stage developmental process has to do with the authority of tradition and the authority of the prophet Isaiah. If the original tradition is at such odds with the later view, why did it gain any hearing at all? Why was the prophet Isaiah judged to have been a true prophet? To say simply that he was and that, as such, later traditionists had to reinterpret his message, is to beg the question. Such a view also raises questions about the nature of prophecy as such, as though it were self-authenticating and required no validation through time and community. Apparently prophets existed who spoke a word at odds with that of Isaiah (28:7ff.). What prevented the later community from saying the prophet Isaiah was just plain wrong about God's planned attack on Zion and his positive commissioning of Assyria, views that were rendered problematic by Jerusalem's deliverance in 701 B.C.? Is it not more likely that the prophet's Zion and Assyria preaching was vindicated by the wondrous events of 701? Quite apart from one's understanding of the nature and function of prophecy, does the text of Isaiah not reveal a more complex word concerning Zion and Assyria than any two-stage scheme would have it?

In the context of our discussion of chapter 29, similar problems arose. There too we saw God encamped against Ariel (29:1–4) but also zealous for Zion's welfare amidst the onslaught of the nations (29:5–8). Rather than divide the text into two sections, one "original" and one "corrective," we sought an understanding of the text as a composite whole. It is not to be ruled out in every instance that the deliverance of Jerusalem in 701 B.C. has influenced the text in its present form. At stake is the question of continuity and discontinuity between the prophetic word of Isaiah and later hearings of that word, which now form part of the present text. In our judgment, Isaiah's proclamation concerning Zion is neither unequivocally positive nor unequivocally negative. The same can be said of his proclamation concerning Assyria.

Within the presentation of chapters 1—12, Assyria emerges 223
as Yahweh's instrument of judgment. In that role, Assyria serves as the embodiment of Yahweh's outstretched hand (5:25). Grad-

ually the vineyard comes under assault, first the northernmost sections, then Samaria itself (9:12, 17, 21). The hand is out-stretched still, we are told, beyond the fall of the Northern Kingdom (10:4). And indeed we learn later at 36:1 that the king of Assyria eventually succeeds in taking all the fortified cities of Judah. At the same time, God will not permit the total desola-tion of his vineyard at the hands of Assyria (10:5–19). The limit set in Assyria is not a secondary development made in the light of Jerusalem's wondrous 701 B.C. deliverance, and neither is it solely the consequence of Assyria's gradual downfall and defeat in the seventh century. An integral dimension of the prophet's Assyria proclamation involves God's plan and purpose for Zion and all the nations. Assyria is not to overstep its role within God's plan; the same is true for all the nations.

It is within the context of this same plan that the prophet's Zion teaching is to be interpreted. God's judgment of the vine-yard and of Zion is not to be set over against his limiting of the nations, as though these were two distinct and opposing themes. Chapter 29 makes clear that God's judgment of Zion extends to and includes his judgment of the nations. Something of this same perspective can be noted in chapter 31.

The opening indictment is aimed at those who seek political alliances with Egypt (31:1–3). These alliances are not con-demned because they stand in opposition to a policy of submis-sion to Assyria. Nothing is ever said of such a policy, neither here nor anywhere else in the Book of Isaiah. Those who go down to Egypt are condemned for not turning in the first in-stance to the Holy One of Israel. Utopian or realistic—neither of these characterizations plays any role in the prophet's word. The prophet simply judges attempts to link up with Egypt as refusals to consult Israel's God.

Neither is Hezekiah mentioned as the target of the indict-ment. The comparison with Isaiah 7—8, with its focus on Ahaz and his house, is revealing at this point. Consistently, a plural, anonymous group of individuals is the object of the prophet's condemnation. Is this a pro-Egyptian group, royal counselors, political advisers? The text does not identify them any more specifically. Obviously, foreign policy and political alignment were not solely the concern of the king. Throughout Israel's experience of government by dynastic kingship, numerous other forces came into play in the affairs of state. One thinks of the queen mother (I Kings 1:11–31; II Kings 11:1–3), "the people of the land" (II Kings 23:30), the one "who was in charge of the palace" (II Kings 18:18, 37; Isa. 22:15), not to mention prophets and priests, minor government officials and counselors (II Sam. 16:20–23), and military leaders (II Sam. 19:1–8). The text does not stipulate exactly who warranted the prophet's rebuke, but there are good grounds, as we shall see, for seeing the failure to mention Hezekiah as no accident.

The prophet condemns these efforts at treaties with Egypt and announces that both helper and helped "will fall" together (31:3). The following verse (31:4) has been the subject of much discussion because of the ambiguity of its depiction of Yahweh's descent onto Mount Zion. The image of a lion growling over its prey, undaunted by rescuing shepherds, would suggest hostile action against Zion, God's prey. At the same time, the following verse depicts God as the undisputed guardian of Zion, an image bolstered by the fivefold repetition of verbs for protection (31:5). How are these two images to be understood juxtaposed in the present text?

The opening conjunction "for" *(kî)* in 31:4 clearly intends to link the preceding indictment against Egypt (helper) and those who go to Egypt (helped) with a scene of judgment in which Yahweh, undaunted by attempts at rescue, growls over his prey. The metaphorical judgment of verse 4 is simply an amplification of the preceding scene, where Yahweh's hand is stretched out against helper and helped, and they "all perish together" (31:3). Yahweh will destroy the Egyptians who come to Israel's defense, and he will crush those who seek Egyptian help rather than look to him. Given this description of verses 1–4, should we understand Yahweh's fighting as "against" or "upon" Mount Zion? The matter cannot be determined on grammatical grounds alone.

In our judgment, the more neutral rendering "upon" is to be preferred, yet this does not mean that Yahweh comes down to Mount Zion only in a positive sense. He fights upon Mount Zion against those who refuse to consult him, that is, first against those within Zion whose trust and reliance is a rejection of the "returning and rest" of chapter 30, in favor of the strength and numbers of chariots and horses; and second, against the Egyptians themselves, who, like Israel, have chosen a false mode of "defense." Precisely in this action of hostility against helper and helped, Yahweh's chief aim is not to destroy Zion but to protect, deliver, spare, and rescue Zion from the plans of humankind.

225

As in chapter 29, Yahweh's "hostility" toward Zion is aimed at exposing the false trust of those who seek alliance with Egypt, and as such it intends Zion's deliverance and rescue. Alliances with Egypt are not condemned because they threaten a policy of submission to Assyria but because they seek strength and salvation in a source other than the Holy One of Israel. They are a concrete embodiment of rejection of the counsel of 30:15.

The following appeal to return in verses 6–7, ostensibly a secondary addition, has also interpreted the opening unit along these lines. That is, the introductory exhortation "return" (šûbû) picks up the same language of "returning and rest" from 30:15: those in Zion who have revolted become a cipher for the wider people of Israel who trust, not in Egyptian aid, but in idols. The identification of false political alliances with false religious allegiance is thus made, again driving home that the choice is not between Egypt and Assyria but between "returning and rest" and going "down to Egypt."

The final unit (31:8–9), which tells of the defeat of Assyria, may well have been composed in the light of the events of 701 B.C. In particular, the reference to Assyria's downfall by "a sword, not of humans" links quite nicely to the outcome of the 701 B.C. debacle: "Then the angel of the LORD set out and struck down one hundred eighty-five thousand in the camp of the Assyrians" (37:36). What is more intriguing is the placement of the unit in this particular context and at this particular point in the presentation of chapters 28—39. First, God's defense of Zion from those who seek false help has been extended to include God's defeat of the Assyrians as well. From the image of lion growling over prey (31:4) to birds hovering in protection (31:5), we move in conclusion to Yahweh's fire and furnace in Zion, which now defends Zion specifically against the assault of Assyria, ostensibly in the events of 701 B.C. Yahweh's rescue of Zion is from helper (Egypt) and helped (Israel), and from the one they both feared (Assyria). As we learn in chapters 36—37, the Assyrian official regards reliance with Egypt as a false hope (36:6). He is of course right, but for the wrong reasons: not because Assyria is stronger than any alliance—which may in fact be true—but because Yahweh has a plan for Zion that excludes of necessity any trust in foreign aid. What the Rabshakeh must learn is that the fate in store for those who trust in Egypt, and for Egypt itself, is the same fate Assyria will share. Chapter 31 has deftly woven all three of these themes together:

God's defense of Zion against helper, against helped, and against the one for whom such treaties are allegedly designed.

The content and the placement of the final unit of chapter 31 make reasonably clear that the presentation of chapters 28—32, in particular, has been constructed with attention to the final 701 B.C. narratives in chapters 36—39. Chapter 29 introduced the notion that Yahweh would fight both against Ariel and against the nations, as one undivided action in defense of Zion's final integrity—as paradoxical as that might seem. Isaiah 31:1–5 anticipates the challenge of the Rabshakeh concerning trust in foreign aid (36:4–6), and it condemns such trust, both internally (helped) and externally (helper). When the Rabshakeh repeats the key word "rely" (= "trust," *bth*) four times in the space of three verses (36:4–6), are we not to see a clear pointer to the issue raised in chapter 30, where returning and rest, quietness and confidence *(bth)* were commended by the prophet to God's people? The Rabshakeh sees what options exist for God's people in Zion: trust in Egypt or trust in Israel's God. Yet he regards both as false trusts, and even claims to have been sent on a mission of destruction at Yahweh's very behest—a distortion of Isaiah's prophecy clearly in the realm of blasphemy.

Isaiah 31:8–10 serves the function of underscoring that God's cleansing of Zion, within and without, is not simply equivalent with any and all Assyrian onslaught. The Rabshakeh's speech is a precisely constructed example of just the sort of hubris that was condemned by Isaiah back in 10:10–11: "As my hand has reached to the kingdoms of the idols whose images were greater than those of Jerusalem and Samaria, shall I not do to Jerusalem and her idols what I have done to Samaria and her images?" Wrong. Yahweh commands the destruction of images for his own sake (31:7), and the Assyrian will be destroyed by a "sword, not of humans" precisely because he has arrogated to himself a task that belongs to God alone. Here the metaphor of Assyria as Yahweh's instrument (10:5) reaches its outer limit. The ax shall not vaunt itself over him who hews with it (10:15); rather, the sword not of humans will slay the blasphemous Assyrian. The Rabshakeh's speech reveals an Assyria no longer worthy to bear the title "rod of my anger." Isaiah 31:8–9 clarifies that now God's judgment against Zion, and against Egypt, is to be directed more fundamentally to Assyria. It is the same action of cleansing justice

227

meted out to all. Assyria's role as Yahweh's instrument has been consigned to the past. As chapters 28—32 look to the future, they anticipate God's wondrous defense of Zion, most dramatically against the Assyrian foe.

Isaiah 32:1-20
A King Will Reign in Righteousness

In our judgment, the coordination with narratives that report Jerusalem's deliverance (chaps. 36—38) is particularly well evidenced in chapter 32. We have witnessed a string of five woe oracles, directed at the Northern Kingdom (28:1), Ariel (29:1), those who hide counsel (29:15), and those who prefer alliances with Egypt over "quietness and confidence" (30:1; 31:1). That string, reminiscent of a similar presentation in chapter 5, is broken here at 32:1 with the single opening phrase, "See." At 33:1 we return to the woe refrain, as the "destroyer" is singled out for destruction. In the case of chapter 5, we saw that many argued for a similar split of an original sequence, whose continuation can now be spotted at 10:1. So too the theme of the outstretched hand is introduced at 5:25 and picked up again at 9:12, 17, 21; 10:4 (14:27). The intervening material (6:1—9:7) introduced the figure of Ahaz, the king who refused to believe and was disestablished. Assyria becomes an agent of judgment against the entire vineyard, not just the Northern Kingdom (5:26-30). Assyria is likened to a lion that growls over its prey (5:29-30), an image strikingly familiar in the present context, where Yahweh growls like a lion over Zion (31:4).

The woe refrain is also broken here in order to introduce a royal figure, who, unlike Ahaz, however, is not named. Clements quite rightly notes: "What is especially striking about the basic section [vv. 1–5] is that the introduction of the king ruling justly in v. 1 does not foretell his advent, as is usual in the case of the promises of the restoration of the Davidic monarchy (cf. 11:1–5), but simply describes him as a present figure" (Clements, *Isaiah 1—39,* p. 259). This is striking for Clements, because he, and many other interpreters, regard the royal figure who shall reign in righteousness as representing "an almost idyllic hope" (p. 259). Such hopes attach either to a postexilic figure who will restore kingship along proper lines or to King

228

Josiah, around whom a preexilic edition of First Isaiah took shape as the Assyrian empire began to collapse.

In our view, the observation that the reigning king is a present figure is correct, but the royal scion who is "like streams of water in a dry place" is not Josiah, who plays no named role whatsoever in the Book of Isaiah. We prefer to follow the lead that an intentional structure has been given to chapters 28—33 that anticipates and is fulfilled by the narratives of Jerusalem's deliverance (chaps. 36—38). As such, the king who reigns in righteousness is King Hezekiah, as the later narratives of Isaiah 36—38 will clearly reveal. The king's advent is not foretold, as has been noted, precisely because we already know of it (see 7:14; 9:1-7). Neither Hezekiah nor the royal house is explicitly mentioned in the foregoing indictments (chaps. 28—31), because they do not apply to them. The woe pattern is broken here with the sudden "see" (32:1) in order to set Hezekiah apart as the pattern of righteousness and wisdom (32:8).

Throughout chapters 28—31 suggestions of a different attitude of wisdom and firm trust have emerged, alternatives to the patterns of behavior warranting indictment and judgment: the wise farmer (28:23-29); the understanding spirit (29:24); the choice for returning and rest (30:15). Now the figure of the king emerges embodying these traits: eyes and ears are opened (32:3), good judgment appears (32:4), and the noble one stands firm (32:8). What a contrast to Ahaz, who does not stand firm and therefore does not stand at all (7:9).

The second half of the chapter (32:9-20) depicts the coming judgment, which lies just on the horizon (32:10). The familiar image of thorns and briers (5:6; 7:23-25) is reintroduced here (32:13): the final assault on the vineyard is about to take place. Cities and palaces will be deserted in the coming debacle (32: 14), a scene surely fulfilled by the assault of the Assyrians in 701 B.C., when every fortified city of Judah is taken (36:1). Yet precisely this scene of judgment and assault produces the effect called for by the prophet in his Zion proclamation. Zion is utterly cleansed. The images of righteous weal are literally piled up on top of one another in verses 16-18: justice *(mišpāṭ)*, righteousness *(ṣĕdāqāh)*, peace *(šālôm)*, quietness *(hašqēṭ)*, and trust *(beṭaḥ)*. The counsel of the prophet, calling for quietness and confidence, is finally achieved precisely through this act of judgment, precisely as the city is laid utterly low (32:19). The final verse speaks of a day of proverbial blessedness (32:20).

Can the identification of the king who rules in righteousness

229

with Hezekiah, and the coming judgment with the 701 B.C. assault, be firmed up to any greater degree? Does the portrait of Hezekiah in chapters 36—39 coincide with the description given in chapter 32 in such a way as to urge a reading that would see the two as intentionally linked, the general picture fulfilled by the details of the 701 B.C. narratives? The answer to that question must await our fuller treatment of Isaiah 36—39. But several observations can be made here.

First, it is striking that the Rabshakeh's speech consistently addresses the figure of Hezekiah, on almost personal terms. The speech of the Assyrian official has been crafted in such a way as to pick up themes already introduced in the preaching of Isaiah (Smelik). Thus, these speeches are the result of thoroughgoing editorial efforts by those familiar with the Isaiah tradition. There is the interest in proper trust, already mentioned (32:4–6); the possibility of Egyptian aid; the ironic twist put on the reforms of Hezekiah, as though centralization of the cult implied a diminution of Yahweh's true clout (32:7); and the claim that Sennacherib is the agent of Yahweh, again an ironic twisting of the prophet Isaiah's own proclamation.

To all of this the king's only response is, "Do not answer him" (36:21). Hezekiah knows there can be no true conversation with a blasphemer; God alone must give answer to the boasts of the Assyrian (Smelik). In precisely the correct mode of behavior, the king tears his clothes and puts on sackcloth—just as Josiah does when the Book of the Law is read (II Kings 22:11) and as Jehoiakim disdainfully refuses to do upon hearing the word of Jeremiah (Jer. 36:24). The king makes appeal to the prophet, again as does the righteous Josiah through the agency of his servants (II Kings 22:13). When the blasphemy of the Rabshakeh increases (Isa. 37:9–13), Hezekiah himself makes personal appeal in the temple (37:14–20). The prophet's response clearly indicates that it was Hezekiah's prayer that saved the city (37:21). The divine word at 37:35 concludes: "I will defend this city to save it, for my own sake and for the sake of my servant David." A more fitting contrast to Ahaz could not be conceived.

The portrayal of chapter 38 continues this contrast and enhances it even further. Again, the details of our interpretation will be left to the side for the moment. There is, however, one feature of the story of Hezekiah's illness that bears notice here. The fate of the king is said to be linked to the fate of the city, so that his resuscitation embraces the city's resuscitation (38:6). Again, as in chapters 36—37, what comes to the fore is the *intercessory* power of the king. The prophet pronounces a death sentence, parabolically implying the death of the city as well (38:2, 6). The king prays and weeps bitterly (38:2–3). The death sentence is reversed, and the king is granted new life. The sign received by the king, in contrast to his predecessor Ahaz, literally "turns back the clock" on the dial of Ahaz (38:7–8). It is as though Zion has been granted new life in spite of the failure of the royal house in the days of Ahaz. Responsible for this new lease on life is King Hezekiah. The inclusion of a final psalm of Hezekiah (37:9–21) is surely modeled on the figure of David, exemplary supplicant of the Psalter.

The concluding chapter (chap. 39) presents a seemingly straightforward picture of Hezekiah, and on the surface it seems none too flattering. The king shows to a Babylonian embassy everything in his realm; the prophet announces that it will all be carried off. Is the purpose of the story to link the king's action to the subsequent Babylonian exile, or are other factors more significant? Is the portrayal of Hezekiah a sudden departure from what we have seen in chapters 36—38, or can elements of continuity be seen that, far from condemning Hezekiah, commend him to posterity as one who "trusted in the LORD the God of Israel; so that there was no one like him among all the kings of Judah after him, or among those who were before him"? After all, this commendation of the Deuteronomistic Historian—the highest possible praise, bestowed otherwise only on Josiah (II Kings 23:25)—is made with full knowledge of the visit of Babylonian emissaries (II Kings 20:12–19; Isa. 39:1–8). The Chronicler too shares in the view that this episode did not tarnish Hezekiah's record; rather, the king was left alone so that God might "know all that was in his heart" (II Chron. 32:31). The clear implication, reinforced by the following reference to "his good deeds" (II Chron. 32:32), is that Hezekiah passed the test. In sum, we will need to examine the story in more detail below in order to determine wherein lay the righteous action of the king "in the matter of the envoys of the officials of Babylon" (II Chron. 32:31). Both the Chronicler and the Deuteronomistic Historian view the entire record in as positive a light as is possible for Judah's kings.

Although the chapters that close First Isaiah have frequently been referred to as "Isaiah legends" or "Isaiah narratives," a far more appropriate designation would be "Hezekiah narratives." It is Hezekiah who consistently holds center stage across this four-chapter tradition complex. Unlike his predecessor Ahaz, he and the prophet work together as a team, each fulfilling the duties and obligations appropriate to his office. There is no hint of contention or strife, as in the days of Ahaz. For once there is complementarity between prophet and king, with the consequence that Zion is delivered. The king, by dint of prayer and petition, can even reverse a sentence of death uttered by the prophet (38:1). It is his prayer that saves the city from the Assyrian foe (37:21). The king puts his life on the line, as one who has "walked before you in faithfulness with a whole heart" (38:3). God saves the city for his own sake—and in fulfillment of the divine word uttered in chapters 28—33 through the prophet—and for the sake of the royal house (37:35).

Any one of the following factors might suggest that the "king who reigns in righteousness" is none other than Hezekiah: the comprehensive portrayal of Hezekiah as righteous king in chapters 36—39; the unsurpassability evaluations of the Chronicler and the Deuteronomistic Historian; the nonmention of Hezekiah in the indictments of chapters 28—32; the strong likelihood that the contrast between Ahaz and the Immanuel child and royal figure of Isa. 9:1–7 is meant to point to Hezekiah; and the obvious way in which Hezekiah and Ahaz are set in contrast to each other in chapters 7—8 and 36—39. Taken together, they make for a convincing total picture. The coming judgment that leads to a new endowment of God's spirit (32:15), to justice, righteousness, peace, quietness, and trust— the Assyrian assaults of 701 B.C. paradoxically produce this effect, as embodied in King Hezekiah. The countryside of Judah proper is overrun and, from the single-verse description of Isa. 36:1, all but wiped out by Assyrian onslaught. But Zion is delivered. Consequently, the preaching of Isaiah and the deportment of the king stand in clear judgment over all previous attempts at foreign alliance, secret counsel, drunken prophetic vision, covenants with death, and the like.

It cannot be proven that Hezekiah is the object of the prophetic word at 32:1–8, however much Hezekiah does emerge in chapters 36—39 as the noble one who devises "noble things, and by noble things [he] stands" (32:8). The text does not admit of such airtight conclusions. We would appeal in the end to the larger structure of chapters 28—33, with their series of six woes

232

broken here by the single "See" and the portrayal of a righteous king. In chapters 28—31 we have a comprehensive presentation of indictment leveled at every section of Israelite society (most especially the leadership) and an emergent Zion theology that speaks both of Zion's cleansing and God's justice over Egypt, Assyria, and the nations. The latter clearly points ahead to the 701 B.C. crisis, as a singular example of divine justice visited upon Assyria, in defense of divine word and royal petition. As such, the royal figure of 32:1–8 anticipates the figure of Hezekiah, who holds center stage in the presentation of chapters 36—39.

Isaiah 33:1–24
Woe to You, Destroyer

What has been said in the previous section must be taken into consideration in our interpretation of chapter 33, where the woe cycle is resumed and directed at the (equally anonymous) "destroyer, who yourself have not been destroyed." The language of this opening phrase is familiar from the nations section (24:16), where it is applied to Babylon. The notion of the final treacherous dealing with the one who has been treacherous is also a familiar motif as applied to Babylon in the nations section (see 14:3–11; 27:7).

Chapter 33 has been frequently lost in larger structural schemes that seek to identify patterns and complexes in the Book of Isaiah. On the one hand, chapters 28—32 are considered a distinct cycle of prophecies; on the other hand, chapters 34—35 have been interpreted as a "small apocalypse" on analogy with the "large apocalypse" in chapters 24—27. Chapter 33 shares with the following complex (chaps. 34—35) an interest in God's judgment over the nations (33:1–6) and with the previous chapter (chap. 32) a glimpse at righteous kingship in the aftermath of God's judgment (33:17–24).

In our judgment, chapter 33 gives no convincing signal that would oblige us to seek a historical setting much later than Isaiah's own historical period, when the content alone is considered. The destroyer of 33:1 need not be Babylon; the passages in the nations section that utilize similar language may have taken shape on the basis of this text. The image of the nations scattered before the Lord's justice and righteousness (33:3-6) is by no means a postexilic or later apocalyptic notion and in fact is well attested in the section under discussion (28:17-22; 29:5-8; 30:27-28; 31:5). We see as well in chapter 33 the same concern to underscore that God's exaltation over the nations has distinct repercussions for those in Zion who have placed their trust and confidence elsewhere and tremble at the thought of God's judgment (33:14). So that while some in Zion await God's promised exaltation over the nations (33:2; 33:15-16), for others in Zion that exaltation is a source of grave concern.

The final unit (33:17-24) again introduces the king as the figure who emerges from the debacle, in much the same manner as in the previous chapter. The eyes of the faithful will see him in his splendor, while others disappear from view, including those who trusted in military strength ("who counted the towers"), those who sought through treaty to ward off danger (who "counted" and "weighed the tribute"), and a people of obscure and insolent speech (v. 19). This last reference has a parallel at 28:11 ("men of strange lips and with an alien tongue" [RSV]) where the Assyrians are clearly intended. If our inclination to view chapters 28—32 as culminating in the presentation of chapters 36—39 is correct, then an identification with the Assyrians is further bolstered. The Rabshakeh is certainly a man of insolent speech (36:4-10), and the appeal by Hezekiah's servants that he speak Aramaic rather than the language of Judah (36:11) is a clear reminder that the mother tongue of the besieging Assyrians fits well with the description at 33:19 of "an obscure speech that you cannot comprehend, stammering in a language that you cannot understand."

A further compelling factor that urges an interpretation of the "destroyer" as the Assyrians is the larger structure of this section. In our view, the repetition of five introductory woes *(hôy)* at 28:1; 29:1; 30:1; 31:1; and now 33:1, offset by the single "see" *(hēn)* at 32:1, can hardly be coincidental. Those looking for a place to locate chapter 33 within the larger complex of chapters 28—39 need only consider this obvious structural devise, which has grouped chapter 33 together with chapters 28—32. The woes of chapters 28—31, involving the Northern and the Southern Kingdom, priest and prophet, false counsel and false treaty, failed leaders and rebellious people, also ex-

234

tend to the nations in general and Assyria specifically. Especially in chapter 31 we saw how God's judgment over helper (Egypt) and helped (Israel) culminated in his routing of the Assyrians by "a sword, not of humans" (31:8). The larger structural evidence points in the direction of an identification of the Assyrians with the "destroyer, who yourself have not been destroyed" (33:1) and "the people of an obscure speech" (33:19). In the nations section, where Assyria is replaced by Babylon in God's purpose concerning the whole earth (14:26), Babylon becomes the "treacherous [ones who] deal treacherously, . . . very treacherously" (24:16). But this is a secondary development based on the initial identification of the treacherous destroyer with Assyria.

What is most striking is the emphasis on the judgment of God, against Israel and the nations, that serves to inaugurate a new period of royal justice and secure habitation in Zion. Rather than annihilating Zion, God's exaltation accomplishes God's will on behalf of Zion, scattering the nations without and routing the "sinners" and "the godless" within (33:14). The Zion theology of chapters 28—31 had prepared us for such a scene, and here it is fulfilled in the 701 B.C. onslaught of the Assyrians.

Older scholars referred to chapter 33 as a "prophetic liturgy" on the grounds of its internal structure (vv. 1–6, threat; vv. 7–9, lament; vv. 10–13, oracle; vv. 14–16, liturgy; vv. 17–24, promise of salvation), with attendant speculation about its situation in life and historical setting. We would prefer to tie the interpretation of the chapter more closely to its "situation in context," which in this instance involves the broader presentation of chapters 28—33 as a whole. These chapters prepare us for the deliverance of Zion and the exaltation of Yahweh over the Assyrians. Hezekiah will emerge as a king who reigns in righteousness, whose prayer seals Zion's deliverance. But the conclusion of that four-chapter complex also gives us an ominous and unequivocal look into the future, when the Babylonians will come from afar and carry off the royal house and its treasures (39:1–8). In so doing, the wider historical lens of the nations section, with its emphasis on a world judgment accomplished by—and then including—the Babylonians, is put into place. The deliverance of Zion in the 701 B.C. debacle, then, only foreshadows God's final forgiveness and restoration of Zion 235 following the desolation of Jerusalem in 587 B.C.

It is precisely because the Book of Isaiah as a whole has

chosen to link the destiny of Zion in 701 B.C. with the ultimate fate of Zion following 587 that chapters 28—33 do not now directly introduce the logical culmination in chapters 36—38. Instead, in chapters 34—35 we return to the perspective of the nations section, and especially that of its conclusion (chaps. 24—27), before learning of God's gracious deliverance of Zion in 701 B.C. That deliverance becomes, then, a "type" that foreshadows God's final restoration of Zion and comforting of Jerusalem spoken of in chapters 40—66.

Isaiah 34:1—35:10
The Ransomed of the Lord Shall Return

Though some scholars would separate the interpretation of chapter 34 from 35 on redaction-critical grounds (Steck, *Heimkehr*), there is a long-standing consensus for treating them as a single tradition complex. As noted, older scholars following Duhm spoke of chapters 34—35 as a small apocalypse to be compared with the larger apocalypse of chapters 24—27. Our reservations about employing the genre designation "apocalypse" for chapters 24—27 also apply here. By the same token, more general comparisons between the two sections may well be apt, on literary and historical grounds.

Both sections keep before the reader's eye a much broader geographical sweep than is evidenced, for example, in chapters 28—33. As in chapters 24—27, we also hear of nations and peoples, as well as earth *(hā'āreṣ)* and world *(tēbēl)*, right from the outset (34:1). All the nations merit God's fierce wrath, and the hosts of heaven will feel the effect of his massive judgment. The opening scene of chapter 24 comes readily to mind in the depiction of 34:1-4.

It is not entirely clear why, following this clearly international and cosmic perspective, the text suddenly shifts to focus on Edom alone, maintaining this narrower focus for the remainder of the chapter (34:5-17). Historical explanations have been given: Edom may have played a role in the overthrow of Jerusalem in 587 B.C., thus meriting special condemnation here in a text where the 587 assault on Jerusalem is presupposed (see Obadiah; Jer. 49:7-22; Ezek. 25:12-17). The Ezekiel text reports that "Edom acted revengefully against the house of Judah and has grievously offended in taking vengeance" (Ezek. 25:12). It is also to be noted that in the role of the nations in Isaiah 13—24, while oracles are included for Babylon, Assyria, Moab, Syria, Ethiopia, Egypt, Dumah, and Arabia, there is no reference to Edom. On the other hand, as the references to Jeremiah and Ezekiel above make clear, these two other prophetic books with nations collections have not forgotten Edom. Whatever the reason for the omission of Edom from the nations section in Isaiah, that omission is more than covered here. Edom serves as representative type for all the nations that merit God's judgment (34:1–4).

The chapter describes a thoroughgoing destruction of Edom. The image of sword and sacrifice and slaughter (34:5–7) gives way to that of an enduring fire (34:8–10) and finally to a return to thorns and thistles, where all varieties of animals replace princes and former inhabitants of the kingdom now called "No Kingdom" (34:11–15). There is a curious reference to reading from "the book of the LORD" for confirmation about no animal—or its mate—being missing (34:16), and there does seem to be an emphasis on the abundance of different types of animal life: hawk, porcupine, owl, raven, jackals, ostriches, wild beasts, hyenas, satyrs, night hag, and kites. We would speculate that what is being depicted with this animal roster is a scene like that prior to Noah's entering the ark (Gen. 6:19—7:3)—or better, like that after the flood when all had been destroyed and only Noah and his animal collection remained. This might explain the threefold reference to the animal and his or her mate (34:14, 15, 16), as in the case of Noah, "two of every kind . . . male and female" (Gen. 6:19–20). Edom has been returned to a state similar to the one after the flood, but with only animals and their mates as inhabitants. The reference to "the book of the LORD" would then be a reference to the "book" in which the Noah story appeared (where reference to animals is found—"none shall be without its mate"; cf. Isa. 34:14–15 and Gen. 6:17–22).

The imagery of return to chaos and the explicit reference to the Noah story are of course familiar motifs from chapters 24—27 (see above). But what of the other images in chapter 34 of slaughter and burning? For the latter, is the story of Sodom and Gomorrah to be regarded as exercising some direct influence, as several commentators have suggested? It is striking

237

when one returns to chapters 24—27 that several of these same images are also strung together there. More specifically, in chapter 27 we have the sword that punishes the beast Leviathan (27:1), thorns and briers as battle weapons (27:4), and the threat of wholesale burning (27:4)—all this if any nation refuses to make peace (27:5) and threatens the security of the vineyard. In chapter 34 we see a sword descending for judgment (34:5), slaughtering not Leviathan but the beasts of Edom (34:6–7), the streams of Edom becoming pitch, the soil brimstone, and the land burning pitch (34:10), leading to utter desolation (34:11), and finally thorns overwhelming Edom's strongholds (34:13).

We would conclude, then, that one possible interpretation of chapter 34 is that here Edom is being depicted as representative of any nation that might choose to violate God's restored vineyard, over which God now stands watch "night and day so that no one can harm it" (27:3). This warning was directed to the nations at large in chapter 27, and Edom's fate is given as an example of what happens when the restored vineyard is violated. Hence the fierce judgment along the lines sketched out in 27:1–5. If this reading is correct, then we have in chapter 34 a fairly clear instance of inner-biblical exegesis, where a prior text (27:1–6) is interpreted as being fulfilled in a new situation. It remains unclear why Edom was chosen as representative of the nations, or whether specific historical circumstances influenced the choice of Edom in this context. A combination of factors—historical and literary—probably accounted for Edom's portrayal here: that is, it was not spoken of in the nations roster and could therefore be included at this juncture; and it may have played a concrete historical role as violator of God's vineyard in the aftermath of 587 B.C.

The new Song of the Vineyard in chapter 27 concluded with the promise:

> In days to come Jacob shall take root,
> Israel shall blossom and put forth shoots,
> and fill the whole world with fruit.
> (Isa. 27:6)

Obviously the fate of Edom is depicted as precisely the reverse of this: a return to wilderness, with nettles and thistles, a haunt of jackals (34:13). What is more striking, however, is the opening verse of chapter 35:

238

The wilderness and the dry land shall be glad,
    the desert shall rejoice and blossom;
like the crocus it shall blossom abundantly.
                          (Isa. 35:1–2)

This looks for all the world like an exact fulfillment of the promise of the new Song of the Vineyard at 27:6, thus further
strengthening the notion of inner-biblical interpretation playing a key role in both chapters 34 and 35. The violator Edom
goes from fat to "no kingdom." The desolated Israel blossoms
once again. Instead of slaughter and burning, we hear of waters
breaking forth in the desert and of dry ground becoming
springs (35:7).

The language parallels with Second Isaiah, which scholars
have pointed out, have urged some to regard the author of
chapters 34—35 and the author of chapters 40—55 as one and
the same. In point of fact, any true resemblance really only
exists in chapter 35, where the predominant images of blossoming wilderness (35:1–2, 6*b*–7), restored health (35:3–6*a*), and the
return of the ransomed dispersed (35:8–10) are familiar from
Second Isaiah. It is notoriously difficult to determine the direction of influence when language parallels are tallied up and thus
to conjecture about authorship and redactional development (is
chap. 35 based on Second Isaiah? vice versa? both by the same
author?). Moreover, frequently such reconstructions fail to deal
with the function of the present arrangement of the material.

The more recent emphasis on the relationship of chapters
34—35 forward in the direction of Second Isaiah has tended to
mute the older view of a relationship back to chapters 24—27
(so-called little and big apocalypses). In our judgment, both
views have a measure of truth to commend them. The contrast
between Edom and Zion is quite strong in the present text—
one moving toward wilderness, the other away from it (compare the "haunt of jackals" image in 34:13 and 35:7)—and this
contrast takes its cue from themes developed in chapters 24—
27. Edom as violator of the vineyard is destroyed, while Jacob
and Israel blossom and put forth fruit. At the same time, the
special relationship between chapter 35 and Second Isaiah is
also to be noted. Indeed, as one interpreter has put it, Isaiah 35
is the "redactional bridge" linking the two Isaiahs. In the depiction of a restored Israel, the highway for the dispersed, the
blossoming wilderness, the opened eyes and strengthened

239

limbs, we are given a glimpse of the joy that will obtain in days to come. Chapter 35 tells of sorrow and sighing fleeing away (35:10) in the language of First Isaiah (25:8) and of a highway for the dispersed (35:8) in the language of Second Isaiah.

We come to the question, What is the function of these two chapters in their present location? Or, to state it another way, If one were building a bridge from First to Second Isaiah, why not place the bridge *after* the chapters of First Isaiah were completed, following chapters 36—39? Why move from a vision of restored sight and a highway for the dispersed straight into the account of Sennacherib's invasion of Judah and Jerusalem? A later redactorial hand presumably could have inserted chapters 34—35 wherever wished, and a position prior to chapters 36—39, separated from chapters 40—55, has been chosen. If, on the other hand, one author or circle was responsible for both chapters 34—35 and chapters 40—55, then a conscious decision must have been made to separate the first two chapters from the remaining sixteen by the Hezekiah narratives in chapters 36—39.

In a very general sense, one can see that by prefacing the narratives that tell of Zion's deliverance in 701 B.C. with chapters 34—35, the specific historical instance of Zion's protection in the days of Sennacherib has been placed within a much broader framework of God's ongoing attention and care for his vineyard amidst the nations at large. The wondrous deliverance of 701 B.C. foreshadows Zion's final triumph as God's chosen place of exaltation and return. The Assyrian destroyer about to be destroyed (chap. 33) becomes a type of the nations at large (34:1–4); God's gracious sparing of the old vineyard, after the Assyrian waters had reached to the very neck, becomes a type of God's total protection of the new vineyard from any and all violation, as promised in 27:2–6. Still, such typology might have been executed equally well with chapters 34—35 *following* the account of Zion's deliverance in chapters 36—39 rather than preceding it.

We would seek the primary explanation for the present location of chapters 34—35 in a slightly different realm, as having to do with the merger of First Isaiah and Second Isaiah chapters into one synthetic presentation whose combined portrayal is greater than the sum of its parts. I have argued in another context for a First Isaiah collection that once ended dramatically with the account of Zion's deliverance in 701 B.C.,

240

as the culmination and vindication of the prophet's complex Zion and royal theology. The presentation of chapters 28—33 would have led logically into chapters 36—39 (a similar argument has been set forth above in briefer form). The effect of the placement of chapters 34—35 has been to "enclose" this dramatic finale with material from Second Isaiah on either side. Zion's deliverance is no longer an act of historical significance validating Isaiah preaching; it is that, and more: the Hezekiah narratives in chapters 36—39 point ahead to God's final defense of his new vineyard, with a new and restored Zion at its center. The violators of the new vineyard will come to the same end as the Assyrian destroyer in Isaiah's day.

One other major effect is achieved. The sharpness of the distinction between "First" and "Second" Isaiah is blurred by the placement of chapters 34—35. It is impossible to link these two "halves" of the book neatly with fixed historical periods, one fluctuating around the key date of 701 B.C. and the other around the key date of 587 B.C. Already "First" Isaiah has a major level of tradition under the influence of the events of 587, namely, the nations section (chaps. 13—27). Now those "First" Isaiah chapters most closely connected to historical events in the period of Isaiah's preaching, concerning the deliverance of Jerusalem in "the fourteenth year of King Hezekiah" (36:1), have been enclosed within "Second" Isaiah chapters. To be sure, the final chapter (chap. 39) eases the transition to the "Babylonian" half of the book, with its reference to coming Babylonian assault. But that transition is effected not just by means of prophecy-fulfillment schemes (39:5-7) but also by the present arrangement of chapters 34—39 as such.

Moreover, it is now a striking fact that the first half of the book, strictly speaking (what the Masoretes mark in the margin of the Hebrew text as "midpoint of the book according to verse count"), comes precisely at the twentieth verse of chapter 33, practically where chapter 34 picks up with its vision of the new vineyard's protection. While scholarship may prefer to speak of a division of the Book of Isaiah into two or three sections, marked at chapters 39/40 and 55/56, a more significant division in the final shaping of the tradition may now be found at 33/34, at the halfway point of the sixty-six-chapter full presentation. In a manner of speaking, chapters 34—35 introduce a "second" Isaiah: sustained speech concerned with the aftermath of Babylonian desolation and Zion's restoration (chaps. 40—66). In so

241

doing, they "enclose" the record of Zion's deliverance and royal triumph in the days of Assyrian assault (chaps. 36—39) within a broader framework of God's care for Zion against all assaults of the nations.

One other factor is to be considered in this context, regarding the "merger" of two Isaiahs. In chapters 1—33, texts abound that point to or presuppose the destruction of Jerusalem in 587 B.C. But as was noted above, we have no formal record of that desolation, such as we find in the Books of Jeremiah or Ezekiel. What remains of paramount concern to those who have shaped the present tradition is not Zion's defeat but rather *God's fundamental, abiding concern for Zion's final triumph and permanent fortification against the nations.* Chapters 34—35 speak of that triumph; chapters 36—39 give a concrete example of God's care at one moment in Zion's history; and chapters 40—66 pursue the same line of interest. We do not move from "first" to "second" Isaiah by way of a record of Zion's defeat but, more mysteriously, from the promise of victory amidst the nations (chaps. 34—35), to one miraculous victory in the past (chaps. 36—38), to foreseen exile (chap. 39), and finally to bold words of comfort and forgiveness (chap. 40). First and Second Isaiah are not distinguished merely as preexilic and postexilic blocks of tradition but rather as promised and revealed phases of Zion's ongoing destiny, as God's place of exaltation and Israel's place of return.

Isaiah 36:1—37:38
Hezekiah Reigns in Righteousness

We have spoken at some length about the presentation of Hezekiah in Isaiah 36—37 in the context of our discussion of the king who reigns in righteousness (32:1), whom eyes will see in his beauty (33:17). Traditionally, interpretation of the story of Jerusalem's deliverance in 701 B.C. has been carried out within certain very specific historical and literary-critical parameters, which unfortunately have led the interpreter away from any serious engagement with the Isaiah text in its present form. As such, the positive portrayal of Hezekiah, for example, has taken a backseat to questions of a more strictly historical character.

What happened in 701 B.C.? How was the city delivered? What happened to the army of Sennacherib?

Several other matters have governed discussion of these two chapters, and these should be mentioned briefly. The roughly parallel account in II Kings 18:13—19:37 has been granted priority over the Isaiah tradition on the theory that the fuller Isaiah record (chaps. 36—39) has been brought over from its original position in Kings to serve as the formal conclusion to a "First Isaiah Book," on analogy with the Book of Jeremiah, which likewise concludes with a historical appendix from Kings (Jeremiah 52 // II Kings 25). Second, the brief notice in Kings that is lacking in Isaiah (II Kings 18:14–16) has been judged the most reliable historical bit of tradition, further enhancing the claim to priority for the Kings account over against Isaiah (Isaiah 36—37 is judged to be an abbreviation, while Isaiah 38 is an expanded and disjointed version of II Kings 20:1–11). Third, since the late nineteenth century scholars have talked of the 701 B.C. traditions in Kings and Isaiah as comprised of three evolving reports: a record of Hezekiah's tribute payment, located in II Kings 18:(13)14–16, judged to be historically accurate (Account A); a mildly historical report of the Rabshakeh's speech and Assyrian withdrawal, whose conclusion has been lost, truncated, or dislocated, found at II Kings 18:13, 17—19:8 (Account B1); and a parallel but highly theologized version of the same story, composed at a later period, which tells of the miraculous deliverance of Jerusalem, located at II Kings 19:9–37 (Account B2). A fuller summary and discussion of this theory is readily available and need not be further rehearsed here.

One consequence of the theory has been that the question of the function and purpose of the Isaiah traditions in their present form has often been treated as strictly derivative of more important historical questions. Only recently has an interest been shown in examining the Isaiah material in its own right. The assumed priority of the Kings tradition has also been called into question. The present order of the accounts (701 B.C. deliverance; sickness and recovery; the prophecy of Babylonian exile) has a certain logic in Isaiah, given the continuation into chapters 40—55, while in the more sequential presentation in Kings the visit of Merodach-baladan should have preceded the 701 B.C. narratives, with the sickness and recovery story holding the initial position (Smelik). An extended narrative with an

243

appearance by an individual canonical prophet is in fact rare in the context of the Books of Kings, while narratives with an interest in the deportment of the royal house are already attested in the Book of Isaiah (chaps. 7—8). Smelik has also shown how the theory of parallel accounts (B1 and B2) is similarly flawed and has interpreted the Isaiah narratives as a unified record (so too II Kings 18:13, 17—19:37). The undisputed claim to "historicality" for the brief notice of Hezekiah's submission (II Kings 18:14–16) has also been called into question (Provan). The notice functions within the larger schema of the Deuteronomistic History and is probably a redactional—not a supremely historical—piece of tradition, concerned with the effect of foreign rapprochement on the downfall of the kingdom. In sum, an interpretation of the Isaiah traditions on their own terms—not simply as a task derivative of historical questions more properly handled in the context of II Kings 18:13—19:37—need no longer appear idiosyncratic or requiring lengthy justification.

The theory of parallel accounts (in Isa. 36:1—37:8 and 37:9–38) was based on the observation that Isaiah prophesies the turning back of Assyria at 37:7, and yet this does not happen until the end of chapter 37. Bernhard Stade theorized that the rumor that caused Sennacherib to turn back, as prophesied by Isaiah (37:7), involved the sudden appearance of the army of Tirhakah (37:9). Account B1 once ended with a report of Assyria's departure, but that conclusion was disturbed when account B2 was merged with the original story. As we shall see, the fulfillment of the prophecy at 37:7 has been delayed intentionally until the conclusion of the story (37:36–38), in part for dramatic effect and in part to set before the reader the possibility that Jerusalem might be delivered by foreign aid after all.

The account as it now appears in Isaiah 36—37 is to be divided as follows:

1. Situation (36:1–3): Only Jerusalem is left
2. Rabshakeh's Speech (36:4–10): A question of trust
3. Dramatic Interlude (36:11–12): Request denied
4. Rabshakeh's Speech (36:13–20): Hezekiah is a deceiver
5. Delegation Response (36:21–22): Not a word
6. Royal Response and Request (37:1–4): Let God answer

7. Prophetic Response (37:5–7): Return and death
8. Assyrian Speech (37:8–13): God and king are useless
9. Royal Appeal (37:14–20): Thou art God alone
10. Prophetic Response (37:21–29): Divine plan will be fulfilled
11. Continuation (37:30–35): Sign and promise
12. Conclusion (37:36–38): Death in camp and temple

The genre of the account is narrative short story (Lohfink), with situation (assault), complication (delay; foreign aid?), and resolution (royal prayer heard; Assyrians slain) governing the dramatic movement. Repeated elements are not signs of parallel accounts having been clumsily merged; instead, these serve to produce dramatic tension until the final resolution, briefly stated, comes (37:36–38).

Chapter 36 opens quite suddenly (36:1–3), with a situation of threat from Assyrian forces well under way: all the fortified cities of Judah have been taken. It is already the fourteenth year of Hezekiah. Among other things, with this reference we are given a signal that the king has been on the throne for some time. This is a necessary bit of data, since the Rabshakeh spends the bulk of his "air time" referring to Hezekiah and his established record as king—as rebel (36:5), cult reformer (36:7), stout defender of God's ability to deliver the city (36:15), misleader of Israel (36:18), and deceived of God (37:10). We are also most certainly to be put in mind of another similarly phrased narrative introduction, when, in the days of Ahaz, king of Judah, the kings of Syria and Israel "went up to attack Jerusalem, but could not mount an attack against it" (7:1). Only here, the army of the king of Assyria, far more terrifying than the combined forces of Syria and Israel, has not failed to conquer anything! Rabshakeh has the right to boast as he does—or so it would seem. The question for the reader is: How can Zion and king possibly survive?

We are not told why Sennacherib stays at Lachish, preferring to send the Rabshakeh in his stead, together with a great army (36:2). Presumably the Assyrian king feels that his personal presence is unnecessary. He is requesting (and anticipating) surrender of Hezekiah, not a full-scale assault. The dramatic effect achieved thereby is enormous: the bulk of the account now focuses on the speeches of the Assyrian Rab-

245

shakeh, as he sues for surrender and, getting no response (37:21), must dig himself deeper and deeper into a position of blasphemous disrespect, for which there can be no answer except from the Holy One of Israel (37:16).

If the opening verse failed to evoke the earlier scene of crisis and threat against Jerusalem in the days of Ahaz, we have an unmistakable signal at 36:2. The Rabshakeh takes his stand at the "conduit of the upper pool on the highway to the Fuller's Field" (cf. 7:3). Yet this time the fateful meeting place finds not king and prophet pitted against each other, as in the days of Ahaz, but an Assyrian official and a triad dispatched by the king, comprised of Hilkiah, Shebna, and Joah (36:22). The fact that the latter two are clearly scribal figures (secretary, recorder), and that all three function as messengers for king and prophet (36:22; 37:2, 6), might suggest that their role as the composers of this narrative short story is being hinted at. They are the faithful transmitters of information from king to prophet, from prophet to king, and from king to Rabshakeh; they are indispensable within the dramatic action of the story, and the reference to them in such specific terms may well be a signal of their greater importance behind the composition of these narratives.

In his role as emissary for the Assyrian king, the Rabshakeh uses speech forms reminiscent of those employed by Israel's prophets, who speak on behalf of the true king, the Holy One of Israel (Isa. 6:5). His first two addresses open with the words: "Thus says the great king" (36:4) and "Hear the words of the great king" (36:13). He wastes no time getting to the matter at hand, namely, trust (= "rely," *bth*, repeated six times within vv. 4–7)—the same trust commended by the prophet Isaiah when he spoke of "returning and rest, quietness and confidence *(bth)*" (30:15). From the mouth of a blasphemous Assyrian official we learn that Hezekiah has been following the counsel of the prophet Isaiah. The Rabshakeh regards this as foolishness, and the question must also arise for the reader: Will the prophet's counsel bear fruit? The stakes are awfully great at this juncture. Shall we trust the "Thus says the LORD" of Isaiah or the "Thus says the great king" of the Rabshakeh?

We mention the matter of authorship for chapters 36—37 above because it is clear that the report of Assyrian siege, including the long address of the Rabshakeh, has been composed with an eye toward the preaching of Isaiah. The Rabshakeh speaks of matters well known to those sitting on the wall within earshot (36:11), and his knowledge is not derived from inside information, as some have suggested (Rabshakeh as "secret agent"). Through and through, the speeches of the Rabshakeh reflect matters of burning importance for the people of Judah, and they have been shaped with those concerns in mind by an author from within Isaiah's circle. So, for example, while the speeches are ostensibly addressed to Hezekiah (36:4), from one king to another, they are in fact addressed to the people of Judah, and their main burden concerns Hezekiah's trust—is it misplaced or not? Hezekiah is on trial here. He is not just the eventual hearer of a message brokered by one emissary to another, a threesome of his own servants. There can be no answer to the Rabshakeh's appeal, because it is no appeal. It is a speech about proper trust (Hezekiah's) and the one who has been trusted (God). God will have to answer for himself. Hezekiah will have to be vindicated or exposed.

The first charge leveled by the Rabshakeh is that Hezekiah has placed false trust in Egypt. Is this charge based on accurate information? Has Hezekiah enlisted the Egyptians in his cause? As the story unfolds, the clear answer is no. Hezekiah never refers to such trust, and the Rabshakeh himself quickly moves away from this topic to another (36:7). If one charge fails, he moves to the next without regard for the larger consistency of his argument. He is right that trust in Egypt would be misplaced and would offer no security. But perhaps such trust might have seemed to be the right policy for those listening on the wall, and the Rabshakeh's chief concern is to discredit Hezekiah by any means possible. We learn that such trust, while it might delay the Assyrians (37:9), cannot decide the issue finally. The final issue—and this is the issue to which the speeches of the Rabshakeh quickly move—concerns Hezekiah's trust in Yahweh. On the way, the Rabshakeh tries to use Hezekiah's cult reforms against him (36:7), as signs of his putative lack of religious zeal (the more altars the better)—an ironic ploy that again reveals the sarcastic logic of an author from within Israel (viz., Assyrians believe gods prefer as many altars as possible). A similar irony is displayed in the final assertion, that the king of Assyria has come up to destroy Jerusalem at Yahweh's own command (36:10). As Smelik points out, this is nothing less than a blasphemous distortion of Isaiah's own Assyrian proclamation—the flattening out of a complex prophetic teaching (see 10:5–19) for the purpose of exploitation and propaganda.

247

The following unit (36:11–12) makes absolutely clear that the Rabshakeh has more in mind than the simple transmission of a message from Sennacherib to Hezekiah. The true audience for his message is already assembled, and he is literally seeking to speak their language. The Rabshakeh's address is for those sitting on the wall as much as for Hezekiah or the threesome (36:12). With this, the Rabshakeh raises his voice and repeats the language of royal—and for those sitting on the wall divine— address: "Hear the words of the great king, the king of Assyria! Thus says the king" (36:13–14a).

Now the illusion of a word from one king to another is dropped altogether, as the assembled Jerusalemites are directly addressed (36:14–20). What is striking is that Hezekiah is here characterized as one who fully trusts the Lord and the promise that the king of Assyria will be halted and Jerusalem delivered by God (36:15). At no point in the subsequent account does Isaiah the prophet indicate that he takes issue with Hezekiah's trust in Zion's deliverance. The enemy considers such trust deception, but we are clearly to regard it as proper trust congruent with the prophet's own teaching. The ever-resourceful Rabshakeh next moves to distort a known picture of šālôm by conflating it with the fruits of surrender: exile to Assyria, here depicted as a sort of new promised land (36:16–17).

The final charge is the culmination of all that precedes (36:18–20). Hezekiah's trust in Yahweh's ability to save is functionally equivalent to the claims of all the other nations and their gods. Now the blasphemy is revealed in all its virulence: Yahweh is not Lord of the nations but just another national god, about to suffer defeat as did the gods of Hamath, Arpad, and Sepharvaim. The final reference to Samaria's fallen deity might have caused the Jerusalemites on the wall to shudder—precisely the intention of the Rabshakeh's blasphemous charge— but all that the threesome do is fall obediently silent, according to the command of Hezekiah (36:21).

The rending of clothes, by Hezekiah's servants (36:22) and by Hezekiah himself, is a sign of distress at the content of the Rabshakeh's speech, similar to King Josiah's action at hearing the words of the Book of the Law read before him, aware of the disobedience of his people (II Kings 22:11–13; cf. Jer. 36:24). In Hezekiah's trip to the temple and in his revealed speech to the prophet Isaiah (37:3–4), the king's primary concern is not for his own welfare or for the fate of the city and its inhabitants. It is a day of distress, of rebuke, and of disgrace—because the Rab-shakeh has rebuked and mocked the living God! God has heard the blasphemous speech (37:4). The prophet Isaiah is asked to lift up a prayer for the surviving remnant. Here we touch upon the promise of a remnant as articulated at 6:13; 10:20–21. The question is, Will this surviving remnant take root downward and bear fruit upward (37:31)? We must still wait for the verdict.

The prophet's first response to the royal appeal is for Hezekiah not to be afraid (37:5–6). Again, similar counsel was given by Isaiah to King Ahaz (7:4). Will Hezekiah obey the prophet's exhortation and be established? Or will Israel again suffer because of the failure of the royal house to believe and stand firm? The prophet promises that Assyria's revilings will be judged and that the king of Assyria will himself meet a tragic end (cf. 7:8–9). He will hear a report and will return to his own land, and will fall there.

Bernhard Stade rightly noted that the fulfillment of the prophecy seemed to be delayed, if the concluding notice of Sennacherib's return and death was intended as that fulfillment (37:37–38). But Stade was wrong in therefore identifying the hearing by Sennacherib of the approach of Tirhakah (37:9) as a nearer fulfillment. The advance of Tirhakah is mentioned at this juncture to raise the possibility that Jerusalem might be saved by outside help after all. This would mean a victory over Sennacherib and a squelching of the boasting remarks of his servant the Rabshakeh (36:6), but it would be a defeat for Isaiah and Hezekiah. For the issue at hand is the blasphemy of the Assyrians, not the physical removal of danger from military assault. If the Assyrians were to retreat, and Jerusalem be freed from military threat, there would still be the matter of the Rabshakeh's speeches, which God has heard. And the prophet has promised more than retreat or return: he has promised death for a blasphemer, precisely where that blasphemer believes he can escape, gods being only national deities with national loyalties and national sovereignty. No, the retreat of Sennacherib is not enough. Nor is his death enough. At issue is the character of God's sovereignty, over Israel and over every nation on earth. Sennacherib must fall in his own land and, as we shall see, at an even more specific place within his country. In sum, the delay in the final denouement has been intentionally constructed.

249

In the final speech of the Assyrians (37:8–13) the true audience is at last King Hezekiah. The citizens of Jerusalem who were assembled on the wall have disappeared. The Rabshakeh has been replaced by anonymous messengers (was he judged a failure?) whose speech becomes in the end a letter, capable of personal reception by Hezekiah (37:14). Two points are made: God is a deceiver; no king has delivered. The final verse shows the shift from the charge of divine to royal impotence: "Where is the *king* of Hamath, the *king* of Arpad, the *king* of the city of Sepharvaim, the *king* of Hena, or the *king* of Ivvah?" (cf. 36:20). In this manner, King Hezekiah is left in the spotlight. What about the *king* of Jerusalem? Will he meet the same fate as these other kings? Another king comes to mind: Ahaz. Hezekiah had turned to the prophet Isaiah with a request for a prayer "for the remnant that is left" (37:4). Instead, he received a prophetic promise whose fulfillment has not yet come. We hear nothing of Isaiah's prayer on behalf of the remnant. The Assyrians are dealing with the king, not Isaiah the prophet. And so finally Hezekiah must act.

The next unit (37:14–20) shows a king who, unlike Ahaz, is willing to take action. Hezekiah receives the letter of abuse (including the charge "Do not let your God on whom you rely [*bṭḥ*] deceive you," 37:10) and heads for the temple. The only answer to these charges is from God, but first a swift and appropriate action by God's agent the king is required. By depicting Hezekiah at prayer on behalf of God's honor and in defense of the remnant, a royal figure accomplishes what was asked of a prophetic figure (37:4). No judgment is passed on Isaiah—he has responded already to the request of Hezekiah by means of a prophetic word (37:6–7). But the intercessory role is taken up by Hezekiah himself, in the temple. King and prophet work in tandem, and the contrast with Ahaz is further enhanced.

The formal prayer of the king is similar to his earlier appeal (37:3–4) in that what is chiefly of concern is the sovereignty of Yahweh over all the nations. Sennacherib has mocked Yahweh by likening him to the gods of the nations. But Hezekiah addresses Yahweh as God of Israel and God of all the kingdoms on earth (37:16), a confession underscored by the presentation of chapters 13—27. Hezekiah mentions his own deliverance and the saving of Jerusalem only in the context of God's honor and wider recognition by all the kingdoms of the earth (37:20).

The critical opinion is frequently rendered that these statements of God's fundamental uniqueness on the lips of Hezekiah belong to the later monotheistic logic of Second Isaiah and are therefore intrusive additions. But the theme of God's plan and purpose for the nations is well rooted in Isaiah's own oracles and derives from the prophet's statements regarding the role of Assyria, instrument of God's fury (10:5) yet functional only within the parameters of God's sovereign justice over all the earth (10:33–34; 14:24–27). We regard the appeal to Yahweh's fundamental uniqueness and control over the nations in Second Isaiah as based on just such a text as this; that is, the relationship is the reverse of that held by critical opinion, forward from "First" to "Second" Isaiah. This is why the confession of God's uniqueness in chapters 40—55 is so frequently accompanied by an appeal to "former things" (esp. 43:8–13; 44:6–8; 45:20–21). By "enclosing" the narratives of Jerusalem's deliverance in 701 B.C. within the broader "second" Isaiah perspective (chaps. 33—34; 40—66), Jerusalem's deliverance becomes a trustworthy example of God's ongoing care and concern for Zion. It is a "former thing" that testifies to God's sovereignty over the nations; to his uniqueness as a God who fulfills his word spoken beforehand, revealed to Israel alone; and to his abiding concern for Zion's welfare.

Similar language and concepts are to be found in the prophet's word (37:22–29), which accompanies and complements the royal prayer (37:15–20). Yet the issuance of a prophetic word is predicated on the prayer of Hezekiah, as Isaiah makes clear: "Because you have prayed to me concerning King Sennacherib of Assyria" (37:21). King and prophet work in tandem, each fulfilling the responsibilities appropriate to his office. The prophet, too, focuses not on Jerusalem's deliverance but on the hubris of Sennacherib and his royal Assyrian predecessors. Again the language of 10:5–19 lies close at hand: Assyria has felled the greatest forests, but in so doing the ax has vaunted itself over the one who hews it (10:15). It was the God of Israel who sent Assyria on a mission of judgment (37:26) in accordance with a plan set long ago. We heard of Assyria's arrogance earlier (10:13), but this time Assyria's words of rebuke have been uttered in Yahweh's own hearing (37:29) and in the hearing of his people, his king, and his prophet. The prophet repeats his earlier word: Sennacherib will be forcibly turned back (37:7; 37:29).

251

A following sign is given (37:30–32) as an assurance to King

Hezekiah. God will attend to the remnant, as Hezekiah had requested (37:4). Royal prayer and prophetic word converge. A sign is given for its own sake, and also to reinforce the contrast with Ahaz in the Syro-Ephraimite crisis, who refused to accept a sign when one was offered "deep as Sheol or high as heaven" (7:11). Now what is deep are the roots of the surviving remnant; what is high is the fruit borne upward (37:31).

The word of assurance regarding the fate of Sennacherib and his army concludes the prophetic address (37:33–35). What is striking is that, while we are accustomed to speaking of the "701 siege of Jerusalem," the final prophetic word understands the Assyrian assault somewhat differently. No siege has or ever will take place (37:33). Sennacherib remains with his army somewhere outside the city's environs, at Lachish (36:2) or Libnah (37:8), thus far attacking only by means of blasphemous speech. The city will be defended for the sake of God's own honor, which was called into question, and because of God's promises to David (37:35).

When in the final verses we hear of the Assyrian defeat (37:36–38), the episode is reported with an air of finality but also with a degree of mystery. We are not told exactly how 185,000 Assyrians are slain, only that when those in the camp arose in the morning, "they were all dead bodies" (37:36). It is striking that the Bible resists full explanation of a sort demanded by modern readers and is content with the more important confession that God was at work in the defeat. Then the final verses tell of the fulfillment of the prophet's word regarding Sennacherib. It is difficult to judge which the author of the story regards as more dramatic: the death of thousands of Assyrians in the camp or the death of one Sennacherib. The Assyrian king not only falls "by the sword in his own land" (37:7), as promised. He is slain by his own sons (37:38). He is not just back in Nineveh: he dies while worshiping Nisroch his god. As one scholar has put it: Sennacherib and the reader learn "A blasphemer is nowhere safe from the power of the omnipotent God" (Smelik, *Distortion*, p. 84).

In our judgment, because modern scholarship has been chiefly interested in determining how the army of Sennacherib was felled in the events of 701 B.C. (or if it was felled at all), the design of the narrative in its present form has often been ignored in the name of sifting out "objective" records uncontaminated by theological bias (here the Annals of Sennacherib

252

are curiously regarded as more "historical" than biblical records, although the former's thoroughgoing tone of bombast and exaggeration certainly bears out the truth of the latter's presentation of Assyrian hubris). If any one statement could characterize the chapters before us, it is that they are relentlessly theological. The chief issue at every point is the sovereignty of Yahweh over all the kingdoms of the earth.

In this regard it is a striking fact that the actual report of Assyrian defeat is given in as compressed a fashion as possible: one verse tells the whole story (37:36). The defeat is accompanied by no lengthy peroration, no gloating, and, as noted above, no explanation as to what really happened or how the Assyrians died. The verse is left to relate a wonder, and that is all that it does. In our judgment, the defeat of the Assyrian army was never as important a datum as the death of Sennacherib for the composers of Isaiah 36—37. The defeat served the purpose of leading to the Assyrian king's withdrawal (confirmed by Assyrian records)—this is the report that Sennacherib was to hear that would cause him to return to his own land (37:7). But the attention of the narrator remains with Sennacherib and his fate in Assyria: a matter of grave concern, given the prophecy by Isaiah at 37:7. The defeat of the army releases Jerusalem from danger, but the story is not over until the divine word spoken by Isaiah is fulfilled.

It remains an ironic fact, given the interest of historians in the events of 701 B.C., that the one historical datum generally agreed upon is that Sennacherib was assassinated by his own sons (not immediately upon return but subsequently). It is toward that historical datum that the narrative in its present form strains, not willing to halt at the defeat of the Assyrian army, however dramatic. Sennacherib's death in Nineveh, the narrative argues, was prophesied by Isaiah and came about as a result of his blasphemy against the God of Israel, God of all the kingdoms on earth. With his death, Jerusalem was not forever freed from Assyrian threat. Esar-haddon, son of Sennacherib, reigned in his stead (37:38) and with a vigor that would have made his father proud and that Judah would soon experience in full measure. But the blasphemous words of Sennacherib and his officials are rebuked, and the theological point the narrative wishes to make is made: Jerusalem is saved from the hand of Sennacherib   253
so that all the kingdoms on earth might know that Yahweh is God alone (37:20).

Isaiah 38:1–22
The Power of Prayer

As should be clear from the title of the preceding section, the story of Jerusalem's deliverance in 701 B.C. not only charts the fall of a blasphemer, it also plots the rise of the king of Judah, Hezekiah. The king's prayer and appeal lead to Jerusalem's salvation and Yahweh's vindication before the nations. At every point along the way he is set in contrast to his father, Ahaz. Moreover, the composition of the narrative points to Hezekiah as the fulfillment of promises uttered by Isaiah in the days of the Syro-Ephraimite crisis. Assyria defeats the Northern Kingdom and assaults the vineyard even to the neck (8:8), but the counsel of the nations comes to naught, "for God is with us" (8:10). Hezekiah reigns in righteousness, and in the language of 33:17, "your eyes will see the king in his beauty."

The curious order of accounts in chapters 36—39 has already been referred to. Merodach-baladan's incursions into the region—searching for assistance against Assyria—most likely preceded the 701 B.C. assault on Judah, even though the present arrangement has the visit of his emissaries last (39:1–8). Moreover, nothing is said in the final chapter about possible political alliance against Assyria, as attractive as this explanation is on historical grounds. The Babylonian visitors come bearing gifts, having heard of Hezekiah's sickness and recovery. As such, in its present form chapter 39 presupposes the account of Hezekiah's sickness now supplied in chapter 38. Similarly, chapter 38 does not flow altogether smoothly from the report of Jerusalem's deliverance, insofar as reference is made at 38:6 to the city's recovery in the same breath as Hezekiah's recovery. God promises to "deliver you and this city out of the hand of the king of Assyria, and defend this city" (38:6).

On formal grounds, there is a great deal of similarity between the story of Sennacherib's fall and the story of Hezekiah's recovery. The former ends with Sennacherib's death, while the latter opens with Hezekiah's near-death (38:1). We see the same sequence of prophetic word (v. 1), royal prayer (vv. 2–3), further prophetic word (vv. 4–6), sign (vv. 7–8), and delivery from death

254

(v. 19) as in the preceding story (word, 37:5–7; prayer, 37:15–20; word, 37:22–29; sign, 37:30–32; deliverance, 37:36–38). The chief difference is that the prophetic word is reversed by the royal prayer, and the deliverance from death is handled through the long psalm of Hezekiah with which the account concludes (38:9–22).

This similar sequencing can hardly be accidental, and indeed it points to a conscious development of chapter 38 on the basis of the preceding narrative of Jerusalem's deliverance. Now the "near-death" of Jerusalem is explored by linking it with the king's fatal illness. What is also explored in more detail in chapter 38 is the power of royal intercessory prayer and the figure of Hezekiah as righteous supplicant (38:9–22). In sum, the relationship between the two accounts in chapters 36—37 and 38 is not simply one of chronological sequence: first, delivery of the city, then royal recovery. The collapsing of the fate of the city and the king's return to health at 38:6 prevent such an interpretation. Rather, the relationship between the two is more typological. Hezekiah is first established as a king with authority as a supplicant on Jerusalem's behalf, and then that authority is explored in detail in chapter 38.

As noted above in our discussion of Isaiah 36—37, the tendency has been to regard chapter 38 as a secondary deviation from a better preserved account in the Books of Kings (II Kings 20:1–11). It is to be noted immediately that the accounts diverge from each other. The psalm of Hezekiah in Isa. 38:9–20 is missing altogether in Kings. But the material held in common is placed in a different sequence. Isaiah receives a special word telling him to return and pronounce a positive word on the king (II Kings 20:4), while there is no indication of the prophet's distance—or proximity—to the king in Isaiah 38. Second, the prophet promises that the king will visit the temple in three days (II Kings 20:5), a theme handled at the end of the Isaiah version (Isa. 38:22). Third, the prophet orders a medical treatment after the promise of recovery (II Kings 20:7), a theme again dealt with after the royal psalm (Isa. 38:21). Fourth, the sign given by the prophet no longer serves to confirm the promise of recovery, as in Isaiah, but is now linked to the king's question about when he should go up to the temple (II Kings 20:8)—even though he had already been told he would go up in three days (II Kings 20:5). Finally, and most radically divergent, when the sign is offered by Isaiah, the king is given an "easier" and a "harder" version to choose from, and he picks the latter. The account ends with the prophet accomplishing what the king had asked, despite its difficulty (II Kings 20:11).

It is fairly easy to spot these divergences between Kings and Isaiah, but how are we to evaluate them? In the past, one searched for an original account and then tried to explain the deviations from the original, in both Kings and Isaiah. It does seem to be the case that the Kings version has enhanced the role of the prophet Isaiah, who cries to the Lord and succeeds in bringing the shadow back ten steps (II Kings 20:11). Can we be sure in every instance that an enhancement of Isaiah also means a demotion of Hezekiah (he asks for the harder sign)? And what about the order of each account taken on its own? Most regard the order of Kings to be more original and more sensible than what we have in Isaiah, which ends, for example, with a question (Isa. 38:22). Yet how is one to interpret the merger of the sign theme with the question about visiting the temple in Kings (II Kings 20:8)? This merger is also confusing, given the three-day reference at II Kings 20:5.

We have also made note already of the fact that the sequence in Isaiah 38 appears to be modeled on a pattern already found in the story of Jerusalem's deliverance. This pattern is not followed in Kings, which goes its own way with the logic of the king's sickness and recovery. In our view, the two accounts have taken slightly different shape because of the influence exercised by their respective contexts. The larger Deuteronomistic History must present a wider view of kingship beyond the reigns of Ahaz and Hezekiah, and it works with a systematic understanding of response (or nonresponse) to the prophetic word. The Book of Isaiah is more specifically interested in the contrast between Ahaz and Hezekiah, the effect of royal petition on the fate of the nation, and the sickness and recovery of city and king.

In the opening chapter of Isaiah, we heard of a nation whose whole head was sick (1:5):

> From the sole of the foot even to the head,
>   there is no soundness in it,
> but bruises and sores
>   and bleeding wounds;
> they have not been drained, or bound up,
>   or softened with oil.
>
> (Isa. 1:6)

Israel, despite its sickness, refuses to turn to Yahweh and as such continues to be smitten (1:5). We conjectured that the opening chapter reflects a situation of refusal, on the wider Israel's part, to heed the gracious deliverance of Jerusalem in 701 B.C. and to change its ways, following the lead of its king. The result can only be a return to the pre-701 B.C. period of warning and renewed threat against Israel's leaders (cf. chaps. 28—31).

Chapter 38 presents a king sick from head to foot, at the point of death (v. 1), consigned to the gates of Sheol for the rest of his days (v. 10). His fate is likened to that of the city itself (v. 6). He has heard the prophetic pronouncement to put his house in order, "for you shall die; you shall not recover" (v. 1). All appears to be lost. What can the king do? The word of the prophet has gone forth, and it is a word of death, not life. The prophet leaves no route open, no possibility of altering the sentence.

But picking up from the portrayal of chapter 37, where the king's prayer also turned back what appeared to be a sentence of death for Zion, so too here Hezekiah follows the only path left: he prays (38:2). He takes a stand on the basis of his faithfulness before God—something the nation cannot do! God hears the prayer, as in chapter 37, and a new prophetic word goes forth: a promise of new life is granted for the king (38:5). But more than this: the royal prayer also saves a city that has no record of faithfulness to fall back on or on the basis of which to appeal to God's mercy. The city is saved by the prayer of the king, by his years of faithful service, and by his walking before God with a whole heart (compare the "whole heart faint" of 1:5). What the city cannot do on its own merit, the king can and does.

Those who regard the order in the Kings account as more logical and more original generally fail to see that Hezekiah has not been healed of his sickness at this point but has only been given a pledge of new life. The same movement can be spotted in chapter 37, where the prophetic word for new life is announced through the promise of removal of the Assyrian threat (37:7, 29), while the reader (and the king and city) must wait patiently for the actual turning back of Sennacherib (37:36–38). What the prophet does grant in the interim is a sign (37:30–32). It is not surprising that so too the prophet issues a sign here (38:7–8). While the image of the sundial and its steps ("hour" markers) is somewhat obscure, and has been differently inter-

257

preted, the mention of Ahaz ought to catch our attention. The moving back of the sun's shadow ten steps may be nothing more than a way of saying that Ahaz's refusal to believe (and accept a sign such as this) is being covered by Hezekiah's righteous deportment. Hezekiah has "turned back the clock" by his prayer and life of faithfulness. The city is delivered and the royal house is given a pledge of additional life. The Kings account has dealt with the sign motif and the healing in a very different way, so that the active intervention of the prophet might be emphasized.

So too the active role of Hezekiah has been diminished in Kings, which does not include the following psalm of the king (38:9–20). The psalm's superscription (v. 9) is most certainly intended to put us in mind of the psalms of King David, whom we are told Hezekiah emulated fully: "He did what was right in the sight of the LORD just as his ancestor David had done" (II Kings 18:3). The omission of the psalm in Kings may have to do with the eventual working out of the relationship between Hezekiah and Josiah, who receive equally high marks (paradoxically, both are "number one" in the class) in the final evaluation of the Deuteronomistic Historian (cf. II Kings 18:5 and 23:25). But in Isaiah, there is no doubt about Hezekiah's quintessential faithfulness. In fact, although the record is much briefer and of an altogether different nature, Hezekiah even threatens to outshine the figure of David.

The psalm's superscription is interpreted by the NRSV as indicating that the following prayer was uttered *after* the king was sick and had recovered. As such, the psalm is interpreted as a thanksgiving for healing, somewhat similar to the psalm of Jonah (Jonah 2:2–9). Yet unlike the prayer of Jonah, Hezekiah's psalm is primarily comprised of a description of distress and lamentation (38:10–15) and an appeal for healing (38:16–18). Only in verse 19 does one have a clear sense of the turning of God in favor toward the supplicant, such that the king in the final verse (v. 20) looks forward to his return to full life and full participation in the worship of God in the temple. Given the content of the psalm, a more appropriate translation of the superscription would read: "A writing *(miktāb)* of Hezekiah, king of Judah, when he was sick and survived his illness." This allows the temporal perspective to move gradually from sickness to health rather than placing all the emphasis on the recovery as a past reality. For, as was stated above, Hezekiah's full

258

recovery has only been promised (38:6). The psalm shows the king in a stance of prayer and lamentation and appeal, out of which new life is granted—not by prophetic promise alone but by a direct divine turning toward the supplicant.

In fact, we regard the function of the psalm of Hezekiah as having to do with the power of prayer in effecting new life. It had already been established in chapter 37 just how vital the prayer of the king was in delivering the city (37:21). In chapter 38 we also see the prayer of the king diverting a sentence of death uttered by the prophet Isaiah (38:2–3). The psalm of Hezekiah continues to pursue the significance of prayer for affecting the will of God. We have heard of God's will in the context of prophetic promise (38:5: "Thus says the LORD"). But the psalm goes yet farther by allowing us to hear of God's gracious turning to the supplicant in the context of his very praying. Moreover, the illness of Hezekiah is taken seriously on its own terms in 38:9–22, quite apart from the fate of the city (38:6).

Using language already quite familiar from the psalter, Hezekiah describes his plight (38:10–15). As indicated in the opening verse (38:1), and here described in a moving, personal way, the king is near to death (38:10). Though he has years remaining in his life, they will be spent apart from the land of the living (38:11), apart from the praise of God. God, the source of all life and health, is also the one whom the psalmist acknowledges as bringing on pain and suffering (38:12–15). At the same time, God is put in mind of the loss of one faithful soul, should Hezekiah be cast down into Sheol forever (cf. Ps. 30:9: "What profit is there in my death . . . ? Will the dust praise you? Will it tell of your faithfulness?"). Hezekiah makes appeal to the one God who holds life and death in his hands (38:16–18). And with the same sort of mysterious movement also to be noted in psalms of lament, suddenly the skies clear and the supplicant knows that his prayer is heard: "The living, the living, they thank you, as I do this day" (38:19). In the final verse the supplicant speaks in the indicative of God's healing (38:20). There is to be a future in the land of the living for Hezekiah, and that future will be spent—as at key moments in the past (see 37:1–4; 37:14–20)—in the house of the Lord. The first-person plural at 38:20 points ahead to a Hezekiah fully rejoined to the company of the faithful.

259

The governing opinion concerning the last two verses

(38:21–22) is that they somehow dropped out of their rightful position (i.e., as evidenced in the Kings version; see II Kings 20:5–8). The sign referred to at verse 22 was therefore first connected to the sign of the dial of Ahaz at verses 7–8, a connection better preserved in Kings. When an editor noticed that the connection had been lost, he decided to drop the verses in at the end so that they would not be lost altogether.

As theories run, this theory is as good as any, if one is prepared to accept that the Isaiah text has disturbed a connection that is better preserved in Kings. In our judgment, the connection between the sign for going to the temple and the sign of the dial of Ahaz is not an original or a better-preserved connection; actually, it introduces a confusing sequence in Kings. The king is told he will go to the temple in three days (II Kings 20:5); he then asks what the sign will be that he should go to the temple (II Kings 20:8); and when the sign is given, it involves the dial of Ahaz and a test for the prophet (II Kings 20:10).

When one returns to the Isaiah version, several factors argue in favor of a logical position at the conclusion of the story. First, as noted above, from Isa. 38:9 onward we are getting essentially a repeat of the royal prayer//prophetic response sequence provided in 38:1–8, only a much more detailed one so far as the royal prayer is concerned. Again the king prays, now following the model provided by King David in the psalms, with full description of distress, lamentation, and appeal; again the prophet responds (the pluperfect "had" in the NRSV is just a grammatical version of the displacement theory and cannot be justified on the basis of the Hebrew alone). The full recovery of the king, in medical terms, still lies in the future (so both 38:5–6 and 38:20). The prophet prescribes the proper medical treatment, to which the king obediently adds a question concerning the proper timetable for his return to the temple, a return spoken of at the conclusion of the psalm ("all the days of our lives, at the house of the LORD"). While the king has received in the psalm a direct divine response to his illness (v. 19), requiring no prophetic intervention (vv. 4–6), nevertheless the prophet takes up what appears to be a priestly role in stipulating the proper period for cleansing before a visit to the temple can occur (see Leviticus 13—14 for the determination of disease and proper cleansing and medical treatments).

260

In sum, the final two verses, far from being dropped in by an editor so as not to be lost, serve an important function in the larger shape and movement of the chapter. The complementary nature of the relationship between Hezekiah and Isaiah is preserved, even as the powerful authority of royal prayer is explored, both in affecting the destiny of Zion and for its own sake, as linked to the health and future of King Hezekiah.

We are accustomed to holding fixed notions about what kingship was all about in Israel: warfare, taxes, the state, government, life at court, civil and religious reform, or the lack of it. The Psalter has recognized another critical royal trait that undergirds all these several aspects of kingship and leads either to commonweal or to the utter dissolution of Israel, nation and royal head. That trait, shared by common Israelite, prophet and priest, but especially notable for its presence or absence in the royal house, is prayer. Hezekiah follows David in all that he does, as we learn at II Kings 18:3. The Book of Isaiah has paid particular attention to the way Hezekiah has emulated David as a man of prayer. Hezekiah's prayers deliver the city in time of crisis, turning back a sentence of death. These prayers also reveal a man after the prophet Isaiah's heart: a man who follows the counsel of returning and rest, quietness and confidence, a counsel that cannot be followed apart from the life of prayer. While the blasphemer goes from life to death, the man of prayer goes from death to life.

Isaiah 39:1–8
The Word of the Lord Is Good

In comparison with the preceding three chapters in this larger Hezekiah presentation, the final chapter presents unique problems for the interpreter. First of all, unlike chapters 36—38 there is no significant variation between the Isaiah narrative and the account in Kings (II Kings 20:12–19). On the surface, this should make the task of interpretation easier. Yet—and herein one faces the second unique feature of chapter 39—both Kings and Isaiah present a portrait of Hezekiah that seems to depart radically from the presentation of him in Isaiah 36—38, and for that matter in II Kings 18:13—20:18. The king appears to be chastised by the prophet for his actions vis-à-vis the delegation of Merodach-baladan (39:2). The prophet announces that

261

everything Hezekiah showed the Babylonian envoys will later be hauled off by them, and in addition some of his own sons will be carried into exile (39:5–7). If the translation "eunuchs" at verse 7 is correct (instead of minor officials), then Isaiah also is made to predict the end of the royal line, or at least the exclusion of some potential candidates. Hezekiah the righteous supplicant either wittingly or unwittingly brings about the exile and the end of the Davidic monarchy through his actions with the envoys of Merodach-baladan.

Yet there are some problems with this essentially straightforward reading, quite apart from the fact of its radical departure from the Hezekiah presentation that precedes. First, the motivation for Hezekiah's decision to show the emissaries his treasure houses and storehouses is never stated explicitly. If one assumes a judgment oracle directed by the prophet to the king on the basis of these actions, then perhaps Hezekiah is judged for gloating over his military and economic strength. But this is never made clear. Second, and related to this, while the prophetic word that tells of Babylonian exile is certainly a negative pronouncement, the link between that pronouncement and the king's action is never explicitly made, namely, "Because *(kî)* you have done this, hear the word of the LORD." Rather, the exile is simply announced as a fact, once the prophet determines from the king *where* the envoys have come from and *what* they said (39:3–4). Third, and derived from this observation, is the curious response of the king recorded at the final verse (39:8). The NRSV translation makes it sound as though the king responds favorably at first, *but then said to himself,* in effect, "At least *I* will not have to be hauled off into exile" (Hebrew reads, "and he said"; NRSV, "for he thought"). The Kings reading is even more extreme: "Why not, if there will be peace and security in my days?" (II Kings 20:19). Not a particularly generous remark on the king's part, given the fact of his prior decision to show these future marauders everything in the realm!

Yet, as Ackroyd has carefully noted, there are problems with this *après moi le déluge* interpretation of Hezekiah's final response (Ackroyd, "Babylonian Exile"). Is it really likely that the king responded positively to the prophetic word, but then said selfishly, as if under his breath: "Well, at least I'm off the hook"? Ackroyd is also puzzled by the report of the Chronicler at this juncture (II Chron. 32:31). While the Chronicler has no access to special records that would shed light on the "matter of the envoys of the officials of Babylon" (II Chron. 32:31), nevertheless his is an early reading of the terse report in Isaiah 39 (II Kings 20:12–19). The Chronicler sees the encounter between the envoys and Hezekiah as a sort of test: the king is left alone so that God might know what is in his heart. Though it is not stated explicitly, the context implies that Hezekiah passed the test (the following verse speaks of his good deeds). Ackroyd conjectures that the test involved Hezekiah's response to the prophetic word. He passes the test in that he responds positively to the divine judgment: "The word of the LORD that you have spoken is good" (Isa. 39:8).

Several other observations can be added to those of Ackroyd. First, the Chronicler is by no means interested in whitewashing Hezekiah or eliminating the negative features of the record as found in Kings (and Isaiah). The Chronicler, for example, regards the king's chief crime to have been his refusal to deal appropriately with the prophetic sign granted him during his illness (II Kings 20:8–11): "Hezekiah did not respond according to the benefit done to him, for his heart was proud" (II Chron. 32:25). As a consequence, "wrath came upon him and upon Judah and Jerusalem" (32:25). The Chronicler can spot wrongdoing in the royal house during Hezekiah's tenure, but he sees the sign incident as more critical than the visit of the envoys, which was a test that the king passed.

Second, as to the king's final response, "And he said, 'There will be peace and security in my days'" (Isa. 39:8), a similar handling of royal exemption from a larger judgment can also be noted during the reign of Josiah, Hezekiah's only righteous peer before the fall of the state. Because Judah has sinned grievously against the law of God, God's wrath is kindled against them (II Kings 23:15–17)—this is the judgment of the prophet Huldah, who functions on analogy to the prophet Isaiah. Because Josiah responded appropriately to the Book of the Law (as did Hezekiah upon hearing the blasphemous speech of the Assyrians), the prophet exempts him from the judgment: "I will gather you to your ancestors, and you shall be gathered to your grave in peace; your eyes shall not see all the disaster that I will bring on this place" (II Kings 22:20). A similar exemption is provided for Hezekiah, and in that sense his response is no selfish *après moi le déluge* but a realistic appraisal of God's mercy directed to him, similar to the mercy granted to Josiah in his day.

The question still remains, What was Hezekiah doing with the envoys of the prince of Babylon? What is the point the author of the story wishes to make? It is interesting to note that the Chronicler has compressed the entire account into a single-verse appraisal, emphasizing the motif of a test for the king (II Chron. 32:31). Or so it would seem. For the single-verse appraisal is now placed at the end of a larger unit dealing with Hezekiah's wealth (32:27–30), in which Hezekiah's treasuries and storehouses are referred to. Isaiah 39 also speaks of the royal treasuries and of Hezekiah's accumulated goods (39:2, 6). The Chronicler may well be suggesting that precisely by showing the Babylonian envoys his great wealth, and all that was in his realm, he passed the test for which God had left him to himself.

The reference to having been left alone may more specifically refer to Hezekiah's having acted apart from prophetic counsel in the matter of the envoys, and this in contrast to the other episode in which foreign emissaries played an important role (chaps. 36—37). The prophet Isaiah does not appear until 39:3, and then with the question, "From where did they come to you?" Quite apart from the question under discussion—that is, how do we evaluate the actions of Hezekiah in this chapter?—the narrative also seeks to portray the prophet Isaiah as a man who makes a discovery, Hezekiah having been left to himself (as the Chronicler puts it) for the beginning of the episode.

Several factors are becoming clearer about this terse report of visitors from the Babylonian prince in Isaiah 39. First, the Chronicler has understood Hezekiah's treasuries and storehouses as signs of divine blessing (II Chron. 32:27–30), and he speaks of this in the same context as the report of Babylonian envoys (II Chron. 32:31). He does not negatively judge the king's decision to display these treasures—nothing is said about this—and if anything he appears to regard the king's action favorably. Second, in the context of Isaiah 39, the prophet Isaiah is depicted as making a discovery, because the king was left by himself (as the Chronicler puts it) at the beginning of the chapter. Third, the final response of the king need not be read in a negative light. Rather, the response functions to make clear that Hezekiah, like Josiah after him, will, as righteous king, be exempted from the coming judgment over Judah.

On the basis of these observations, can a coherent view of

Isaiah 39 be put forward? The opening verse depicts the envoys of Merodach-baladan coming to Jerusalem for the express purpose of presenting King Hezekiah with a gift. In and of itself, this action is significant. Where once we had envoys bearing blasphemous speech, here we have envoys bearing gifts. Rather than Israel paying tribute to Egypt or Assyria, here Babylon pays tribute to Jerusalem and its king. It is precisely in this spirit that Hezekiah welcomes them; the Hebrew at verse 2 reads, "and Hezekiah rejoiced because of them." In this mood of rejoicing he shows them all his treasures and everything in the realm. There is no suggestion that such a display is being portrayed negatively. Here the Chronicler has caught the right tone: these treasures are—like his recovery from illness that the envoys have come to honor—signs of God's blessing. It should not be forgotten, when one considers the wider context of the Hezekiah presentation, that the treasures are also a sign of Jerusalem's victory: the Assyrian assault on Jerusalem failed miserably.

Ackroyd is right in emphasizing the relationship between the king's action and the following prophetic word, but the difficult issue is how to understand the nature of the relationship. Hezekiah shows them everything; Isaiah indicates that everything shown will be carried off. But before he makes this prediction, he must ask the king a question, since he was not present during the envoys' visit (so the narrative would have it). He asks two questions, and the latter is answered first (39:3). Because no answer is given to the former, we can safely assume the prophet had received the answer he really wanted. Nothing more needed to be said.

The word order of the king's answer is significant. The Hebrew can be translated: "and Hezekiah said, from a country far off they came to me, from Babylon." The reference to "country far off" (Heb.: *mē'ereṣ rĕḥôqāh*) is general, but it may have a more significant ring for the prophet, as the narrative is presently constructed. We know from the larger nations section, and especially its introductory chapters (chaps. 13—14), that Assyria will be replaced by Babylon in days to come as part of God's larger plan concerning the whole earth (14:26). In chapter 13 a nation is summoned "from a distant land" *(mē'ereṣ merḥāq).* Is the narrative trying to say here that the larger purpose of God is unfolding now, even during the reign of King Hezekiah, through this mysterious visit of Babylonian envoys?

265

If so, the emphasis need not be on the disobedient actions of Hezekiah—which would represent an obvious departure from his portrayal elsewhere—but solely on the divine purpose mysteriously unfolding. Hezekiah is not condemned by the prophet. Rather, Isaiah inquires from what region the envoys came, and he hears first, "from afar," and then, "from Babylon."

The author of chapter 39 has used this visit of tribute-bearing Babylonians to point to a future beyond Hezekiah's responsibility or even apprehension. He hears the divine word of coming judgment, but in the end he can say without a hint of gloating or selfish disregard, "There will be peace and security in my days." The king's actions—never condemned by the prophet—merely point to days beyond his knowing, days to come (v. 5). The address of the prophet is ostensibly directed to the king, but in fact it is directed to the reader. God has not forgotten his plan of old in the jubilant aftermath of Zion's deliverance and in days of recovery and tribute. But it is finally a plan that does not concern King Hezekiah: there will be peace and security in his days.

It would probably be going beyond the narrative to regard, as does the Chronicler, Hezekiah's display of his treasures as a sign of his righteousness, though such a reading cannot be ruled out. But the narrative is simply too terse at this point and is finally concerned with a more important issue than Hezekiah's deportment, namely, the coming transition from Assyrian defeat to Babylonian fulfillment of the larger plan of God concerning the whole earth.

BIBLIOGRAPHY

1. For further study

BECKER, JOACHIM. *Isaias—der Prophet und sein Buch.* STUTTGARTER BIBELSTUDIEN 30 (Stuttgart: Katholisches Bibelwerk, 1968).

CHILDS, BREVARD S. *Isaiah and the Assyrian Crisis.* STUDIES IN BIBLICAL THEOLOGY 3 (Naperville, Ill.: Alec R. Allenson, 1967).

CLEMENTS, RONALD. *Isaiah 1—39.* NEW CENTURY BIBLE COMMENTARIES (Grand Rapids: Wm. B. Eerdmans Publishing Co., 1980).

———. *Isaiah and the Deliverance of Jerusalem.* JOURNAL FOR THE STUDY OF THE OLD TESTAMENT—SUPPLEMENT SERIES 13 (Sheffield: JSOT Press, 1980).

CONRAD, EDGAR W. *Reading Isaiah.* OVERTURES TO BIBLICAL THEOLOGY (Minneapolis: Fortress Press, 1991).

DUHM, BERNHARD. *Das Buch Jesaia* (Göttingen: Vandenhoeck & Ruprecht, 1892).

GITAY, YEHOSHUA. *Isaiah and His Audience: The Structure and Meaning of Isaiah 1—12* (Assen: Van Gorcum, 1991).

GOTTWALD, NORMAN K. "Immanuel as the Prophet's Son." *Vetus Testamentum* 8:36–47 (1958).

HARDMEIER, CHRISTOF. *Prophetie im Streit vor dem Untergang Judas.* BEIHEFTE ZUR ZEITSCHRIFT FÜR DIE ALTTESTAMENTLICHE WISSENSCHAFT 187 (Berlin: Walter de Gruyter, 1990).

JONES, DOUGLAS R. "The Traditio of the Oracles of Isaiah of Jerusalem." *Zeitschrift für die alttestamentliche Wissenschaft* 26:226–246 (1955).

KAISER, OTTO. *Isaiah 1—12.* OLD TESTAMENT LIBRARY. 2nd ed. (Philadelphia: Westminster Press, 1983).

———. *Isaiah 13—39.* OLD TESTAMENT LIBRARY (Philadelphia: Westminster Press, 1974).

SEITZ, CHRISTOPHER R., ed. *Reading and Preaching the Book of Isaiah* (Philadelphia: Fortress Press, 1988).

SHEPPARD, GERALD T. "Isaiah 1—39." In *Harper's Bible Commentary,* ed. by James L. Mays (San Francisco: Harper & Row, 1988), pp. 542–570.

VERMEYLEN, JACQUES, ed. *The Book of Isaiah* (Louvain: University Press, 1989).

WATTS, JOHN D. W. *Isaiah 1—33.* WORD BIBLICAL COMMEN-
TARY (Waco, Tex.: Word Books, 1985).
———. *Isaiah 34 66.* WORD BIBLICAL COMMENTARY (Waco,
Tex.: Word Books, 1987).
WILDBERGER, H. *Isaiah: A Commentary.* CONTINENTAL
COMMENTARIES (Minneapolis: Fortress Press, 1990).

2. Literature cited

ACKROYD, PETER R. "An Interpretation of the Babylonian
Exile." *Scottish Journal of Theology* 27:328–352 (1974).
———. "Isaiah I—XII: Presentation of a Prophet." *Vetus Tes-
tamentum,* Supplement 29:16–48 (1978).
———. "Isaiah 36—39: Structure and Function." In *Von Kana-
an bis Kerala. Festschrift für Prof. Mag. Dr. Dr. J. P. M. van
der Ploeg, O. P. zur Vollendung des siebzigsten Lebens-
jahres am 4. Juli 1979,* ed. by W. C. Delsman, J. T. Nelis, J.
R. T. M. Peters, W. H. Ph. Romer, and A. S. Van der Woude
(Neukirchen-Vluyn: Neukirchener Verlag, 1982), pp. 3–21.
ANDERSON, BERNHARD W. " 'God with Us'—In Judgment
and in Mercy: The Editorial Structure of Isaiah 5—10 (11)."
In *Canon, Theology, and Old Testament Interpretation.*
Festschrift B. S. Childs (Philadelphia: Fortress Press, 1988).
BARTH, HERMANN. *Die Jesaja-Worte in der Josiazeit: Israel
und Assur als Thema einer produktiven Neuinterpretation
der Jesajaüberlieferung.* WISSENSCHAFTLICHE MONOGRA-
PHIEN ZUM ALTEN UND NEUEN TESTAMENT 48 (Neukir-
chen-Vluyn: Neukirchener Verlag, 1977).
CHILDS, BREVARD S. *Introduction to the Old Testament as
Scripture* (Philadelphia: Fortress Press, 1979).
CLEMENTS, RONALD. "The Prophecies of Isaiah and the Fall
of Jerusalem in 587 B.C." *Vetus Testamentum* 30:421–436
(1980).
———. *Isaiah 1—39.* (See Bibliography 1.)
———. "Beyond Tradition-History: Deutero-Isaianic Development of First Isaiah's Themes." *Journal for the Study of the
Old Testament* 31:95–113 (1985).
———. "The Immanuel Prophecy of Isa. 7:10–17 and Its Mes-
sianic Interpretation." In *Die Hebräische Bibel und ihre
zweifache Nachgeschichte. Festschrift für Rolf Rendtorff
zum 65. Geburtstag,* ed. by E. Blum, C. Macholz, and E. W.
Stegemann (Neukirchen-Vluyn: Neukirchener Verlag,
1991), pp. 225–240.

CONRAD, EDGAR W. (See Bibliography 1.)

DAVIES, GRAHAM. "The Destiny of the Nations in the Book of Isaiah." In *The Book of Isaiah*, ed. by Jacques Vermeylen (Louvain: University Press, 1989).

ERLANDSSON, S. *The Burden of Babylon: A Study of Isaiah 13:2—14:23.* CONIECTANEA BIBLICA OLD TESTAMENT SERIES 4 (Lund: CWK Gleerup, 1970).

GESE, HARMUT. "Natus ex Virgine." In *Probleme biblischer Theologie. Gerhard von Rad zum 70. Geburtstag* (Munich: Chr. Kaiser Verlag, 1971), pp. 73–89.

GESENIUS, W. *Philologisch-kritischer und historischer Commentar über den Jesaia* (Leipzig: F. C. W. Vogel, 1821).

HAMBORG, G. R. "Reasons for Judgement in the Oracles Against the Nations of the Prophet Isaiah." *Vetus Testamentum* 31:145–159 (1981).

HAYES, JOHN. "The Usage of Oracles Against Foreign Nations in Ancient Israel." *Journal of Biblical Literature* 87:81–92 (1968).

HAYES, JOHN, and STUART IRVINE. *Isaiah, the Eighth-Century Prophet: His Times and His Preaching* (Nashville: Abingdon Press, 1987).

JENKINS, A. K. "The Development of the Isaiah Tradition in Isaiah 13—23." In *The Book of Isaiah*, ed. by Jacques Vermeylen (Louvain: University Press, 1989).

JOHNSON, DAN G. *From Chaos to Restoration: An Integrative Reading of Isaiah 24—27.* JOURNAL FOR THE STUDY OF THE OLD TESTAMENT—SUPPLEMENT SERIES 61 (Sheffield: JSOT Press, 1988).

KAISER, OTTO. (See Bibliography 1.)

KEIL, KARL FRIEDRICH. *Manual of Historico-Critical Introduction to the Canonical Scriptures of the Old Testament*, trans. from the 2nd ed. by C. M. Douglas. 2 vols. (Edinburgh: T. & T. Clark, 1870–1871), pp. 281–332.

LAATO, ANTTI. *Who Is Immanuel? The Rise and Foundering of Isaiah's Messianic Expectations.* (Turku, Finland: Åbo Academy Press, 1988).

LOHFINK, NORBERT. "Die Gattung der 'Historischen Kurzgeschichte' in den letzten Jahren von Juda und in der Zeit des Babylonischen Exils." *Zeitschrift für die alttestamentliche Wissenschaft* 90:319–347 (1986).

MACINTOSH, A. A. *Isaiah XXI. A Palimsest* (Cambridge: Cambridge University Press, 1980).

MEADE, DAVID G. *Pseudonymity and Canon: An Investiga-*

tion Into the Relationship of Authorship and Authority in Jewish and Earliest Christian Tradition. WISSENSCHAFTLICHE UNTERSUCHUNGEN ZUM NEUEN TESTAMENT 39 (Tübingen: J. C. B. Mohr [Paul Siebeck], 1986).

PLÖGER, OTTO. Theocracy and Eschatology (Richmond: John Knox Press, 1968 [German 1959]).

PROVAN, IAIN W. Hezekiah and the Book of Kings: A Contribution to the Debate About the Composition of the Deuteronomistic History. BEIHEFTE ZUR ZEITSCHRIFT FÜR DIE ALTTESTAMENTLICHE WISSENSCHAFT 172 (Berlin: Walter de Gruyter, 1988).

RAD, GERHARD VON. Old Testament Theology, vol. 2 (New York: Harper & Row, 1965).

RENDTORFF, ROLF. The Old Testament: An Introduction (Philadelphia: Fortress Press, 1986).

ROBERTS, J. J. M. "Isaiah and His Children." In Biblical and Related Studies Presented to Samuel Iwry, ed. by A. Kort and S. Morschauser (Winona Lake, Ind.: Eisenbrauns, 1985), pp. 193–203.

SCHOORS, A. "Isaiah, the Minister of Royal Anointment?" Oudtestamentische Studiën 20:85–107 (1977).

SEITZ, CHRISTOPHER R. "The Prophet Moses and the Canonical Shape of Jeremiah." Zeitschrift für die alttestamentliche Wissenschaft 101:3–27 (1989).

Zion's Final Destiny: The Development of the Book of Isaiah (Minneapolis: Augsburg Fortress Press, 1991).

———. "Isaiah, Book of (First Isaiah)." The Anchor Bible Dictionary, ed. by D. N. Freedman (New York: Doubleday & Co., 1992), 3:472–488.

SMELIK, KLAAS A. D. "Distortion of Old Testament Prophecy: The Purpose of Isaiah xxxvi and xxxvii." Oudtestamentische Studiën 24:70–93 (1989).

STADE, BERNHARD. "Miscellen. Anmerkungen zu 2 Kön. 15—21." Zeitschrift für die alttestamentliche Wissenschaft 6:156–192 (1886).

STANSELL, GARY. "The Structure and Redaction of Isaiah 28—33." Unpublished paper read at the 1989 Society of Biblical Literature meeting in Anaheim, Calif. (Cited with permission of the author.)

STECK, ODIL HANNES. "Bemerkungen zu Jesaja 6." Biblische Zeitschrift 16:188–206 (1972).

———. Bereitete Heimkehr: Jesaja 35 als redactionelle Brücke

270

zwischen dem Ersten und dem Zweiten Jesaja. STUTTGAR-
TER BIBELSTUDIEN 121 (Stuttgart: Katholisches Bibelwerk,
1985).

SWEENEY, MARVIN A. *Isaiah 1—4 and the Post-Exilic Understanding of the Isaianic Tradition* (Berlin: Walter de
Gruyter, 1988).

———. "Textual Citations in Isaiah 24—27: Toward an Understanding of the Redactional Function of Chapters 24—27 in
the Book of Isaiah." *Journal of Biblical Literature*
107:39–52 (1988).

VAN WINKLE, DWIGHT W. "The Relationship of the Nations
to Yahweh and Israel in Isaiah XL—LV." *Vetus Testamentum* 35:446–458 (1985).

WILDBERGER, H. (See Bibliography 1.)

271